CELEBRATING THE EUCHARIST

Holy Week

LITURGICAL PRESS
Collegeville, Minnesota

www.litpress.org

CONTENTS

A publication of LITURGICAL PRESS, Collegeville, Minnesota 56321
ISBN: 978-0-8146-3447-9

The Order of Mass

THE INTRODUCTORY RITES

ENTRANCE CHANT STAND

SIGN OF THE CROSS

Priest: In the name of the Father, and of the Son, and of the Holy Spirit.

People: **Amen.**

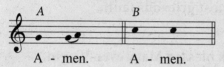

A - men. A - men.

GREETING

A Priest: The grace of our Lord Jesus Christ,
and the love of God,
and the communion of the Holy Spirit
be with you all.

People: **And with your spirit.**

B Priest: Grace to you and peace from God our Father
and the Lord Jesus Christ.

People: **And with your spirit.**

C Priest: The Lord be with you.

People: **And with your spirit.**

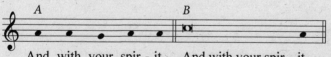

And with your spir - it. And with your spir - it.

PENITENTIAL ACT

Priest: Brethren (brothers and sisters), let us acknowledge our sins,
and so prepare ourselves to celebrate the sacred mysteries. (Pause)

3

A   All: **I confess to almighty God**
and to you, my brothers and sisters,
that I have greatly sinned,
in my thoughts and in my words,
in what I have done and in what I have failed
to do,

And, striking their breast, they say:

through my fault, through my fault,
through my most grievous fault;

Then they continue:

therefore I ask blessed Mary ever-Virgin,
all the Angels and Saints,
and you, my brothers and sisters,
to pray for me to the Lord our God.

B   Priest: Have mercy on us, O Lord.
People: **For we have sinned against you.**

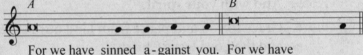

Priest: Show us, O Lord, your mercy.
People: **And grant us your salvation.**

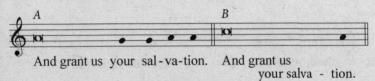

C   Priest (Deacon or another minister):
You were sent to heal the contrite of heart:
Lord, have mercy.   Or: Kyrie, eleison.
People: **Lord, have mercy.**   Or: **Kyrie, eleison.**

Priest: You came to call sinners:
Christ, have mercy.   Or: Christe, eleison.
People: **Christ, have mercy.**   Or: **Christe, eleison.**

Priest: You are seated at the right hand of the Father to
intercede for us:

Lord, have mercy.　**Or:** Kyrie, eleison.

People: **Lord, have mercy.**　**Or:** **Kyrie, eleison.**

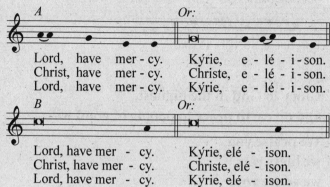

A　　　　　　　　　　　　　*Or:*

Lord,　have　mer - cy.　　Kýrie,　e - lé - i - son.
Christ,　have　mer - cy.　　Christe,　e - lé - i - son.
Lord,　have　mer - cy.　　Kýrie,　e - lé - i - son.

B　　　　　　　　　　　　　*Or:*

Lord, have mer - cy.　　Kýrie, elé - ison.
Christ, have mer - cy.　　Christe, elé - ison.
Lord, have mer - cy.　　Kýrie, elé - ison.

Priest: May almighty God have mercy on us,
forgive us our sins,
and bring us to everlasting life.

People: **Amen.**

KYRIE

The Kyrie, eleison (Lord, have mercy) invocations follow, unless they have
just occurred in a formula of the Penitential Act.

℣. Lord, have mercy.　　　℞. **Lord, have mercy.**

℣. Christ, have mercy.　　℞. **Christ, have mercy.**

℣. Lord, have mercy.　　　℞. **Lord, have mercy.**

Or:

℣. Kyrie, eleison.　　　℞. **Kyrie, eleison.**

℣. Christe, eleison.　　℞. **Christe, eleison.**

℣. Kyrie, eleison.　　　℞. **Kyrie, eleison.**

Ký - ri - e,　e - lé - i - son.　Lord,　have　mer - cy.

Chri - ste,　e - lé - i - son.　Christ,　have　mer - cy.

Or:

Ký - ri - e,   e - lé - i - son.   Lord,   have   mer - cy.

Alternate ending

Ký - ri - e,   e - lé - i - son.

GLORIA

All: **Glory to God in the highest,**
and on earth peace to people of good will.

We praise you,
we bless you,
we adore you,
we glorify you,
we give you thanks for your great glory,
Lord God, heavenly King,
O God, almighty Father.

Lord Jesus Christ, Only Begotten Son,
Lord God, Lamb of God, Son of the Father,
you take away the sins of the world,
have mercy on us;
you take away the sins of the world,
receive our prayer;
you are seated at the right hand of the Father,
have mercy on us.

For you alone are the Holy One,
you alone are the Lord,
you alone are the Most High,
Jesus Christ,
with the Holy Spirit,
in the glory of God the Father.
Amen.

Glo-ry to God in the high-est, and on earth peace
to peo-ple of good will. We praise you, we bless you,
we a-dore you, we glo-ri-fy you, we give you thanks
for your great glo-ry, Lord God, heav-en-ly King,
O God, al-might-y Fa-ther. Lord Je-sus Christ, On-ly
Be-got-ten Son, Lord God, Lamb of God, Son of the Fa-ther,
you take a-way the sins of the world, have mer-cy on us;
you take a-way the sins of the world, re-ceive our prayer;
you are seat-ed at the right hand of the Fa-ther,
have mer-cy on us. For you a-lone are the Ho-ly One,
you a-lone are the Lord, you a-lone are the Most High,
Je-sus Christ, with the Ho-ly Spir-it, in the glo-ry
of God the Fa-ther. A-men.

COLLECT (OPENING PRAYER)

Priest: **Let us pray.**

All pray in silence with the Priest for a while.

Then the Priest, with hands extended, says the Collect prayer, at the end of which the people acclaim:

Amen.

THE LITURGY OF THE WORD

FIRST READING   **SIT**

Then the reader goes to the ambo and reads the First Reading, while all sit and listen.

To indicate the end of the reading, the reader acclaims:

The word of the Lord.

All: **Thanks be to God.**

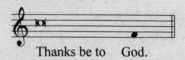

RESPONSORIAL PSALM

The psalmist or cantor sings or says the Psalm, with the people making the response.

SECOND READING

After this, if there is to be a Second Reading, a reader reads it from the ambo, as above.

To indicate the end of the reading, the reader acclaims:

The word of the Lord.

All: **Thanks be to God.**

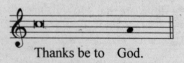

ACCLAMATION BEFORE THE GOSPEL   **STAND**

There follows the **Alleluia** or another chant laid down by the rubrics, as the liturgical time requires.

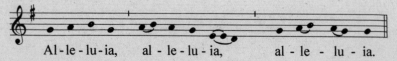

or:

Praise and hon-or to you, Lord Je-sus Christ.

GOSPEL DIALOGUE

Deacon or Priest: The Lord be with you.

People: **And with your spirit.**

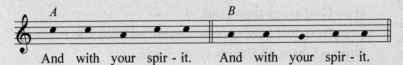

And with your spir - it.   And with your spir - it.

Deacon or Priest: A reading from the holy Gospel according to N.

People: **Glory to you, O Lord.**

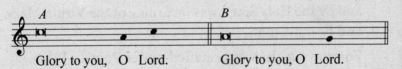

Glory to you, O Lord.   Glory to you, O Lord.

GOSPEL READING

At the end of the Gospel, the Deacon, or the Priest, acclaims:
The Gospel of the Lord.

All: **Praise to you, Lord Jesus Christ.**

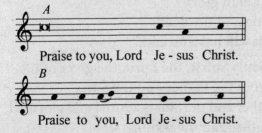

Praise to you, Lord Je-sus Christ.

Praise to you, Lord Je-sus Christ.

HOMILY   SIT

PROFESSION OF FAITH   **STAND**

All: **I believe in one God,**
  the Father almighty,
  maker of heaven and earth,
  of all things visible and invisible.

  I believe in one Lord Jesus Christ,
  the Only Begotten Son of God,
  born of the Father before all ages.
  God from God, Light from Light,
  true God from true God,
  begotten, not made, consubstantial with the Father;
  through him all things were made.
  For us men and for our salvation
  he came down from heaven,

At the words that follow, up to and including and became man,
all bow.

  and by the Holy Spirit was incarnate of the Virgin Mary,
  and became man.

  For our sake he was crucified under Pontius Pilate,
  he suffered death and was buried,
  and rose again on the third day
  in accordance with the Scriptures.
  He ascended into heaven
  and is seated at the right hand of the Father.
  He will come again in glory
  to judge the living and the dead
  and his kingdom will have no end.

  I believe in the Holy Spirit, the Lord, the giver of life,
  who proceeds from the Father and the Son,
  who with the Father and the Son is adored and glorified,
  who has spoken through the prophets.

  I believe in one, holy, catholic and apostolic Church.
  I confess one Baptism for the forgiveness of sins
  and I look forward to the resurrection of the dead
  and the life of the world to come. Amen.

I be-lieve in one God, the Fa-ther al-might-y,

mak-er of heav-en and earth, of all things vis-i-ble and

in-vis-i-ble. I be-lieve in one Lord Je-sus Christ,

the On-ly Be-got-ten Son of God, born of the Fa-ther

be-fore all a-ges. God from God, Light from Light,

true God from true God, be-got-ten, not made, con-sub-stan-tial

with the Fa-ther; through him all things were made.

For us men and for our sal-va-tion he came down from heav-en,

At the words that follow, up to and including and became man, *all bow.*

and by the Ho-ly Spir-it was in-car-nate

of the Vir-gin Mar-y, and be-came man.

For our sake he was cru-ci-fied un-der Pon-tius Pi-late,

he suf-fered death and was bur-ied, and rose a-gain

on the third day in ac-cord-ance with the Scrip-tures.

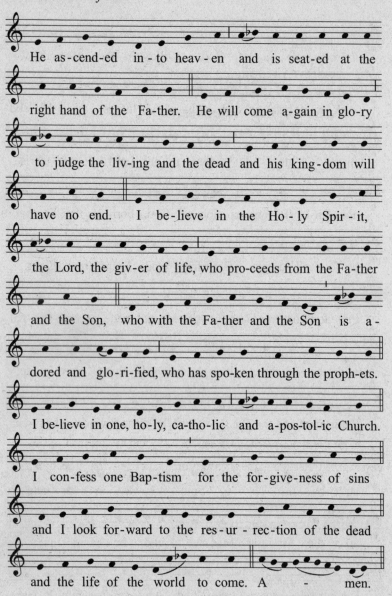

He as-cend-ed in - to heav-en and is seat-ed at the

right hand of the Fa-ther. He will come a-gain in glo-ry

to judge the liv-ing and the dead and his king-dom will

have no end. I be-lieve in the Ho-ly Spir-it,

the Lord, the giv-er of life, who pro-ceeds from the Fa-ther

and the Son, who with the Fa-ther and the Son is a-

dored and glo-ri-fied, who has spo-ken through the proph-ets.

I be-lieve in one, ho-ly, ca-tho-lic and a-pos-tol-ic Church.

I con-fess one Bap-tism for the for-give-ness of sins

and I look for-ward to the res-ur - rec-tion of the dead

and the life of the world to come. A - men.

Instead of the Niceno-Constantinopolitan Creed, especially during Lent and Easter Time, the baptismal Symbol of the Roman Church, known as the Apostles' Creed, may be used.

All: **I believe in God,**
the Father almighty,
Creator of heaven and earth,
and in Jesus Christ, his only Son, our Lord,

At the words that follow, up to and including the Virgin Mary, all bow.

who was conceived by the Holy Spirit,
born of the Virgin Mary,
suffered under Pontius Pilate,
was crucified, died and was buried;
he descended into hell;
on the third day he rose again from the dead;
he ascended into heaven,
and is seated at the right hand of God the Father
almighty;
from there he will come to judge the living and the
dead.

I believe in the Holy Spirit,
the holy catholic Church,
the communion of saints,
the forgiveness of sins,
the resurrection of the body,
and life everlasting. Amen.

UNIVERSAL PRAYER
(*or* PRAYER OF THE FAITHFUL *or* BIDDING PRAYERS)

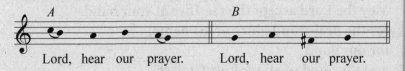

A   B
Lord, hear our prayer.   Lord, hear our prayer.

The Liturgy of the Eucharist

Presentation and Preparation of the Gifts SIT

The Priest, standing at the altar, takes the paten with the bread and holds it
slightly raised above the altar with both hands, saying in a low voice:

Blessed are you, Lord God of all creation,
for through your goodness we have received
the bread we offer you:
fruit of the earth and work of human hands,
it will become for us the bread of life.

If, however, the Offertory Chant is not sung, the Priest may speak these words
aloud; at the end, the people may acclaim:

Blessed be God for ever.

The Priest then takes the chalice and holds it slightly raised above the altar
with both hands, saying in a low voice:

Blessed are you, Lord God of all creation,
for through your goodness we have received
the wine we offer you:
fruit of the vine and work of human hands,
it will become our spiritual drink.

If, however, the Offertory Chant is not sung, the Priest may speak these words
aloud; at the end, the people may acclaim:

Blessed be God for ever.

Standing at the middle of the altar, facing the people, extending and then
joining his hands, he says:

Pray, brethren (brothers and sisters),
that my sacrifice and yours
may be acceptable to God,
the almighty Father.

The people rise and reply: STAND

May the Lord accept the sacrifice at your hands
for the praise and glory of his name,
for our good
and the good of all his holy Church.

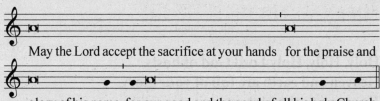

May the Lord accept the sacrifice at your hands   for the praise and glory of his name, for our good and the good of all his holy Church.

PRAYER OVER THE OFFERINGS

Then the Priest, with hands extended, says the Prayer over the Offerings, at the end of which the people acclaim:

Amen.

THE EUCHARISTIC PRAYER

Priest: The Lord be with you.

People: **And with your spirit.**

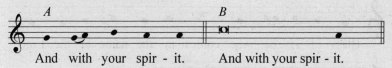

And with your spir - it.   And with your spir - it.

Priest: Lift up your hearts.

People: **We lift them up to the Lord.**

We lift them up to the Lord.   We lift them up to the Lord.

Priest: Let us give thanks to the Lord our God.

People: **It is right and just.**

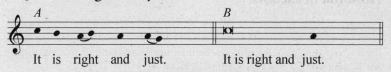

It is right and just.   It is right and just.

PREFACE

PREFACE ACCLAMATION

At the end of the Preface he joins his hands and concludes the Preface with the people, singing or saying aloud:

Holy, Holy, Holy Lord God of hosts.
Heaven and earth are full of your glory.
Hosanna in the highest.
Blessed is he who comes in the name of the Lord.
Hosanna in the highest.

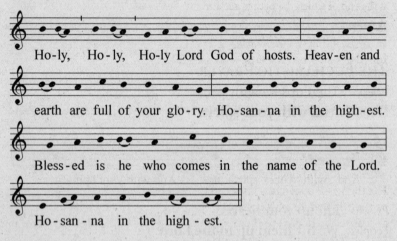

Ho-ly,   Ho-ly,   Ho-ly Lord God of hosts. Heav-en and
earth are full of your glo-ry. Ho-san-na in the high-est.
Bless-ed is he who comes in the name of the Lord.
Ho-san-na in the high-est.

Or:

Sanctus, Sanctus, Sanctus Dominus Deus Sabaoth.
Pleni sunt cæli et terra gloria tua.
Hosanna in excelsis.
Benedictus qui venit in nomine Domini.
Hosanna in excelsis.

A common bodily posture, to be observed by all those taking part, is a sign of the unity of the members of the Christian community gathered together for the Sacred Liturgy, for it expresses the intentions and spiritual attitude of the participants and also fosters them (GIRM no. 42).

In the dioceses of the United States of America, they [the faithful] should kneel beginning after the singing or recitation of the Sanctus (Holy, Holy, Holy) until after the Amen of the Eucharistic Prayer, except when prevented on occasion by ill health, or for reasons of lack of space, of the large number of people present, or for another reasonable cause. However, those who do not kneel ought to make a profound bow when the Priest genuflects after the Consecration (GIRM no. 43).

Eucharistic Prayer I (The Roman Canon) **KNEEL**

Priest:

To you, therefore, most merciful Father,
we make humble prayer and petition
through Jesus Christ, your Son, our Lord:
that you accept
and bless ✠ these gifts, these offerings,
these holy and unblemished sacrifices,
which we offer you firstly
for your holy catholic Church.
Be pleased to grant her peace,
to guard, unite and govern her
throughout the whole world,
together with your servant N. our Pope
and N. our Bishop,*
and all those who, holding to the truth,
hand on the catholic and apostolic faith.

Commemoration of the Living

Remember, Lord, your servants N. and N.
and all gathered here,
whose faith and devotion are known to you.
For them, we offer you this sacrifice of praise
or they offer it for themselves
and all who are dear to them:
for the redemption of their souls,
in hope of health and well-being,
and paying their homage to you,
the eternal God, living and true.

Within the Action

In communion with those whose memory we venerate,
especially the glorious ever-Virgin Mary,
Mother of our God and Lord, Jesus Christ,
† and blessed Joseph, her Spouse,
your blessed Apostles and Martyrs,
Peter and Paul, Andrew,
(James, John,
Thomas, James, Philip,
Bartholomew, Matthew,
Simon and Jude;
Linus, Cletus, Clement, Sixtus,
Cornelius, Cyprian,

---

* Mention may be made here of the Coadjutor Bishop, or Auxiliary Bishops,
as noted in the *General Instruction of the Roman Missal*, no. 149.

Lawrence, Chrysogonus,
John and Paul,
Cosmas and Damian)
and all your Saints;
we ask that through their merits and prayers,
in all things we may be defended
by your protecting help.
(Through Christ our Lord. Amen.)

From the Mass of the Easter Vigil until the Second Sunday of Easter
Celebrating the most sacred night (day)
of the Resurrection of our Lord Jesus Christ in the flesh,
and in communion with those whose memory we venerate,
especially the glorious ever-Virgin Mary,
Mother of our God and Lord, Jesus Christ, †

Therefore, Lord, we pray:
graciously accept this oblation of our service,
that of your whole family;
order our days in your peace,
and command that we be delivered from eternal damnation
and counted among the flock of those you have chosen.
(Through Christ our Lord. Amen.)

From the Mass of the Easter Vigil until the Second Sunday of Easter
Therefore, Lord, we pray:
graciously accept this oblation of our service,
that of your whole family,
which we make to you
also for those to whom you have been pleased to give
the new birth of water and the Holy Spirit,
granting them forgiveness of all their sins:
order our days in your peace,
and command that we be delivered from eternal damnation
and counted among the flock of those you have chosen.
(Through Christ our Lord. Amen.)

Be pleased, O God, we pray,
to bless, acknowledge,
and approve this offering in every respect;
make it spiritual and acceptable,
so that it may become for us
the Body and Blood of your most beloved Son,
our Lord Jesus Christ.

On the day before he was to suffer,
he took bread in his holy and venerable hands,
and with eyes raised to heaven

to you, O God, his almighty Father,
giving you thanks, he said the blessing,
broke the bread
and gave it to his disciples, saying:

TAKE THIS, ALL OF YOU, AND EAT OF IT,
FOR THIS IS MY BODY,
WHICH WILL BE GIVEN UP FOR YOU.

In a similar way, when supper was ended,
he took this precious chalice
in his holy and venerable hands,
and once more giving you thanks, he said the blessing
and gave the chalice to his disciples, saying:

TAKE THIS, ALL OF YOU, AND DRINK FROM IT,
FOR THIS IS THE CHALICE OF MY BLOOD,
THE BLOOD OF THE NEW AND ETERNAL COVENANT,
WHICH WILL BE POURED OUT FOR YOU AND FOR MANY
FOR THE FORGIVENESS OF SINS.

DO THIS IN MEMORY OF ME.

The mystery of faith.

And the people continue, acclaiming:

A **We proclaim your Death, O Lord,
and profess your Resurrection
until you come again.**

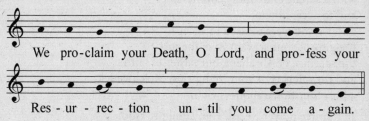

We pro-claim your Death, O Lord, and pro-fess your
Res - ur - rec - tion   un - til you come a - gain.

B **When we eat this Bread and drink this Cup,
we proclaim your Death, O Lord,
until you come again.**

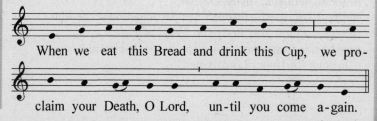

When we eat this Bread and drink this Cup, we proclaim your Death, O Lord, un-til you come a-gain.

C **Save us, Savior of the world,**
for by your Cross and Resurrection
you have set us free.

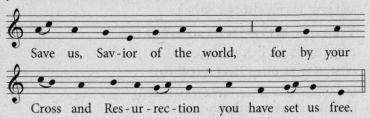

Save us, Sav-ior of the world,   for by your

Cross and Res-ur-rec-tion   you have set us free.

Priest:
Therefore, O Lord,
as we celebrate the memorial of the blessed Passion,
the Resurrection from the dead,
and the glorious Ascension into heaven
of Christ, your Son, our Lord,
we, your servants and your holy people,
offer to your glorious majesty
from the gifts that you have given us,
this pure victim,
this holy victim,
this spotless victim,
the holy Bread of eternal life
and the Chalice of everlasting salvation.

Be pleased to look upon these offerings
with a serene and kindly countenance,
and to accept them,
as once you were pleased to accept
the gifts of your servant Abel the just,
the sacrifice of Abraham, our father in faith,
and the offering of your high priest Melchizedek,
a holy sacrifice, a spotless victim.

In humble prayer we ask you, almighty God:
command that these gifts be borne
by the hands of your holy Angel
to your altar on high
in the sight of your divine majesty,
so that all of us, who through this participation at the altar
receive the most holy Body and Blood of your Son,
may be filled with every grace and heavenly blessing.
(Through Christ our Lord. Amen.)

Commemoration of the Dead
Remember also, Lord, your servants N. and N.,
who have gone before us with the sign of faith
and rest in the sleep of peace.

Grant them, O Lord, we pray,
and all who sleep in Christ,
a place of refreshment, light and peace.
(Through Christ our Lord. Amen.)

To us, also, your servants, who, though sinners,
hope in your abundant mercies,
graciously grant some share
and fellowship with your holy Apostles and Martyrs:
with John the Baptist, Stephen,
Matthias, Barnabas,
(Ignatius, Alexander,
Marcellinus, Peter,
Felicity, Perpetua,
Agatha, Lucy,
Agnes, Cecilia, Anastasia)
and all your Saints;
admit us, we beseech you,
into their company,
not weighing our merits,
but granting us your pardon,
through Christ our Lord.

Through whom
you continue to make all these good things, O Lord;
you sanctify them, fill them with life,
bless them, and bestow them upon us.

Through him, and with him, and in him,
O God, almighty Father,
in the unity of the Holy Spirit,
all glory and honor is yours,
for ever and ever.

People: **Amen.**

Then follows the Communion Rite (*See* p. 27).

Eucharistic Prayer II   **KNEEL**

Preface
It is truly right and just, our duty and our salvation,
always and everywhere to give you thanks, Father most holy,
through your beloved Son, Jesus Christ,
your Word through whom you made all things,

whom you sent as our Savior and Redeemer,
incarnate by the Holy Spirit and born of the Virgin.

Fulfilling your will and gaining for you a holy people,
he stretched out his hands as he endured his Passion,
so as to break the bonds of death and manifest the resurrection.

And so, with the Angels and all the Saints
we declare your glory,
as with one voice we acclaim:

Holy, Holy, Holy Lord God of hosts.
Heaven and earth are full of your glory.
Hosanna in the highest.
Blessed is he who comes in the name of the Lord.
Hosanna in the highest.

Priest:
You are indeed Holy, O Lord,
the fount of all holiness.
Make holy, therefore, these gifts, we pray,
by sending down your Spirit upon them like the dewfall,
so that they may become for us
the Body and ✠ Blood of our Lord Jesus Christ.

At the time he was betrayed
and entered willingly into his Passion,
he took bread and, giving thanks, broke it,
and gave it to his disciples, saying:

TAKE THIS, ALL OF YOU, AND EAT OF IT,
FOR THIS IS MY BODY,
WHICH WILL BE GIVEN UP FOR YOU.

In a similar way, when supper was ended,
he took the chalice
and, once more giving thanks,
he gave it to his disciples, saying:

TAKE THIS, ALL OF YOU, AND DRINK FROM IT,
FOR THIS IS THE CHALICE OF MY BLOOD,
THE BLOOD OF THE NEW AND ETERNAL COVENANT,
WHICH WILL BE POURED OUT FOR YOU AND FOR MANY
FOR THE FORGIVENESS OF SINS.

DO THIS IN MEMORY OF ME.

The mystery of faith.

People:

A **We proclaim your Death, O Lord,
and profess your Resurrection
until you come again.**

B **When we eat this Bread and drink this Cup,
we proclaim your Death, O Lord,
until you come again.**

C **Save us, Savior of the world,
for by your Cross and Resurrection
you have set us free.**

Priest:

Therefore, as we celebrate
the memorial of his Death and Resurrection,
we offer you, Lord,
the Bread of life and the Chalice of salvation,
giving thanks that you have held us worthy
to be in your presence and minister to you.

Humbly we pray
that, partaking of the Body and Blood of Christ,
we may be gathered into one by the Holy Spirit.

Remember, Lord, your Church,
spread throughout the world,
and bring her to the fullness of charity,
together with N. our Pope and N. our Bishop*
and all the clergy.

In Masses for the Dead, the following may be added:
Remember your servant N.,
whom you have called (today)
from this world to yourself.
Grant that he (she) who was united with your Son in a death like his,
may also be one with him in his Resurrection.

Remember also our brothers and sisters
who have fallen asleep in the hope of the resurrection,
and all who have died in your mercy:
welcome them into the light of your face.
Have mercy on us all, we pray,
that with the Blessed Virgin Mary, Mother of God,
with the blessed Apostles,

---

* Mention may be made here of the Coadjutor Bishop, or Auxiliary Bishops,
as noted in the *General Instruction of the Roman Missal*, no. 149.

and all the Saints who have pleased you throughout the ages,
we may merit to be coheirs to eternal life,
and may praise and glorify you
through your Son, Jesus Christ.

Through him, and with him, and in him,
O God, almighty Father,
in the unity of the Holy Spirit,
all glory and honor is yours,
for ever and ever.

People: **Amen.**

Then follows the Communion Rite (*See* p. 27).

Eucharistic Prayer III   **KNEEL**

Priest:
You are indeed Holy, O Lord,
and all you have created
rightly gives you praise,
for through your Son our Lord Jesus Christ,
by the power and working of the Holy Spirit,
you give life to all things and make them holy,
and you never cease to gather a people to yourself,
so that from the rising of the sun to its setting
a pure sacrifice may be offered to your name.

Therefore, O Lord, we humbly implore you:
by the same Spirit graciously make holy
these gifts we have brought to you for consecration,
that they may become the Body and ✠ Blood
of your Son our Lord Jesus Christ,
at whose command we celebrate these mysteries.

For on the night he was betrayed
he himself took bread,
and, giving you thanks, he said the blessing,
broke the bread and gave it to his disciples, saying:

Take this, all of you, and eat of it,
for this is my Body,
which will be given up for you.

In a similar way, when supper was ended,
he took the chalice,
and, giving you thanks, he said the blessing,
and gave the chalice to his disciples, saying:

TAKE THIS, ALL OF YOU, AND DRINK FROM IT,
FOR THIS IS THE CHALICE OF MY BLOOD,
THE BLOOD OF THE NEW AND ETERNAL COVENANT,
WHICH WILL BE POURED OUT FOR YOU AND FOR MANY
FOR THE FORGIVENESS OF SINS.

DO THIS IN MEMORY OF ME.

The mystery of faith.

People:

A **We proclaim your Death, O Lord,
and profess your Resurrection
until you come again.**

B **When we eat this Bread and drink this Cup,
we proclaim your Death, O Lord,
until you come again.**

C **Save us, Savior of the world,
for by your Cross and Resurrection
you have set us free.**

Priest:

Therefore, O Lord, as we celebrate the memorial
of the saving Passion of your Son,
his wondrous Resurrection
and Ascension into heaven,
and as we look forward to his second coming,
we offer you in thanksgiving
this holy and living sacrifice.

Look, we pray, upon the oblation of your Church
and, recognizing the sacrificial Victim by whose death
you willed to reconcile us to yourself,
grant that we, who are nourished
by the Body and Blood of your Son
and filled with his Holy Spirit,
may become one body, one spirit in Christ.

May he make of us
an eternal offering to you,
so that we may obtain an inheritance with your elect,
especially with the most Blessed Virgin Mary, Mother of God,
with your blessed Apostles and glorious Martyrs
(with Saint N.: the Saint of the day or Patron Saint)
and with all the Saints,
on whose constant intercession in your presence
we rely for unfailing help.

May this Sacrifice of our reconciliation,
we pray, O Lord,
advance the peace and salvation of all the world.
Be pleased to confirm in faith and charity
your pilgrim Church on earth,
with your servant N. our Pope and N. our Bishop,*
the Order of Bishops, all the clergy,
and the entire people you have gained for your own.

Listen graciously to the prayers of this family,
whom you have summoned before you:
in your compassion, O merciful Father,
gather to yourself all your children
scattered throughout the world.

† To our departed brothers and sisters
and to all who were pleasing to you
at their passing from this life,
give kind admittance to your kingdom.
There we hope to enjoy for ever the fullness of your glory
through Christ our Lord,
through whom you bestow on the world all that is good. †

Through him, and with him, and in him,
O God, almighty Father,
in the unity of the Holy Spirit,
all glory and honor is yours,
for ever and ever.

People: **Amen.**

Then follows the Communion Rite (*See* p. 27).

When this Eucharistic Prayer is used in Masses for the Dead, the following
may be said:
† Remember your servant N.
whom you have called (today)
from this world to yourself.
Grant that he (she) who was united with your Son in a death like his,
may also be one with him in his Resurrection,
when from the earth
he will raise up in the flesh those who have died,
and transform our lowly body
after the pattern of his own glorious body.
To our departed brothers and sisters, too,

---

* Mention may be made here of the Coadjutor Bishop, or Auxiliary Bishops,
  as noted in the *General Instruction of the Roman Missal*, no. 149.

and to all who were pleasing to you
at their passing from this life,
give kind admittance to your kingdom.
There we hope to enjoy for ever the fullness of your glory,
when you will wipe away every tear from our eyes.
For seeing you, our God, as you are,
we shall be like you for all the ages
and praise you without end,
through Christ our Lord,
through whom you bestow on the world all that is good. †

THE COMMUNION RITE　　　　　　　　　　**STAND**

THE LORD'S PRAYER

Priest:　At the Savior's command
　　　　and formed by divine teaching,
　　　　we dare to say:

All:　　**Our Father, who art in heaven,**
　　　　hallowed be thy name;
　　　　thy kingdom come,
　　　　thy will be done
　　　　on earth as it is in heaven.
　　　　Give us this day our daily bread,
　　　　and forgive us our trespasses,
　　　　as we forgive those who trespass against us;
　　　　and lead us not into temptation,
　　　　but deliver us from evil.

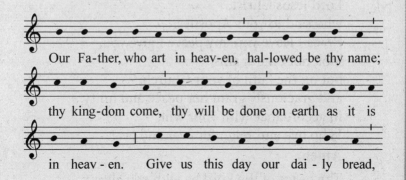

Our Fa-ther, who art in heav-en, hal-lowed be thy name;
thy king-dom come, thy will be done on earth as it is
in heav-en. Give us this day our dai-ly bread,

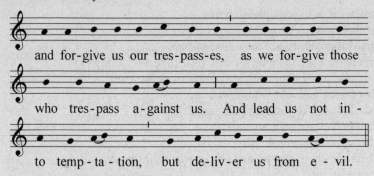

and for-give us our tres-pass-es, as we for-give those who tres-pass a-gainst us. And lead us not in-to temp-ta-tion, but de-liv-er us from e-vil.

Priest: Deliver us, Lord, we pray, from every evil,
graciously grant peace in our days,
that, by the help of your mercy,
we may be always free from sin
and safe from all distress,
as we await the blessed hope
and the coming of our Savior, Jesus Christ.

All: **For the kingdom,**
the power and the glory are yours
now and for ever.

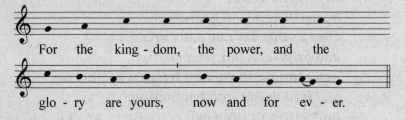

For the king-dom, the power, and the glo-ry are yours, now and for ev-er.

Priest: Lord Jesus Christ,
who said to your Apostles:
Peace I leave you, my peace I give you,
look not on our sins,
but on the faith of your Church,
and graciously grant her peace and unity
in accordance with your will.
Who live and reign for ever and ever.

People: **Amen.**

Priest: The peace of the Lord be with you always.

People: **And with your spirit.**

And with your spir - it.   And with your spir - it.

Then, if appropriate, the Deacon, or the Priest, adds:

Let us offer each other the sign of peace.

Lamb of God

All: **Lamb of God, you take away the sins of the world, have mercy on us.**
Lamb of God, you take away the sins of the world, have mercy on us.
Lamb of God, you take away the sins of the world, grant us peace.

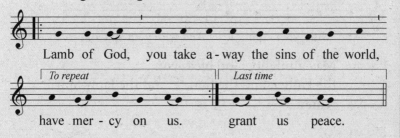

Lamb of God,   you take a - way the sins of the world,

have mer - cy on us.   grant us peace.

The faithful kneel after the Agnus Dei (Lamb of God) unless the Diocesan Bishop determines otherwise (GIRM no. 43).

Invitation to Communion

Priest: Behold the Lamb of God,
behold him who takes away the sins of the world.
Blessed are those called to the supper of the Lamb.

All: **Lord, I am not worthy**
that you should enter under my roof,
but only say the word
and my soul shall be healed.

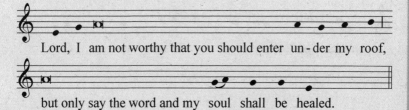

Lord, I am not worthy that you should enter un - der my roof,

but only say the word and my soul shall be healed.

COMMUNION

The Priest says to each of the communicants: **The Body of Christ.**

The communicant replies: **Amen.**

PRAYER AFTER COMMUNION   **STAND**

The Priest says: Let us pray.

At the end the people acclaim: **Amen.**

THE CONCLUDING RITES

FINAL BLESSING

Priest: The Lord be with you.

People: **And with your spirit.**

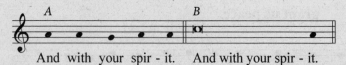

And with your spir - it.   And with your spir - it.

Priest: May almighty God bless you,
the Father, and the Son, ✠ and the Holy Spirit.

People: **Amen.**

DISMISSAL

The Deacon, or the Priest himself:

Go forth, the Mass is ended.

Or:

Go and announce the Gospel of the Lord.

Or:

Go in peace, glorifying the Lord by your life.

Or:

Go in peace.

People: **Thanks be to God.**

Thanks   be   to   God.   Thanks   be   to   God.

Celebration of the Liturgy of the Word
[With Holy Communion]

INTRODUCTORY RITES

INTRODUCTION

SIGN OF THE CROSS   STAND

GREETING
Response: **Blessed be God for ever.**

COLLECT

LITURGY OF THE WORD   SIT

FIRST READING

RESPONSORIAL PSALM

SECOND READING

GOSPEL ACCLAMATION   STAND

GOSPEL

HOMILY OR REFLECTION ON THE READINGS   SIT

PERIOD OF SILENCE

PROFESSION OF FAITH   STAND
[The Nicene Creed can be found on page 10]
[The Apostles' Creed can be found on page 13]

PRAYER OF THE FAITHFUL

31

COMMUNION RITE

LORD'S PRAYER, page 27

INVITATION TO COMMUNION   **KNEEL**

Response: **Lord, I am not worthy**
that you should enter under my roof,
but only say the word
and my soul shall be healed.

COMMUNION

ACT OF THANKSGIVING   **STAND**

CONCLUDING RITES

INVITATION TO PRAY FOR VOCATIONS TO THE PRIESTHOOD

BLESSING

SIGN OF PEACE

Palm Sunday
of the Lord's Passion

The Commemoration of the Lord's Entrance into Jerusalem

FIRST FORM: THE PROCESSION

At an appropriate hour, a gathering takes place at a smaller church or other suitable place other than inside the church to where the procession will go. The faithful hold branches in their hands.

Antiphon

Hosanna to the Son of David;
blessed is he who comes in the name of the Lord, the King
  of Israel.
Hosanna in the highest.

Acc. 1

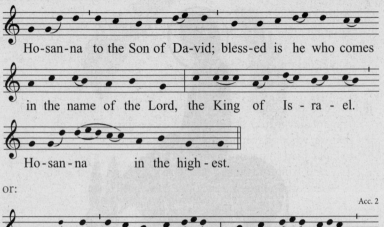

Ho-san-na to the Son of Da-vid; bless-ed is he who comes

in the name of the Lord, the King of Is - ra - el.

Ho-san-na in the high - est.

or:

Acc. 2

Ho - san - na fi - li - o Da-vid: be - ne - dí - ctus

qui ve - nit in nó - mi - ne Dó - mi - ni.

Rex Is - ra - el: Ho-san-na in ex - cél-sis.

Priest: In the name of the Father, and of the Son, and of the Holy Spirit.

All: **Amen.**

Dear brethren (brothers and sisters),
since the beginning of Lent until now
we have prepared our hearts by penance and charitable works.
Today we gather together to herald with the whole Church
the beginning of the celebration
of our Lord's Paschal Mystery,
that is to say, of his Passion and Resurrection.
For it was to accomplish this mystery
that he entered his own city of Jerusalem.
Therefore, with all faith and devotion,
let us commemorate
the Lord's entry into the city for our salvation,
following in his footsteps,
so that, being made by his grace partakers of the Cross,
we may have a share also in his Resurrection and in his life.

A Let us pray.
Almighty ever-living God,
sanctify ✢ these branches with your blessing,
that we, who follow Christ the King in exultation,
may reach the eternal Jerusalem through him.
Who lives and reigns for ever and ever. All: **Amen.**

B Increase the faith of those who place their hope in you, O God,
and graciously hear the prayers of those who call on you,
that we, who today hold high these branches
to hail Christ in his triumph,
may bear fruit for you by good works accomplished in him.
Who lives and reigns for ever and ever. All: **Amen.**

Year A (L 37-A): 2014, 2017, 2020, etc.

GOSPEL   Matthew 21:1-11

✢ **A reading from the holy Gospel according to Matthew**

All: **Glory to you, O Lord.**

**When Jesus and the disciples drew near Jerusalem
and came to Bethphage on the Mount of Olives,
Jesus sent two disciples, saying to them,
"Go into the village opposite you,
and immediately you will find an ass tethered,
and a colt with her.
Untie them and bring them here to me.
And if anyone should say anything to you, reply,
'The master has need of them.'
Then he will send them at once."
This happened so that what had been spoken through
the prophet
might be fulfilled:
"Say to daughter Zion,
'Behold, your king comes to you,
meek and riding on an ass,
and on a colt, the foal of a beast of burden.'"
The disciples went and did as Jesus had ordered them.**

They brought the ass and the colt and laid their cloaks
> over them,
>> and he sat upon them.

The very large crowd spread their cloaks on the road,
> while others cut branches from the trees
> and strewed them on the road.

The crowds preceding him and those following
> kept crying out and saying:
>> "Hosanna to the Son of David;
>>> blessed is he who comes in the name of the Lord;
>> hosanna in the highest."

And when he entered Jerusalem
> the whole city was shaken and asked, "Who is this?"

And the crowds replied,
> "This is Jesus the prophet, from Nazareth in Galilee."

The Gospel of the Lord. All: **Praise to you, Lord Jesus Christ.**

Year B (L 37-B): 2012, 2015, 2018, etc.

GOSPEL (Option A)   Mark 11:1-10

☩ **A reading from the holy Gospel according to Mark**

All: **Glory to you, O Lord.**

When Jesus and his disciples drew near to Jerusalem,
> to Bethphage and Bethany at the Mount of Olives,
> he sent two of his disciples and said to them,
>> "Go into the village opposite you,
>> and immediately on entering it,
>> you will find a colt tethered on which no one has ever sat.

Untie it and bring it here.

If anyone should say to you,
> 'Why are you doing this?' reply,
> 'The Master has need of it
> and will send it back here at once.'"

So they went off
> and found a colt tethered at a gate outside on the street,
> and they untied it.

Some of the bystanders said to them,
"What are you doing, untying the colt?"
They answered them just as Jesus had told them to,
and they permitted them to do it.
So they brought the colt to Jesus
and put their cloaks over it.
And he sat on it.
Many people spread their cloaks on the road,
and others spread leafy branches
that they had cut from the fields.
Those preceding him as well as those following kept
crying out:
"Hosanna!
Blessed is he who comes in the name of the Lord!
Blessed is the kingdom of our father David that
is to come!
Hosanna in the highest!"

The Gospel of the Lord. All: Praise to you, Lord Jesus Christ.

Or:

GOSPEL (Option B)   John 12:12-16

✝ A reading from the holy Gospel according to John

All: Glory to you, O Lord.

When the great crowd that had come to the feast heard
that Jesus was coming to Jerusalem,
they took palm branches and went out to meet him,
and cried out:
"Hosanna!
Blessed is he who comes in the name of the Lord,
the king of Israel."

Jesus found an ass and sat upon it, as is written:
Fear no more, O daughter Zion;
see, your king comes, seated upon an ass's colt.
His disciples did not understand this at first,
but when Jesus had been glorified

they remembered that these things were written about
    him
and that they had done this for him.

The Gospel of the Lord. All: **Praise to you, Lord Jesus Christ.**

Year C (L 37-C): 2013, 2016, 2019, etc.

GOSPEL   Luke 19:28-40

✠ **A reading from the holy Gospel according to Luke**

All: **Glory to you, O Lord.**

Jesus proceeded on his journey up to Jerusalem.
As he drew near to Bethphage and Bethany
    at the place called the Mount of Olives,
    he sent two of his disciples.
He said, "Go into the village opposite you,
    and as you enter it you will find a colt tethered
    on which no one has ever sat.
Untie it and bring it here.
And if anyone should ask you,
    'Why are you untying it?'
    you will answer,
    'The Master has need of it.'"
So those who had been sent went off
    and found everything just as he had told them.
And as they were untying the colt, its owners said to them,
    "Why are you untying this colt?"
They answered,
    "The Master has need of it."
So they brought it to Jesus,
    threw their cloaks over the colt,
    and helped Jesus to mount.
As he rode along,
    the people were spreading their cloaks on the road;
    and now as he was approaching the slope of the
        Mount of Olives,

the whole multitude of his disciples
began to praise God aloud with joy
for all the mighty deeds they had seen.
They proclaimed:
"Blessed is the king who comes
in the name of the Lord.
Peace in heaven
and glory in the highest."
Some of the Pharisees in the crowd said to him,
"Teacher, rebuke your disciples."
He said in reply,
"I tell you, if they keep silent,
the stones will cry out!"

The Gospel of the Lord. All: **Praise to you, Lord Jesus Christ.**

PROCESSION WITH THE BLESSED BRANCHES

After the Gospel, a brief homily may be given. Then, to begin the Procession, an invitation may be given by a Priest or a Deacon or a lay minister, in these or similar words:

Dear brethren (brothers and sisters),
like the crowds who acclaimed Jesus in Jerusalem,
let us go forth in peace.

or:

Let us go forth in peace

In this latter case, all respond:
In the name of Christ. Amen.

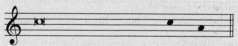

In the name of Christ.   A - men.

As the Procession moves forward, suitable chants in honor of Christ the King are sung by the choir and people.

Acc. 3

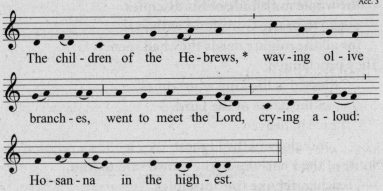

The chil-dren of the He-brews, * wav-ing ol-ive branch-es, went to meet the Lord, cry-ing a-loud: Ho-san-na in the high-est.

or:

Acc. 4

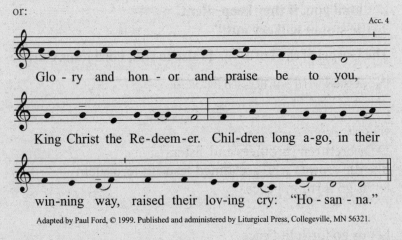

Glo-ry and hon-or and praise be to you, King Christ the Re-deem-er. Chil-dren long a-go, in their win-ning way, raised their lov-ing cry: "Ho-san-na."

or:

Acc. 5

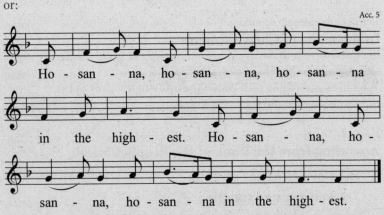

Ho-san-na, ho-san-na, ho-san-na in the high-est. Ho-san-na, ho-san-na, ho-san-na in the high-est.

SECOND FORM: THE SOLEMN ENTRANCE

When a procession outside the church cannot take place, the entrance of the Lord is celebrated inside the church by means of a Solemn Entrance before the principal Mass.

THIRD FORM: THE SIMPLE ENTRANCE

At all other Masses of this Sunday at which the Solemn Entrance is not held, the memorial of the Lord's entrance into Jerusalem takes place by means of a Simple Entrance.

ENTRANCE ANTIPHON (Cf. John 12:1, 12-13; Psalm 24[23]:9-10)

Six days before the Passover,
when the Lord came into the city of Jerusalem,
the children ran to meet him;
in their hands they carried palm branches
and with a loud voice cried out:
* Hosanna in the highest!
Blessed are you, who have come in your abundant mercy!

O gates, lift high your heads;
grow higher, ancient doors.
Let him enter, the king of glory!
Who is this king of glory?
He, the Lord of hosts, he is the king of glory.
* Hosanna in the highest!
Blessed are you, who have come in your abundant mercy!

COLLECT

Almighty ever-living God,
who as an example of humility for the human race to follow
caused our Savior to take flesh and submit to the Cross,
graciously grant that we may heed his lesson of patient suffering
and so merit a share in his Resurrection.
Who lives and reigns with you in the unity of the Holy Spirit,
one God, for ever and ever. All: **Amen.**

READING I (L 38-ABC)　Isaiah 50:4-7

A reading from the Book of the Prophet Isaiah

The Lord GOD has given me
　a well-trained tongue,
that I might know how to speak to the weary
　a word that will rouse them.

Morning after morning
  he opens my ear that I may hear;
and I have not rebelled,
  have not turned back.
I gave my back to those who beat me,
  my cheeks to those who plucked my beard;
my face I did not shield
  from buffets and spitting.

The Lord GOD is my help,
  therefore I am not disgraced;
I have set my face like flint,
  knowing that I shall not be put to shame.

The word of the Lord. All: **Thanks be to God.**

RESPONSORIAL PSALM 22

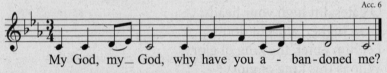

Acc. 6

My God, my— God, why have you a - ban-doned me?

or:

Acc. 7

My God, my God,   why have you a - ban - doned me?

or:

Acc. 8

My   God,   my God,   why have you a -
ban - doned me,——— my   God?

Psalm 22:8-9, 17-18, 19-20, 23-24

R̸. (2a) **My God, my God, why have you abandoned me?**

All who see me scoff at me;
　　they mock me with parted lips, they wag their heads:
"He relied on the LORD; let him deliver him,
　　let him rescue him, if he loves him." R̸.

Indeed, many dogs surround me,
　　a pack of evildoers closes in upon me;
they have pierced my hands and my feet;
　　I can count all my bones. R̸.

They divide my garments among them,
　　and for my vesture they cast lots.
But you, O LORD, be not far from me;
　　O my help, hasten to aid me. R̸.

I will proclaim your name to my brethren;
　　in the midst of the assembly I will praise you:
"You who fear the LORD, praise him;
　　all you descendants of Jacob, give glory to him;
　　revere him, all you descendants of Israel!" R̸.

READING II　　Philippians 2:6-11

A reading from the Letter of Saint Paul to the Philippians

Christ Jesus, though he was in the form of God,
　　did not regard equality with God
　　something to be grasped.
Rather, he emptied himself,
　　taking the form of a slave,
　　coming in human likeness;
　　and found human in appearance,
　　he humbled himself,
　　becoming obedient to the point of death,
　　even death on a cross.
Because of this, God greatly exalted him
　　and bestowed on him the name
　　which is above every name,
　　that at the name of Jesus

every knee should bend,
of those in heaven and on earth and under the earth,
and every tongue confess that
Jesus Christ is Lord,
to the glory of God the Father.

The word of the Lord. All: **Thanks be to God.**

VERSE BEFORE THE GOSPEL (Philippians 2:8-9)
Christ became obedient to the point of death,
even death on a cross.
Because of this, God greatly exalted him
and bestowed on him the name which is above every name.

GOSPEL

Year A: 2014, 2017, 2020, etc. (p. 44)
Year B: 2012, 2015, 2018, etc. (p. 56)
Year C: 2013, 2016, 2019, etc. (p. 66)

YEAR A   Matthew 26:14—27:66 *or* Shorter Form [ ] Matthew 27:11-54

The symbols in the following passion narrative represent:

    C.   Narrator;
    ✠   Christ;
    S.   speakers other than Christ;
    SS.   groups of speakers.

The Passion of our Lord Jesus Christ according to Matthew

C.   **One of the Twelve, who was called Judas Iscariot,**
      went to the chief priests and said,

S.   **"What are you willing to give me**
      if I hand him over to you?"

C.   **They paid him thirty pieces of silver,**
      and from that time on he looked for an opportunity
           to hand him over.

      On the first day of the Feast of Unleavened Bread,
           the disciples approached Jesus and said,

SS.   **"Where do you want us to prepare**
      for you to eat the Passover?"

C. He said,

✝ "Go into the city to a certain man and tell him,
'The teacher says, "My appointed time draws near;
    in your house I shall celebrate the Passover with
        my disciples."'"

C. The disciples then did as Jesus had ordered,
    and prepared the Passover.

When it was evening,
    he reclined at table with the Twelve.
And while they were eating, he said,

✝ "Amen, I say to you, one of you will betray me."

C. Deeply distressed at this,
    they began to say to him one after another,

S. "Surely it is not I, Lord?"

C. He said in reply,

✝ "He who has dipped his hand into the dish with me
    is the one who will betray me.
The Son of Man indeed goes, as it is written of him,
    but woe to that man by whom the Son of Man is
        betrayed.
It would be better for that man if he had never been
    born."

C. Then Judas, his betrayer, said in reply,

S. "Surely it is not I, Rabbi?"

C. He answered,

✝ "You have said so."

C. While they were eating,
    Jesus took bread, said the blessing,
    broke it, and giving it to his disciples said,

✝ "Take and eat; this is my body."

C. Then he took a cup, gave thanks, and gave it to
        them, saying,

✝ "Drink from it, all of you,
    for this is my blood of the covenant,
    which will be shed on behalf of many
    for the forgiveness of sins.

I tell you, from now on I shall not drink this fruit of
 the vine
  until the day when I drink it with you new
  in the kingdom of my Father."

C. Then, after singing a hymn,
  they went out to the Mount of Olives.

Then Jesus said to them,

✠ "This night all of you will have your faith in me
  shaken,
  for it is written:
   I will strike the shepherd,
    and the sheep of the flock will be dispersed;
  but after I have been raised up,
  I shall go before you to Galilee."

C. Peter said to him in reply,

S. "Though all may have their faith in you shaken,
  mine will never be."

C. Jesus said to him,

✠ "Amen, I say to you,
  this very night before the cock crows,
  you will deny me three times."

C. Peter said to him,

S. "Even though I should have to die with you,
  I will not deny you."

C. And all the disciples spoke likewise.

Then Jesus came with them to a place called
  Gethsemane,
  and he said to his disciples,

✠ "Sit here while I go over there and pray."

C. He took along Peter and the two sons of Zebedee,
  and began to feel sorrow and distress.
  Then he said to them,

✠ "My soul is sorrowful even to death.
 Remain here and keep watch with me."

C.   He advanced a little and fell prostrate in prayer,
        saying,
✝   "My Father, if it is possible,
          let this cup pass from me;
          yet, not as I will, but as you will."
C.   When he returned to his disciples he found them
        asleep.
     He said to Peter,
✝   "So you could not keep watch with me for one hour?
     Watch and pray that you may not undergo the test.
     The spirit is willing, but the flesh is weak."
C.   Withdrawing a second time, he prayed again,
✝   "My Father, if it is not possible that this cup pass
        without my drinking it, your will be done!"
C.   Then he returned once more and found them asleep,
        for they could not keep their eyes open.
     He left them and withdrew again and prayed a third
        time,
          saying the same thing again.
     Then he returned to his disciples and said to them,
✝   "Are you still sleeping and taking your rest?
     Behold, the hour is at hand
        when the Son of Man is to be handed over to sinners.
     Get up, let us go.
     Look, my betrayer is at hand."

C.   While he was still speaking,
        Judas, one of the Twelve, arrived,
          accompanied by a large crowd, with swords and
            clubs,
          who had come from the chief priests and the
            elders of the people.
     His betrayer had arranged a sign with them, saying,
S.   "The man I shall kiss is the one; arrest him."
C.   Immediately he went over to Jesus and said,
S.   "Hail, Rabbi!"
C.   and he kissed him.

Jesus answered him,

✠   "Friend, do what you have come for."

C. Then stepping forward they laid hands on Jesus and
       arrested him.
    And behold, one of those who accompanied Jesus
      put his hand to his sword, drew it,
        and struck the high priest's servant, cutting off
          his ear.
    Then Jesus said to him,

✠   "Put your sword back into its sheath,
      for all who take the sword will perish by the sword.
    Do you think that I cannot call upon my Father
      and he will not provide me at this moment
       with more than twelve legions of angels?
    But then how would the Scriptures be fulfilled
      which say that it must come to pass in this way?"

C. At that hour Jesus said to the crowds,

✠ "Have you come out as against a robber,
      with swords and clubs to seize me?
    Day after day I sat teaching in the temple area,
      yet you did not arrest me.
    But all this has come to pass
      that the writings of the prophets may be fulfilled."

C. Then all the disciples left him and fled.

    Those who had arrested Jesus led him away
      to Caiaphas the high priest,
       where the scribes and the elders were assembled.
    Peter was following him at a distance
      as far as the high priest's courtyard,
       and going inside he sat down with the servants to
         see the outcome.
    The chief priests and the entire Sanhedrin
      kept trying to obtain false testimony against Jesus
      in order to put him to death,
      but they found none,
      though many false witnesses came forward.

Finally two came forward who stated,

SS. "This man said, 'I can destroy the temple of God
and within three days rebuild it.'"

C. The high priest rose and addressed him,

S. "Have you no answer?
What are these men testifying against you?"

C. But Jesus was silent.
Then the high priest said to him,

S. "I order you to tell us under oath before the living
God
whether you are the Christ, the Son of God."

C. Jesus said to him in reply,

✠ "You have said so.
But I tell you:
From now on you will see 'the Son of Man
seated at the right hand of the Power'
and 'coming on the clouds of heaven.'"

C. Then the high priest tore his robes and said,

S. "He has blasphemed!
What further need have we of witnesses?
You have now heard the blasphemy;
what is your opinion?"

C. They said in reply,

SS. "He deserves to die!"

C. Then they spat in his face and struck him,
while some slapped him, saying,

SS. "Prophesy for us, Christ: who is it that struck you?"

C. Now Peter was sitting outside in the courtyard.
One of the maids came over to him and said,

S. "You too were with Jesus the Galilean."

C. But he denied it in front of everyone, saying,

S. "I do not know what you are talking about!"

C. As he went out to the gate, another girl saw him
and said to those who were there,

S. "This man was with Jesus the Nazorean."

C.   **Again he denied it with an oath,**

S.   **"I do not know the man!"**

C.   **A little later the bystanders came over and said to Peter,**

S.   **"Surely you too are one of them;**
even your speech gives you away."

C.   **At that he began to curse and to swear,**

S.   **"I do not know the man."**

C.   **And immediately a cock crowed.**
Then Peter remembered the word that Jesus had spoken:
"Before the cock crows you will deny me three times."
He went out and began to weep bitterly.

When it was morning,
all the chief priests and the elders of the people
took counsel against Jesus to put him to death.
They bound him, led him away,
and handed him over to Pilate, the governor.

Then Judas, his betrayer, seeing that Jesus had been condemned,
deeply regretted what he had done.
He returned the thirty pieces of silver
to the chief priests and elders, saying,

S.   **"I have sinned in betraying innocent blood."**

C.   **They said,**

SS. **"What is that to us?**
Look to it yourself."

C.   **Flinging the money into the temple,**
he departed and went off and hanged himself.
The chief priests gathered up the money, but said,

SS. **"It is not lawful to deposit this in the temple treasury,**
for it is the price of blood."

C.   **After consultation, they used it to buy the potter's field**
as a burial place for foreigners.

That is why that field even today is called the Field
of Blood.
Then was fulfilled what had been said through
Jeremiah the prophet,
And they took the thirty pieces of silver,
the value of a man with a price on his head,
a price set by some of the Israelites,
and they paid it out for the potter's field
just as the Lord had commanded me.

Now [Jesus stood before the governor, and he
questioned him,
S. "Are you the king of the Jews?"
C. Jesus said,
✠ "You say so."
C. And when he was accused by the chief priests and
elders,
he made no answer.
Then Pilate said to him,
S. "Do you not hear how many things they are
testifying against you?"
C. But he did not answer him one word,
so that the governor was greatly amazed.

Now on the occasion of the feast
the governor was accustomed to release to the
crowd
one prisoner whom they wished.
And at that time they had a notorious prisoner
called Barabbas.
So when they had assembled, Pilate said to them,
S. "Which one do you want me to release to you,
Barabbas, or Jesus called Christ?"
C. For he knew that it was out of envy
that they had handed him over.
While he was still seated on the bench,
his wife sent him a message,

"Have nothing to do with that righteous man.
I suffered much in a dream today because of him."

The chief priests and the elders persuaded the crowds
    to ask for Barabbas but to destroy Jesus.
The governor said to them in reply,

S.   "Which of the two do you want me to release to
        you?"
C. They answered,
SS. "Barabbas!"
C. Pilate said to them,
S.   "Then what shall I do with Jesus called Christ?"
C. They all said,
SS. "Let him be crucified!"
C. But he said,
S. "Why? What evil has he done?"
C. They only shouted the louder,
SS. "Let him be crucified!"
C. When Pilate saw that he was not succeeding at all,
    but that a riot was breaking out instead,
    he took water and washed his hands in the sight
        of the crowd, saying,
S. "I am innocent of this man's blood.
Look to it yourselves."
C. And the whole people said in reply,
SS. "His blood be upon us and upon our children."
C. Then he released Barabbas to them,
    but after he had Jesus scourged,
    he handed him over to be crucified.

Then the soldiers of the governor took Jesus inside
    the praetorium
    and gathered the whole cohort around him.
They stripped off his clothes
    and threw a scarlet military cloak about him.
Weaving a crown out of thorns, they placed it on his
    head,
    and a reed in his right hand.

And kneeling before him, they mocked him, saying,

SS. "Hail, King of the Jews!"

C. They spat upon him and took the reed
and kept striking him on the head.
And when they had mocked him,
they stripped him of the cloak,
dressed him in his own clothes,
and led him off to crucify him.

As they were going out, they met a Cyrenian named
Simon;
this man they pressed into service
to carry his cross.

And when they came to a place called Golgotha
—which means Place of the Skull—,
they gave Jesus wine to drink mixed with gall.
But when he had tasted it, he refused to drink.
After they had crucified him,
they divided his garments by casting lots;
then they sat down and kept watch over him there.
And they placed over his head the written charge
against him:
This is Jesus, the King of the Jews.
Two revolutionaries were crucified with him,
one on his right and the other on his left.
Those passing by reviled him, shaking their heads
and saying,

SS. "You who would destroy the temple and rebuild it in
three days,
save yourself, if you are the Son of God,
and come down from the cross!"

C. Likewise the chief priests with the scribes and elders
mocked him and said,

SS. "He saved others; he cannot save himself.
So he is the king of Israel!
Let him come down from the cross now,
and we will believe in him.

He trusted in God;
　　let him deliver him now if he wants him.
For he said, 'I am the Son of God.'"

C.　The revolutionaries who were crucified with him
　　　also kept abusing him in the same way.

From noon onward, darkness came over the whole
　　land
　　until three in the afternoon.
And about three o'clock Jesus cried out in a loud voice,

☩　　　*"Eli, Eli, lema sabachthani?"*

C.　which means,

☩　　　"My God, my God, why have you forsaken me?"

C.　Some of the bystanders who heard it said,

SS.　"This one is calling for Elijah."

C.　Immediately one of them ran to get a sponge;
　　　he soaked it in wine, and putting it on a reed,
　　　gave it to him to drink.
But the rest said,

SS.　"Wait, let us see if Elijah comes to save him."

C.　But Jesus cried out again in a loud voice,
　　　and gave up his spirit.

Here all kneel and pause for a short time.

And behold, the veil of the sanctuary
　　was torn in two from top to bottom.
The earth quaked, rocks were split, tombs were opened,
　　and the bodies of many saints who had fallen
　　　asleep were raised.
And coming forth from their tombs after his
　　resurrection,
　　they entered the holy city and appeared to many.
The centurion and the men with him who were
　　　keeping watch over Jesus
　　feared greatly when they saw the earthquake
　　and all that was happening, and they said,

SS.　"Truly, this was the Son of God!"]

C.   There were many women there, looking on from a
           distance,
       who had followed Jesus from Galilee, ministering
           to him.
       Among them were Mary Magdalene and Mary the
           mother of James and Joseph,
       and the mother of the sons of Zebedee.

     When it was evening,
           there came a rich man from Arimathea named
               Joseph,
       who was himself a disciple of Jesus.
     He went to Pilate and asked for the body of Jesus;
           then Pilate ordered it to be handed over.
     Taking the body, Joseph wrapped it in clean linen
           and laid it in his new tomb that he had hewn in
               the rock.
     Then he rolled a huge stone across the entrance to
           the tomb and departed.
     But Mary Magdalene and the other Mary
           remained sitting there, facing the tomb.

     The next day, the one following the day of preparation,
           the chief priests and the Pharisees
       gathered before Pilate and said,

S.   "Sir, we remember that this impostor while still
           alive said,
       'After three days I will be raised up.'
     Give orders, then, that the grave be secured until the
           third day,
       lest his disciples come and steal him and say to
               the people,
       'He has been raised from the dead.'
     This last imposture would be worse than the first."

C.   Pilate said to them,

S.   "The guard is yours;
       go, secure it as best you can."

C.   **So they went and secured the tomb**
     by fixing a seal to the stone and setting the guard.

The Gospel of the Lord. All: **Praise to you, Lord Jesus Christ.**

YEAR B   Mark 14:1—15:47 *or* Shorter Form [ ] Mark 15:1-39

The symbols in the following passion narrative represent:

    C.   Narrator;
    ✝   Christ;
    S.   speakers other than Christ;
    SS. groups of speakers.

The Passion of our Lord Jesus Christ according to Mark

C.   **The Passover and the Feast of Unleavened Bread**
     were to take place in two days' time.
     So the chief priests and the scribes were seeking a way
     to arrest him by treachery and put him to death.
     They said,
SS. **"Not during the festival,**
     for fear that there may be a riot among the people."

C.   **When he was in Bethany reclining at table**
     in the house of Simon the leper,
     a woman came with an alabaster jar of perfumed oil,
     costly genuine spikenard.
     She broke the alabaster jar and poured it on his head.
     There were some who were indignant.
SS. **"Why has there been this waste of perfumed oil?**
     It could have been sold for more than three hundred
     days' wages
     and the money given to the poor."
C.   **They were infuriated with her.**
     Jesus said,
✝   **"Let her alone.**
     Why do you make trouble for her?
     She has done a good thing for me.
     The poor you will always have with you,
     and whenever you wish you can do good to them,
     but you will not always have me.

She has done what she could.
She has anticipated anointing my body for burial.
Amen, I say to you,
> wherever the gospel is proclaimed to the whole
>> world,
> what she has done will be told in memory of her."

C. Then Judas Iscariot, one of the Twelve,
went off to the chief priests to hand him over to them.
When they heard him they were pleased and promised
> to pay him money.
Then he looked for an opportunity to hand him over.

On the first day of the Feast of Unleavened Bread,
> when they sacrificed the Passover lamb,
> his disciples said to him,

SS. "Where do you want us to go
> and prepare for you to eat the Passover?"

C. He sent two of his disciples and said to them,

✝ "Go into the city and a man will meet you,
> carrying a jar of water.
Follow him.
Wherever he enters, say to the master of the house,
> 'The Teacher says, "Where is my guest room
> where I may eat the Passover with my disciples?"'
Then he will show you a large upper room furnished
> and ready.
Make the preparations for us there."

C. The disciples then went off, entered the city,
> and found it just as he had told them;
> and they prepared the Passover.

When it was evening, he came with the Twelve.
And as they reclined at table and were eating,
> Jesus said,

✝ "Amen, I say to you, one of you will betray me,
one who is eating with me."

C. They began to be distressed and to say to him,
      one by one,

S.   "Surely it is not I?"

C. He said to them,

✠   "One of the Twelve, the one who dips with me into
        the dish.
    For the Son of Man indeed goes, as it is written of him,
        but woe to that man by whom the Son of Man is
          betrayed.
    It would be better for that man if he had never been
        born."

C. While they were eating,
      he took bread, said the blessing,
      broke it, and gave it to them, and said,

✠   "Take it; this is my body."

C. Then he took a cup, gave thanks, and gave it to them,
      and they all drank from it.
    He said to them,

✠   "This is my blood of the covenant,
      which will be shed for many.
    Amen, I say to you,
      I shall not drink again the fruit of the vine
      until the day when I drink it new in the kingdom
        of God."

C. Then, after singing a hymn,
      they went out to the Mount of Olives.

    Then Jesus said to them,

✠   "All of you will have your faith shaken, for it is
          written:
      I will strike the shepherd,
        and the sheep will be dispersed.
    But after I have been raised up,
      I shall go before you to Galilee."

C. Peter said to him,

S.   "Even though all should have their faith shaken,
      mine will not be."

C.   Then Jesus said to him,

✠   "Amen, I say to you,
       this very night before the cock crows twice
       you will deny me three times."

C.   But he vehemently replied,

S.   "Even though I should have to die with you,
       I will not deny you."

C.   And they all spoke similarly.

     Then they came to a place named Gethsemane,
          and he said to his disciples,

✠   "Sit here while I pray."

C.   He took with him Peter, James, and John,
          and began to be troubled and distressed.
     Then he said to them,

✠   "My soul is sorrowful even to death.
       Remain here and keep watch."

C.   He advanced a little and fell to the ground and prayed
          that if it were possible the hour might pass by him;
               he said,

✠   "Abba, Father, all things are possible to you.
     Take this cup away from me,
          but not what I will but what you will."

C.   When he returned he found them asleep.
     He said to Peter,

✠   "Simon, are you asleep?
     Could you not keep watch for one hour?
     Watch and pray that you may not undergo the test.
     The spirit is willing but the flesh is weak."

C.   Withdrawing again, he prayed, saying the same thing.
     Then he returned once more and found them asleep,
          for they could not keep their eyes open
          and did not know what to answer him.
     He returned a third time and said to them,

✠   "Are you still sleeping and taking your rest?
     It is enough. The hour has come.
     Behold, the Son of Man is to be handed over to sinners.

Get up, let us go.
See, my betrayer is at hand."

C.   Then, while he was still speaking,
    Judas, one of the Twelve, arrived,
    accompanied by a crowd with swords and clubs
    who had come from the chief priests,
    the scribes, and the elders.
His betrayer had arranged a signal with them, saying,

S.   "The man I shall kiss is the one;
    arrest him and lead him away securely."

C.   He came and immediately went over to him and said,

S.   "Rabbi."

C.   And he kissed him.
At this they laid hands on him and arrested him.
One of the bystanders drew his sword,
    struck the high priest's servant, and cut off his ear.
Jesus said to them in reply,

✠   "Have you come out as against a robber,
    with swords and clubs, to seize me?
Day after day I was with you teaching in the temple
      area,
    yet you did not arrest me;
    but that the Scriptures may be fulfilled."

C.   And they all left him and fled.
Now a young man followed him
    wearing nothing but a linen cloth about his body.
They seized him,
    but he left the cloth behind and ran off naked.

They led Jesus away to the high priest,
    and all the chief priests and the elders and the
      scribes came together.
Peter followed him at a distance into the high priest's
      courtyard
    and was seated with the guards, warming himself
      at the fire.

The chief priests and the entire Sanhedrin
   kept trying to obtain testimony against Jesus
   in order to put him to death, but they found none.
Many gave false witness against him,
   but their testimony did not agree.
Some took the stand and testified falsely against him,
     alleging,

SS. "We heard him say,
   'I will destroy this temple made with hands
   and within three days I will build another
   not made with hands.'"

C. Even so their testimony did not agree.
The high priest rose before the assembly and
     questioned Jesus, saying,

S. "Have you no answer?
What are these men testifying against you?"

C. But he was silent and answered nothing.
Again the high priest asked him and said to him,

S.   "Are you the Christ, the son of the Blessed One?"

C. Then Jesus answered,

✝ "I am;
   and 'you will see the Son of Man
     seated at the right hand of the Power
     and coming with the clouds of heaven.'"

C. At that the high priest tore his garments and said,

S.   "What further need have we of witnesses?
You have heard the blasphemy.
What do you think?"

C. They all condemned him as deserving to die.
Some began to spit on him.
They blindfolded him and struck him and said to him,

SS. "Prophesy!"

C. And the guards greeted him with blows.

While Peter was below in the courtyard,
   one of the high priest's maids came along.

Seeing Peter warming himself,
  she looked intently at him and said,

S.   "You too were with the Nazarene, Jesus."

C.   But he denied it saying,

S.   "I neither know nor understand what you are
    talking about."

C.   So he went out into the outer court.
  Then the cock crowed.
  The maid saw him and began again to say to the
    bystanders,

S.   "This man is one of them."

C.   Once again he denied it.
  A little later the bystanders said to Peter once more,

SS. "Surely you are one of them; for you too are a
    Galilean."

C.   He began to curse and to swear,

S.   "I do not know this man about whom you are
    talking."

C.   And immediately a cock crowed a second time.
  Then Peter remembered the word that Jesus had
    said to him,

✝   "Before the cock crows twice you will deny me
    three times."

C.   He broke down and wept.

[As soon as morning came,
  the chief priests with the elders and the scribes,
  that is, the whole Sanhedrin, held a council.
  They bound Jesus, led him away, and handed him
    over to Pilate.
  Pilate questioned him,

S.   "Are you the king of the Jews?"

C.   He said to him in reply,

✝   "You say so."

C.   The chief priests accused him of many things.
  Again Pilate questioned him,

S.   "Have you no answer?
       See how many things they accuse you of."
C. Jesus gave him no further answer, so that Pilate
           was amazed.

    Now on the occasion of the feast he used to release
           to them
        one prisoner whom they requested.
    A man called Barabbas was then in prison
        along with the rebels who had committed murder
           in a rebellion.
    The crowd came forward and began to ask him
        to do for them as he was accustomed.
    Pilate answered,
S.   "Do you want me to release to you the king of
           the Jews?"
C. For he knew that it was out of envy
        that the chief priests had handed him over.
    But the chief priests stirred up the crowd
        to have him release Barabbas for them instead.
    Pilate again said to them in reply,
S. "Then what do you want me to do
        with the man you call the king of the Jews?"
C. They shouted again,
SS. "Crucify him."
C. Pilate said to them,
S. "Why? What evil has he done?"
C. They only shouted the louder,
SS. "Crucify him."
C. So Pilate, wishing to satisfy the crowd,
        released Barabbas to them and, after he had Jesus
           scourged,
        handed him over to be crucified.

    The soldiers led him away inside the palace,
        that is, the praetorium, and assembled the whole
           cohort.

They clothed him in purple and,
    weaving a crown of thorns, placed it on him.
They began to salute him with,

SS. "Hail, King of the Jews!"

C.   and kept striking his head with a reed and
        spitting upon him.
They knelt before him in homage.
And when they had mocked him,
    they stripped him of the purple cloak,
    dressed him in his own clothes,
    and led him out to crucify him.

They pressed into service a passer-by, Simon,
    a Cyrenian, who was coming in from the country,
    the father of Alexander and Rufus,
    to carry his cross.

They brought him to the place of Golgotha
—which is translated Place of the Skull—.
They gave him wine drugged with myrrh,
    but he did not take it.
Then they crucified him and divided his garments
    by casting lots for them to see what each should take.
It was nine o'clock in the morning when they
        crucified him.
The inscription of the charge against him read,
"The King of the Jews."
With him they crucified two revolutionaries,
    one on his right and one on his left.
Those passing by reviled him,
    shaking their heads and saying,

SS. "Aha! You who would destroy the temple
      and rebuild it in three days,
        save yourself by coming down from the cross."

C. Likewise the chief priests, with the scribes,
      mocked him among themselves and said,

SS. "He saved others; he cannot save himself.

Let the Christ, the King of Israel,
>come down now from the cross
>that we may see and believe."

C. Those who were crucified with him also kept
>abusing him.

At noon darkness came over the whole land
>until three in the afternoon.
And at three o'clock Jesus cried out in a loud voice,

✝ *"Eloi, Eloi, lema sabachthani?"*

C. which is translated,

✝ "My God, my God, why have you forsaken me?"

C. Some of the bystanders who heard it said,

SS. "Look, he is calling Elijah."

C. One of them ran, soaked a sponge with wine, put it
>on a reed
>and gave it to him to drink saying,

S. "Wait, let us see if Elijah comes to take him down."

C. Jesus gave a loud cry and breathed his last.

Here all kneel and pause for a short time.

The veil of the sanctuary was torn in two from top
>to bottom.
When the centurion who stood facing him
>saw how he breathed his last he said,

S. "Truly this man was the Son of God!"]

C. There were also women looking on from a distance.
Among them were Mary Magdalene,
>Mary the mother of the younger James and of Joses,
>and Salome.
These women had followed him when he was in Galilee
>and ministered to him.
There were also many other women
>who had come up with him to Jerusalem.

When it was already evening,
>since it was the day of preparation,
>the day before the sabbath, Joseph of Arimathea,

a distinguished member of the council,
who was himself awaiting the kingdom of God,
came and courageously went to Pilate
and asked for the body of Jesus.
Pilate was amazed that he was already dead.
He summoned the centurion
and asked him if Jesus had already died.
And when he learned of it from the centurion,
he gave the body to Joseph.
Having bought a linen cloth, he took him down,
wrapped him in the linen cloth,
and laid him in a tomb that had been hewn out of
the rock.
Then he rolled a stone against the entrance to the tomb.
Mary Magdalene and Mary the mother of Joses
watched where he was laid.

The Gospel of the Lord. All: **Praise to you, Lord Jesus Christ.**

YEAR C   Luke 22:14—23:56 *or* Shorter Form [ ] Luke 23:1-49

The symbols in the following passion narrative represent:

C.   Narrator;
✛   Christ;
S.   speakers other than Christ;
SS.   groups of speakers.

The Passion of our Lord Jesus Christ according to Luke

C.   **When the hour came,**
     Jesus took his place at table with the apostles.
     He said to them,
✛   **"I have eagerly desired to eat this Passover with**
             you before I suffer,
         for, I tell you, I shall not eat it again
         until there is fulfillment in the kingdom of God."
C.   **Then he took a cup, gave thanks, and said,**
✛   **"Take this and share it among yourselves;**
         for I tell you that from this time on

I shall not drink of the fruit of the vine
until the kingdom of God comes."

C. Then he took the bread, said the blessing,
broke it, and gave it to them, saying,

✠ "This is my body, which will be given for you;
do this in memory of me."

C. And likewise the cup after they had eaten, saying,

✠ "This cup is the new covenant in my blood,
which will be shed for you.

"And yet behold, the hand of the one who is to
betray me
is with me on the table;
for the Son of Man indeed goes as it has been
determined;
but woe to that man by whom he is betrayed."

C. And they began to debate among themselves
who among them would do such a deed.

Then an argument broke out among them
about which of them should be regarded as the
greatest.
He said to them,

✠ "The kings of the Gentiles lord it over them
and those in authority over them are addressed as
'Benefactors';
but among you it shall not be so.
Rather, let the greatest among you be as the youngest,
and the leader as the servant.
For who is greater:
the one seated at table or the one who serves?
Is it not the one seated at table?
I am among you as the one who serves.
It is you who have stood by me in my trials;
and I confer a kingdom on you,
just as my Father has conferred one on me,
that you may eat and drink at my table in my
kingdom;

and you will sit on thrones
 judging the twelve tribes of Israel.

"Simon, Simon, behold Satan has demanded
 to sift all of you like wheat,
  but I have prayed that your own faith may not fail;
 and once you have turned back,
 you must strengthen your brothers."

C. He said to him,

S. "Lord, I am prepared to go to prison and to die
   with you."

C. But he replied,

☩ "I tell you, Peter, before the cock crows this day,
  you will deny three times that you know me."

C. He said to them,

☩ "When I sent you forth without a money bag or
   a sack or sandals,
  were you in need of anything?"

S. "No, nothing,"

C. they replied.
 He said to them,

☩ "But now one who has a money bag should take it,
  and likewise a sack,
  and one who does not have a sword
  should sell his cloak and buy one.
 For I tell you that this Scripture must be fulfilled in me,
  namely, *He was counted among the wicked*;
   and indeed what is written about me is coming to
   fulfillment."

C. Then they said,

SS. "Lord, look, there are two swords here."

C. But he replied,

☩ "It is enough!"

C. Then going out, he went, as was his custom, to the
  Mount of Olives,
  and the disciples followed him.

When he arrived at the place he said to them,

✠   "Pray that you may not undergo the test."

C.   After withdrawing about a stone's throw from them
         and kneeling,
      he prayed, saying,

✠   "Father, if you are willing,
      take this cup away from me;
      still, not my will but yours be done."

C.   And to strengthen him an angel from heaven
         appeared to him.
   He was in such agony and he prayed so fervently
      that his sweat became like drops of blood
      falling on the ground.
   When he rose from prayer and returned to his
         disciples,
      he found them sleeping from grief.
   He said to them,

✠   "Why are you sleeping?
   Get up and pray that you may not undergo the test."

C.   While he was still speaking, a crowd approached
         and in front was one of the Twelve, a man named
            Judas.
   He went up to Jesus to kiss him.
   Jesus said to him,

✠   "Judas, are you betraying the Son of Man with a
         kiss?"

C.   His disciples realized what was about to happen,
         and they asked,

SS.   "Lord, shall we strike with a sword?"

C.   And one of them struck the high priest's servant
         and cut off his right ear.
   But Jesus said in reply,

✠   "Stop, no more of this!"

C.   Then he touched the servant's ear and healed him.
   And Jesus said to the chief priests and temple guards
         and elders who had come for him,

✝   "Have you come out as against a robber, with
swords and clubs?
Day after day I was with you in the temple area,
and you did not seize me;
but this is your hour, the time for the power of
darkness."

C.   After arresting him they led him away
and took him into the house of the high priest;
Peter was following at a distance.
They lit a fire in the middle of the courtyard and sat
around it,
and Peter sat down with them.
When a maid saw him seated in the light,
she looked intently at him and said,

S.   "This man too was with him."

C.   But he denied it saying,

S.   "Woman, I do not know him."

C.   A short while later someone else saw him and said,

S.   "You too are one of them";

C.   but Peter answered,

S.   "My friend, I am not."

C.   About an hour later, still another insisted,

S.   "Assuredly, this man too was with him,
for he also is a Galilean."

C.   But Peter said,

S.   "My friend, I do not know what you are talking
about."

C.   Just as he was saying this, the cock crowed,
and the Lord turned and looked at Peter;
and Peter remembered the word of the Lord,
how he had said to him,
"Before the cock crows today, you will deny me
three times."
He went out and began to weep bitterly.
The men who held Jesus in custody were ridiculing
and beating him.

They blindfolded him and questioned him, saying,

SS.   "Prophesy! Who is it that struck you?"

C.   And they reviled him in saying many other things
          against him.

When day came the council of elders of the people
          met,
      both chief priests and scribes,
      and they brought him before their Sanhedrin.
They said,

SS.   "If you are the Christ, tell us,"

C.   but he replied to them,

✝   "If I tell you, you will not believe,
      and if I question, you will not respond.
But from this time on the Son of Man will be seated
          at the right hand of the power of God."

C.   They all asked,

SS.   "Are you then the Son of God?"

C.   He replied to them,

✝   "You say that I am."

C.   Then they said,

SS.   "What further need have we for testimony?
We have heard it from his own mouth."

C.   Then the whole assembly of them arose and brought
          him before Pilate.

      [(The elders of the people, chief priests and scribes,
          arose and brought Jesus before Pilate.)
They brought charges against him, saying,

SS.   "We found this man misleading our people;
      he opposes the payment of taxes to Caesar
      and maintains that he is the Christ, a king."

C.   Pilate asked him,

S.   "Are you the king of the Jews?"

C.   He said to him in reply,

✝   "You say so."

C.   Pilate then addressed the chief priests and the crowds,

S.   "I find this man not guilty."

C.   But they were adamant and said,

SS.   "He is inciting the people with his teaching
          throughout all Judea,
      from Galilee where he began even to here."

C.   On hearing this Pilate asked if the man was a
        Galilean;
    and upon learning that he was under Herod's
        jurisdiction,
    he sent him to Herod who was in Jerusalem at
        that time.
Herod was very glad to see Jesus;
    he had been wanting to see him for a long time,
    for he had heard about him
    and had been hoping to see him perform some sign.
He questioned him at length,
    but he gave him no answer.
The chief priests and scribes, meanwhile,
    stood by accusing him harshly.
Herod and his soldiers treated him contemptuously
      and mocked him,
    and after clothing him in resplendent garb,
    he sent him back to Pilate.
Herod and Pilate became friends that very day,
    even though they had been enemies formerly.
Pilate then summoned the chief priests, the rulers,
      and the people
    and said to them,

S.   "You brought this man to me
    and accused him of inciting the people to revolt.
I have conducted my investigation in your presence
    and have not found this man guilty
    of the charges you have brought against him,
    nor did Herod, for he sent him back to us.
So no capital crime has been committed by him.
Therefore I shall have him flogged and then release
      him."

C.   But all together they shouted out,

SS.   "Away with this man!
      Release Barabbas to us."

C.   —Now Barabbas had been imprisoned for a rebellion
      that had taken place in the city and for murder.—
    Again Pilate addressed them, still wishing to release
        Jesus,
      but they continued their shouting,

SS.   "Crucify him! Crucify him!"

C.   Pilate addressed them a third time,

S.   "What evil has this man done?
      I found him guilty of no capital crime.
    Therefore I shall have him flogged and then release
        him."

C.   With loud shouts, however,
      they persisted in calling for his crucifixion,
      and their voices prevailed.
    The verdict of Pilate was that their demand should
        be granted.
    So he released the man who had been imprisoned
      for rebellion and murder, for whom they asked,
      and he handed Jesus over to them to deal with as
        they wished.

    As they led him away
      they took hold of a certain Simon, a Cyrenian,
      who was coming in from the country;
      and after laying the cross on him,
      they made him carry it behind Jesus.
    A large crowd of people followed Jesus,
      including many women who mourned and
        lamented him.
    Jesus turned to them and said,

✠   "Daughters of Jerusalem, do not weep for me;
      weep instead for yourselves and for your children
      for indeed, the days are coming when people will
        say,

'Blessed are the barren,
the wombs that never bore
and the breasts that never nursed.'
At that time people will say to the mountains,
'Fall upon us!'
and to the hills, 'Cover us!'
for if these things are done when the wood is green
what will happen when it is dry?"

C. Now two others, both criminals,
were led away with him to be executed.

When they came to the place called the Skull,
they crucified him and the criminals there,
one on his right, the other on his left.
Then Jesus said,

✝ "Father, forgive them, they know not what they do."

C. They divided his garments by casting lots.
The people stood by and watched;
the rulers, meanwhile, sneered at him and said,

SS. "He saved others, let him save himself
if he is the chosen one, the Christ of God."

C. Even the soldiers jeered at him.
As they approached to offer him wine they called out,

SS. "If you are King of the Jews, save yourself."

C. Above him there was an inscription that read,
"This is the King of the Jews."

Now one of the criminals hanging there reviled Jesus,
saying,

S. "Are you not the Christ?
Save yourself and us."

C. The other, however, rebuking him, said in reply,

S. "Have you no fear of God,
for you are subject to the same condemnation?
And indeed, we have been condemned justly,
for the sentence we received corresponds to our
crimes,
but this man has done nothing criminal."

C.   Then he said,

S.   "Jesus, remember me when you come into your
             kingdom."

C.   He replied to him,

✠   "Amen, I say to you,
             today you will be with me in Paradise."

C.   It was now about noon and darkness came over the
             whole land
         until three in the afternoon
         because of an eclipse of the sun.
     Then the veil of the temple was torn down the middle.
     Jesus cried out in a loud voice,

✠   "Father, into your hands I commend my spirit";

C.   and when he had said this he breathed his last.

Here all kneel and pause for a short time.

C.   The centurion who witnessed what had happened
             glorified God and said,

S.   "This man was innocent beyond doubt."

C.   When all the people who had gathered for this
             spectacle
         saw what had happened,
         they returned home beating their breasts;
         but all his acquaintances stood at a distance,
         including the women who had followed him
             from Galilee
         and saw these events.]

Now there was a virtuous and righteous man named
         Joseph who,
     though he was a member of the council,
     had not consented to their plan of action.
He came from the Jewish town of Arimathea
     and was awaiting the kingdom of God.
He went to Pilate and asked for the body of Jesus.
After he had taken the body down,
     he wrapped it in a linen cloth

and laid him in a rock-hewn tomb
in which no one had yet been buried.
It was the day of preparation,
and the sabbath was about to begin.
The women who had come from Galilee with him
followed behind,
and when they had seen the tomb
and the way in which his body was laid in it,
they returned and prepared spices and
perfumed oils.
Then they rested on the sabbath according to the
commandment.

The Gospel of the Lord. All: **Praise to you, Lord Jesus Christ.**

PRAYER OVER THE OFFERINGS
Through the Passion of your Only Begotten Son, O Lord,
may our reconciliation with you be near at hand,
so that, though we do not merit it by our own deeds,
yet by this sacrifice made once for all,
we may feel already the effects of your mercy.
Through Christ our Lord. All: **Amen.**

COMMUNION ANTIPHON (Matthew 26:42)
Father, if this chalice cannot pass without my drinking it,
your will be done.

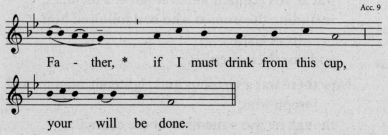

Acc. 9

Fa - ther, * if I must drink from this cup,

your will be done.

Adapted by Paul Ford, © 1999. Published and administered by Liturgical Press, Collegeville, MN 56321.

or:

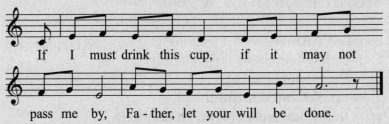

If I must drink this cup, if it may not
pass me by, Fa-ther, let your will be done.

PRAYER AFTER COMMUNION
Nourished with these sacred gifts,
we humbly beseech you, O Lord,
that, just as through the death of your Son
you have brought us to hope for what we believe,
so by his Resurrection
you may lead us to where you call.
Through Christ our Lord. All: **Amen.**

PRAYER OVER THE PEOPLE
Look, we pray, O Lord, on this your family,
for whom our Lord Jesus Christ
did not hesitate to be delivered into the hands of the wicked
and submit to the agony of the Cross.
Who lives and reigns for ever and ever. All: **Amen.**

MONDAY OF HOLY WEEK

ENTRANCE ANTIPHON (Cf. Psalm 35[34]:1-2; 140[139]:8)
Contend, O Lord, with my contenders;
fight those who fight me.
Take up your buckler and shield;
arise in my defense, Lord, my mighty help.

COLLECT
Grant, we pray, almighty God,
that, though in our weakness we fail,
we may be revived through the Passion of your Only Begotten Son.
Who lives and reigns with you in the unity of the Holy Spirit,
one God, for ever and ever. All: **Amen.**

READING I (L 257)   Isaiah 42:1-7

A reading from the Book of the Prophet Isaiah

Here is my servant whom I uphold,
  my chosen one with whom I am pleased,
Upon whom I have put my Spirit;
  he shall bring forth justice to the nations,
Not crying out, not shouting,
  not making his voice heard in the street.
A bruised reed he shall not break,
  and a smoldering wick he shall not quench,
Until he establishes justice on the earth;
  the coastlands will wait for his teaching.

Thus says God, the LORD,
  who created the heavens and stretched them out,
  who spreads out the earth with its crops,
Who gives breath to its people
  and spirit to those who walk on it:
I, the LORD, have called you for the victory of justice,
  I have grasped you by the hand;
I formed you, and set you
  as a covenant of the people,
  a light for the nations,

To open the eyes of the blind,
to bring out prisoners from confinement,
and from the dungeon, those who live in darkness.

The word of the Lord. All: **Thanks be to God.**

RESPONSORIAL PSALM 27

Acc. 11

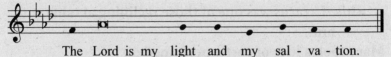

The Lord is my light and my sal - va - tion.

Music: Anthony Ruff, OSB, b. 1963, © 2008, Order of Saint Benedict,
administered by Liturgical Press, Collegeville, MN 56321. All rights reserved.

Psalm 27:1, 2, 3, 13-14

R︎︎. (1a) **The Lord is my light and my salvation.**

The LORD is my light and my salvation;
whom should I fear?
The LORD is my life's refuge;
of whom should I be afraid? R︎︎.

When evildoers come at me
to devour my flesh,
My foes and my enemies
themselves stumble and fall. R︎︎.

Though an army encamp against me,
my heart will not fear;
Though war be waged upon me,
even then will I trust. R︎︎.

I believe that I shall see the bounty of the LORD
in the land of the living.
Wait for the LORD with courage;
be stouthearted, and wait for the LORD. R︎︎.

VERSE BEFORE THE GOSPEL
Hail to you, our King;
you alone are compassionate with our faults.

GOSPEL   John 12:1-11

✠ A reading from the holy Gospel according to John

Six days before Passover Jesus came to Bethany,
    where Lazarus was, whom Jesus had raised from the
        dead.
They gave a dinner for him there, and Martha served,
    while Lazarus was one of those reclining at table with
        him.
Mary took a liter of costly perfumed oil
    made from genuine aromatic nard
    and anointed the feet of Jesus and dried them with
        her hair;
    the house was filled with the fragrance of the oil.
Then Judas the Iscariot, one of his disciples,
    and the one who would betray him, said,
    "Why was this oil not sold for three hundred days'
        wages
    and given to the poor?"
He said this not because he cared about the poor
    but because he was a thief and held the money bag
    and used to steal the contributions.
So Jesus said, "Leave her alone.
Let her keep this for the day of my burial.
You always have the poor with you, but you do not
    always have me."

The large crowd of the Jews found out that he was there
    and came,
    not only because of him, but also to see Lazarus,
    whom he had raised from the dead.
And the chief priests plotted to kill Lazarus too,
    because many of the Jews were turning away
    and believing in Jesus because of him.

The Gospel of the Lord. All: **Praise to you, Lord Jesus Christ.**

PRAYER OVER THE OFFERINGS
Look graciously, O Lord,
upon the sacred mysteries we celebrate here,
and may what you have mercifully provided
to cancel the judgment we incurred
bear for us fruit in eternal life.
Through Christ our Lord. All: **Amen.**

COMMUNION ANTIPHON (Cf. Psalm 102[101]:3)
Do not hide your face from me in the day of my distress.
Turn your ear towards me; on the day when I call, speedily
    answer me.

PRAYER AFTER COMMUNION
Visit your people, O Lord, we pray,
and with ever-watchful love
look upon the hearts dedicated to you by means of these sacred
    mysteries,
so that under your protection
we may keep safe this remedy of eternal salvation,
which by your mercy we have received.
Through Christ our Lord. All: **Amen.**

TUESDAY OF HOLY WEEK

ENTRANCE ANTIPHON (Cf. Psalm 27[26]:12)
Do not leave me to the will of my foes, O Lord,
for false witnesses rise up against me
and they breathe out violence.

COLLECT
Almighty ever-living God,
grant us so to celebrate
the mysteries of the Lord's Passion
that we may merit to receive your pardon.
Through our Lord Jesus Christ, your Son,
who lives and reigns with you in the unity of the Holy Spirit,
one God, for ever and ever. All: **Amen.**

READING I (L 258)   Isaiah 49:1-6

A reading from the Book of the Prophet Isaiah

Hear me, O islands,
listen, O distant peoples.
The LORD called me from birth,
from my mother's womb he gave me my name.
He made of me a sharp-edged sword
and concealed me in the shadow of his arm.
He made me a polished arrow,
in his quiver he hid me.
You are my servant, he said to me,
Israel, through whom I show my glory.

Though I thought I had toiled in vain,
and for nothing, uselessly, spent my strength,
Yet my reward is with the LORD,
my recompense is with my God.
For now the LORD has spoken
who formed me as his servant from the womb,
That Jacob may be brought back to him
and Israel gathered to him;
And I am made glorious in the sight of the LORD,
and my God is now my strength!

It is too little, he says, for you to be my servant,
  to raise up the tribes of Jacob,
   and restore the survivors of Israel;
I will make you a light to the nations,
  that my salvation may reach to the ends of the earth.

The word of the Lord. All: **Thanks be to God.**

RESPONSORIAL PSALM 71

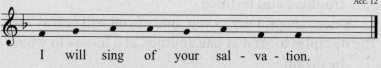

Acc. 12

I   will   sing   of   your   sal - va - tion.

Psalm 71:1-2, 3-4a, 5ab-6ab, 15 and 17

℟. (*See* 15ab) **I will sing of your salvation.**

In you, O LORD, I take refuge;
  let me never be put to shame.
In your justice rescue me, and deliver me;
  incline your ear to me, and save me. ℟.

Be my rock of refuge,
  a stronghold to give me safety,
  for you are my rock and my fortress.
O my God, rescue me from the hand of the wicked. ℟.

For you are my hope, O Lord;
  my trust, O God, from my youth.
On you I depend from birth;
  from my mother's womb you are my strength. ℟.

My mouth shall declare your justice,
  day by day your salvation.
O God, you have taught me from my youth,
  and till the present I proclaim your wondrous deeds. ℟.

Hail to you, our King, obedient to the Father;
you were led to your crucifixion like a gentle lamb to the
   slaughter.

GOSPEL   John 13:21-33, 36-38

✠ **A reading from the holy Gospel according to John**

**Reclining at table with his disciples, Jesus was deeply
      troubled and testified,
   "Amen, amen, I say to you, one of you will betray me."
The disciples looked at one another, at a loss as to whom
      he meant.
One of his disciples, the one whom Jesus loved,
   was reclining at Jesus' side.
So Simon Peter nodded to him to find out whom he meant.
He leaned back against Jesus' chest and said to him,
   "Master, who is it?"
Jesus answered,
   "It is the one to whom I hand the morsel after I have
         dipped it."
So he dipped the morsel and took it and handed it to Judas,
   son of Simon the Iscariot.
After Judas took the morsel, Satan entered him.
So Jesus said to him, "What you are going to do, do
      quickly."
Now none of those reclining at table realized why he
      said this to him.
Some thought that since Judas kept the money bag,
      Jesus had told him,
   "Buy what we need for the feast,"
   or to give something to the poor.
So Judas took the morsel and left at once. And it was night.**

**When he had left, Jesus said,
   "Now is the Son of Man glorified, and God is glorified
         in him.**

If God is glorified in him, God will also glorify him in
  himself,
  and he will glorify him at once.
My children, I will be with you only a little while longer.
You will look for me, and as I told the Jews,
'Where I go you cannot come,' so now I say it to you."

Simon Peter said to him, "Master, where are you going?"
Jesus answered him,
  "Where I am going, you cannot follow me now,
  though you will follow later."
Peter said to him,
  "Master, why can I not follow you now?
  I will lay down my life for you."
Jesus answered, "Will you lay down your life for me?
Amen, amen, I say to you, the cock will not crow
  before you deny me three times."

The Gospel of the Lord. All: **Praise to you, Lord Jesus Christ.**

PRAYER OVER THE OFFERINGS
Look favorably, O Lord, we pray,
on these offerings of your family,
and to those you make partakers of these sacred gifts
grant a share in their fullness.
Through Christ our Lord. All: **Amen.**

COMMUNION ANTIPHON (Romans 8:32)
God did not spare his own Son,
but handed him over for us all.

PRAYER AFTER COMMUNION
Nourished by your saving gifts,
we beseech your mercy, Lord,
that by this same Sacrament,
with which you have fed us in the present age
you may make us partakers of life eternal.
Through Christ our Lord. All: **Amen.**

ENTRANCE ANTIPHON (Cf. Philippians 2:10, 8, 11)
At the name of Jesus, every knee should bend,
of those in heaven and on the earth and under the earth,
for the Lord became obedient to death, death on a cross:
therefore Jesus Christ is Lord, to the glory of God the
Father.

COLLECT
O God, who willed your Son to submit for our sake
to the yoke of the Cross,
so that you might drive from us the power of the enemy,
grant us, your servants, to attain the grace of the resurrection.
Through our Lord Jesus Christ, your Son,
who lives and reigns with you in the unity of the Holy Spirit,
one God, for ever and ever. All: **Amen.**

READING I (L 259)   Isaiah 50:4-9a
A reading from the Book of the Prophet Isaiah

**The Lord GOD has given me
a well-trained tongue,
That I might know how to speak to the weary
a word that will rouse them.
Morning after morning
he opens my ear that I may hear;
And I have not rebelled,
have not turned back.
I gave my back to those who beat me,
my cheeks to those who plucked my beard;
My face I did not shield
from buffets and spitting.**

**The Lord GOD is my help,
therefore I am not disgraced;
I have set my face like flint,
knowing that I shall not be put to shame.
He is near who upholds my right;
if anyone wishes to oppose me,**

let us appear together.
Who disputes my right?
   Let him confront me.
See, the Lord God is my help;
   who will prove me wrong?

The word of the Lord. All: **Thanks be to God.**

RESPONSORIAL PSALM 69

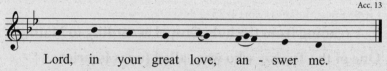

Acc. 13

Lord, in your great love, an - swer me.

Psalm 69:8-10, 21-22, 31 and 33-34

℟. (14c) **Lord, in your great love, answer me.**

For your sake I bear insult,
   and shame covers my face.
I have become an outcast to my brothers,
   a stranger to my mother's sons,
because zeal for your house consumes me,
   and the insults of those who blaspheme you fall
      upon me. ℟.

Insult has broken my heart, and I am weak,
   I looked for sympathy, but there was none;
   for consolers, not one could I find.
Rather they put gall in my food,
   and in my thirst they gave me vinegar to drink. ℟.

I will praise the name of God in song,
   and I will glorify him with thanksgiving:
"See, you lowly ones, and be glad;
   you who seek God, may your hearts revive!
For the LORD hears the poor,
   and his own who are in bonds he spurns not." ℟.

Verse before the Gospel

Hail to you, our King;
you alone are compassionate with our errors.

Or:

Hail to you, our King, obedient to the Father;
you were led to your crucifixion like a gentle lamb to the
    slaughter.

Gospel   Matthew 26:14-25

✛ **A reading from the holy Gospel according to Matthew**

One of the Twelve, who was called Judas Iscariot,
    went to the chief priests and said,
    "What are you willing to give me
    if I hand him over to you?"
They paid him thirty pieces of silver,
    and from that time on he looked for an opportunity
        to hand him over.

On the first day of the Feast of Unleavened Bread,
    the disciples approached Jesus and said,
    "Where do you want us to prepare
    for you to eat the Passover?"
He said,
    "Go into the city to a certain man and tell him,
    'The teacher says, "My appointed time draws near;
    in your house I shall celebrate the Passover with my
        disciples."'"
The disciples then did as Jesus had ordered,
    and prepared the Passover.

When it was evening,
    he reclined at table with the Twelve.
And while they were eating, he said,
    "Amen, I say to you, one of you will betray me."
Deeply distressed at this,
    they began to say to him one after another,
    "Surely it is not I, Lord?"

He said in reply,
"He who has dipped his hand into the dish with me
is the one who will betray me.
The Son of Man indeed goes, as it is written of him,
but woe to that man by whom the Son of Man is
betrayed.
It would be better for that man if he had never been born."
Then Judas, his betrayer, said in reply,
"Surely it is not I, Rabbi?"
He answered, "You have said so."

The Gospel of the Lord. All: **Praise to you, Lord Jesus Christ.**

PRAYER OVER THE OFFERINGS
Receive, O Lord, we pray, the offerings made here,
and graciously grant
that, celebrating your Son's Passion in mystery,
we may experience the grace of its effects.
Through Christ our Lord. All: **Amen.**

COMMUNION ANTIPHON (Matthew 20:28)
The Son of Man did not come to be served but to serve
and to give his life as a ransom for many.

PRAYER AFTER COMMUNION
Endow us, almighty God, with the firm conviction
that through your Son's Death in time,
to which the revered mysteries bear witness,
we may be assured of perpetual life.
Through Christ our Lord. All: **Amen.**

THE SACRED PASCHAL TRIDUUM

Holy Thursday

MORNING PRAYER

All stand and make the sign of the cross as the leader begins:

Leader: God, ✛ come to my assistance.

All: **Lord, make haste to help me.**

Leader: Glory to the Father, and to the Son, and to the Holy Spirit.

All: **As it was in the beginning, is now, and will be for ever. Amen.**

HYMN (See no. 174, p. 274, verses 1–2.)

PSALMODY (All are seated. The recitation or chanting of the psalm stanzas may be alternated between two people or groups of people. The flex measure is only sung on lines beginning with the † symbol.)

Antiphon 1 (*Leader*) Look, O Lord, and see my suffering. Come quickly to my aid.

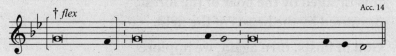

Acc. 14

Music: Bartholomew Sayles, O.S.B., and Cecile Gertken, O.S.B., adapt., © 1977, 1989, Order of Saint Benedict.

Psalm 80

O shepherd of Israel, hear us,
you who lead Joseph like a flock:
† enthroned on the cherubim, shine forth
upon Ephraim, Benjamin, Manasseh.
Rouse up your might and come to save us.

O God, bring us back;
let your face shine on us, and we shall be saved.

How long, O Lord, God of hosts,
will you be angry at the prayer of your people?
You have fed them with tears for their bread,
an abundance of tears for their drink.
You have made us the taunt of our neighbors;
our foes mock us among themselves.

O God of hosts, bring us back;
let your face shine forth, and we shall be saved.

You brought a vine out of Egypt;
you drove out the nations and planted it.
Before it you cleared the ground;
it took root and filled the land.

The mountains were covered with its shadow,
the cedars of God with its boughs.
It stretched out its branches to the sea;
to the River it stretched out its shoots.

Then why have you broken down <u>its</u> walls?
It is plucked by all who pass <u>by</u> the way.
It is ravaged by the boar of <u>the</u> forest,
devoured by the beasts <u>of</u> the field.

God of hosts, turn again, we <u>im</u>plore;
look down from hea<u>ven</u> and see.

† Visit this vine and pro<u>tect</u> it,
the vine your right hand <u>has</u> planted,
the son of man you have claimed <u>for</u> yourself.
They have burnt it with fire and cut <u>it</u> down.
May they perish at the frown <u>of</u> your face.

May your hand be on the man at your <u>right</u> hand,
the son of man you have confirmed <u>as</u> your own.
And we shall never forsake you <u>again</u>;
give us life that we may call up<u>on</u> your name.

O Lord God of hosts, bring <u>us</u> back;
let your face shine forth, and we <u>shall</u> be saved.

Psalm-prayer (*Leader*)
Lord God, eternal shepherd, you so tend the vineyard you
planted that now it extends its branches even to the farthest
coast. Look down on your Church and come to us. Help us
remain in your Son as branches on the vine, that, planted
firmly in your love, we may testify before the whole world
to your great power working everywhere.

Antiphon 1 (*All*) **Look, O Lord, and see my suffering.
Come quickly to my aid.**

Silence

Antiphon 2 (*Leader*) God is my savior; I trust in him and shall not fear.

Canticle   Isaiah 12:1-6

I give you thanks, O Lord;
though you have been angry with me,
your anger has abated, and you have consoled me.

God indeed is my savior;
I am confident and unafraid.
My strength and my courage is the Lord,
and he has been my savior.

With joy you will draw water
at the fountain of salvation, and say on that day:
Give thanks to the Lord, acclaim his name;
among the nations make known his deeds,
proclaim how exalted is his name.

Sing praise to the Lord for his glorious achievement;
let this be known throughout all the earth.

Shout with exultation, O city of Zion,
for great in your midst
is the Holy One of Israel!

Antiphon 2 (*All*) **God is my savior; I trust in him and shall not fear.**

Silence

Antiphon 3 (*Leader*) The Lord has fed us with the finest wheat; he has filled us with honey from the rock.

Music: Bartholomew Sayles, O.S.B., and Cecile Gertken, O.S.B., adapt., © 1977, 1989, Order of Saint Benedict.

Psalm 81

Sing joyfully to God <u>our</u> strength,
shout in triumph to the <u>God</u> of Jacob.

Raise a song and sound <u>the</u> timbrel,
the sweet-sounding harp <u>and</u> the lute;
blow the trumpet at <u>the</u> new moon,
when the moon is full, <u>on</u> our feast.

For this is a statute <u>in</u> Israel,
a command of the <u>God</u> of Jacob.
He made it a decree <u>for</u> Joseph,
when he went out from the <u>land</u> of Egypt.

A voice I did not know said <u>to</u> me:
"I freed your shoulder <u>from</u> the burden;
your hands were freed from the build<u>er's</u> basket.
You called in distress and I de<u>liv</u>ered you.

I answered, concealed in <u>the</u> thunder;
at the waters of Meribah I <u>tested</u> you.
Listen, my people, as <u>I</u> warn you.
O Israel, if only <u>you</u> would heed!

Let there be no strange god <u>among</u> you,
nor shall you worship a <u>foreign</u> god.
† I am the LORD your <u>God</u>,
who brought you up from the land <u>of</u> Egypt.
Open wide your mouth, and <u>I</u> will fill it.

But my people did not heed <u>my</u> voice,
and Israel would <u>not</u> obey me.
So I left them in their stubbornness <u>of</u> heart,
to follow their <u>own</u> designs.

O that my people <u>would</u> heed me,
that Israel would walk <u>in</u> my ways!
At once I would subdue <u>their</u> foes,
turn my hand ag<u>ainst</u> their enemies.

Those who hate the L<small>ORD</small> would cringe <u>be</u>fore him,
and their subjection would <u>last</u> forever.
But Israel I would feed with fin<u>est</u> wheat,
and satisfy with honey <u>from</u> the rock."

All stand.

Glory to the Father, and to <u>the</u> Son,
 and to the <u>Ho</u>ly Spirit.

As it was in the beginning, <u>is</u> now,
 and will be for <u>ev</u>er. Amen.

Psalm-prayer (*Leader*)
Lord God, open our mouths to proclaim your glory. Help us
to leave sin behind and to rejoice in professing your name.

Antiphon 3 (*All*) **The Lord has fed us with the finest wheat;
he has filled us with honey from the rock.**

All are seated.

R<small>EADING</small>   Hebrews 2:9-10
We see Jesus crowned with glory and honor because he
suffered death, that through God's gracious will he might
taste death for the sake of all men. Indeed, it was fitting
that when bringing many sons to glory God, for whom
and through whom all things exist, should make their
leader in the work of salvation perfect through suffering.

R<small>ESPONSORY</small>

Leader: By your own blood, Lord, you brought us back to
         God.
All: **By your own blood, Lord, you brought us back
         to God.**

Leader: From every tribe, and tongue, and people and nation,
All: **you brought us back to God.**

Leader: Glory to the Father, and to the Son, and to the
         Holy Spirit.
All: **By your own blood, Lord, you brought us back
         to God.**

Canticle of Zechariah

All stand. See no. 176 or 177 for sung settings of the Canticle.

Leader: I have longed to eat this meal with you before I
suffer.

Blessed be the Lord, the God of Israel;
he has come to his people and set them free.

He has raised up for us a mighty savior,
born of the house of his servant David.

Through his holy prophets he promised of old
that he would save us from our enemies,
from the hands of all who hate us.

He promised to show mercy to our fathers
and to remember his holy covenant.

This was the oath he swore to our father Abraham:
to set us free from the hands of our enemies,
free to worship him without fear,
holy and righteous in his sight all the days of our life.

You, my child, shall be called the prophet of the Most
High;
for you will go before the Lord to prepare his way,
to give his people knowledge of salvation
by the forgiveness of their sins.

In the tender compassion of our God
the dawn from on high shall break upon us,
to shine on those who dwell in darkness and the shadow
of death,
and to guide our feet into the way of peace.

Glory to the Father, and to the Son, and to the Holy Spirit.

As it was in the beginning, is now, and will be for ever.
Amen.

INTERCESSIONS

Leader: The Father anointed Christ with the Holy Spirit to proclaim forgiveness to those in bondage. Let us humbly call upon the eternal priest:

All: **Lord, have mercy on us.**

Leader: You went up to Jerusalem to suffer and so enter into your glory,

All: **bring your Church to the Passover feast of heaven.**

Leader: You were lifted high on the cross and pierced by the soldier's lance,

All: **heal our wounds.**

Leader: You made the cross the tree of life,

All: **give its fruit to those reborn in baptism.**

Leader: On the cross you forgave the repentant thief,

All: **forgive us our sins.**

Our Father . . .

PRAYER

Leader: God of infinite compassion,
to love you is to be made holy;
fill our hearts with your love.
By the death of your Son
you have given us hope, born of faith;
by his rising again
fulfill this hope
in the perfect love of heaven,
where he lives and reigns with you and the Holy Spirit,
one God, for ever and ever. All: **Amen.**

DISMISSAL

Leader: May the Lord ☩ bless us, protect us from all evil and bring us to everlasting life. All: **Amen.**

MASS OF THE LORD'S SUPPER

ENTRANCE ANTIPHON (Cf. Galatians 6:14)

We should glory in the Cross of our Lord Jesus Christ,
in whom is our salvation, life and resurrection,
through whom we are saved and delivered.

Acc. 16

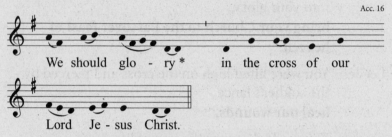

We should glo - ry * in the cross of our
Lord Je - sus Christ.

or:

Acc. 17

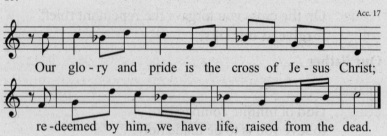

Our glo - ry and pride is the cross of Je - sus Christ;
re - deemed by him, we have life, raised from the dead.

COLLECT

O God, who have called us to participate
in this most sacred Supper,
in which your Only Begotten Son,
when about to hand himself over to death,
entrusted to the Church a sacrifice new for all eternity,
the banquet of his love,
grant, we pray,
that we may draw from so great a mystery,
the fullness of charity and of life.
Through our Lord Jesus Christ, your Son,
who lives and reigns with you in the unity of the Holy Spirit,
one God, for ever and ever. All: **Amen.**

READING I (L 39-ABC)   Exodus 12:1-8, 11-14
A reading from the Book of Exodus

The LORD said to Moses and Aaron in the land of Egypt,
   "This month shall stand at the head of your calendar;
   you shall reckon it the first month of the year.
Tell the whole community of Israel:
   On the tenth of this month every one of your families
   must procure for itself a lamb, one apiece for each
      household.
If a family is too small for a whole lamb,
   it shall join the nearest household in procuring one
   and shall share in the lamb
   in proportion to the number of persons who partake
      of it.
The lamb must be a year-old male and without blemish.
You may take it from either the sheep or the goats.
You shall keep it until the fourteenth day of this month,
   and then, with the whole assembly of Israel present,
   it shall be slaughtered during the evening twilight.
They shall take some of its blood
   and apply it to the two doorposts and the lintel
   of every house in which they partake of the lamb.
That same night they shall eat its roasted flesh
   with unleavened bread and bitter herbs.

"This is how you are to eat it:
   with your loins girt, sandals on your feet and your
      staff in hand,
   you shall eat like those who are in flight.
It is the Passover of the LORD.
For on this same night I will go through Egypt,
   striking down every firstborn of the land, both man
      and beast,
   and executing judgment on all the gods of Egypt—
      I, the LORD!
But the blood will mark the houses where you are.

Seeing the blood, I will pass over you;
   thus, when I strike the land of Egypt,
      no destructive blow will come upon you.

"This day shall be a memorial feast for you,
   which all your generations shall celebrate
      with pilgrimage to the LORD, as a perpetual institution."

The word of the Lord. All: **Thanks be to God.**

RESPONSORIAL PSALM 116

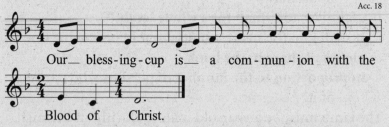

Acc. 18

Our blessing-cup is a communion with the Blood of Christ.

or:

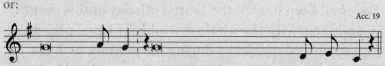

Acc. 19

Our bless-ing-cup is a communion with the Blood of Christ.

or:

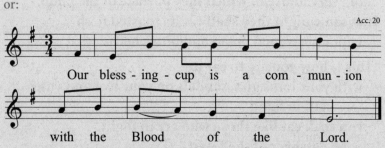

Acc. 20

Our bless-ing-cup is a com-mun-ion with the Blood of the Lord.

Psalm 116:12-13, 15-16bc, 17-18

℟. (*See* 1 Corinthians 10:16) **Our blessing-cup is a communion with the Blood of Christ.**

How shall I make a return to the LORD
   for all the good he has done for me?

The cup of salvation I will take up,
   and I will call upon the name of the LORD. R̷.

Precious in the eyes of the LORD
   is the death of his faithful ones.
I am your servant, the son of your handmaid;
   you have loosed my bonds. R̷.

To you will I offer sacrifice of thanksgiving,
   and I will call upon the name of the LORD.
My vows to the LORD I will pay
   in the presence of all his people. R̷.

READING II   1 Corinthians 11:23-26

A reading from the first Letter of Saint Paul to the Corinthians

Brothers and sisters:
I received from the Lord what I also handed on to you,
   that the Lord Jesus, on the night he was handed over,
   took bread, and, after he had given thanks,
   broke it and said, "This is my body that is for you.
Do this in remembrance of me."
In the same way also the cup, after supper, saying,
   "This cup is the new covenant in my blood.
Do this, as often as you drink it, in remembrance of me."
For as often as you eat this bread and drink the cup,
   you proclaim the death of the Lord until he comes.

The word of the Lord. All: **Thanks be to God.**

VERSE BEFORE THE GOSPEL (John 13:34)
I give you a new commandment, says the Lord:
love one another as I have loved you.

GOSPEL   John 13:1-15

✠ **A reading from the holy Gospel according to John**

All: **Glory to you, O Lord.**

Before the feast of Passover, Jesus knew that his hour
   had come
   to pass from this world to the Father.

He loved his own in the world and he loved them to
      the end.
The devil had already induced Judas, son of Simon the
      Iscariot, to hand him over.
So, during supper,
   fully aware that the Father had put everything into
      his power
   and that he had come from God and was returning
      to God,
   he rose from supper and took off his outer garments.
He took a towel and tied it around his waist.
Then he poured water into a basin
   and began to wash the disciples' feet
   and dry them with the towel around his waist.
He came to Simon Peter, who said to him,
   "Master, are you going to wash my feet?"
Jesus answered and said to him,
   "What I am doing, you do not understand now,
   but you will understand later."
Peter said to him, "You will never wash my feet."
Jesus answered him,
   "Unless I wash you, you will have no inheritance
      with me."
Simon Peter said to him,
   "Master, then not only my feet, but my hands and
      head as well."
Jesus said to him,
   "Whoever has bathed has no need except to have his
      feet washed,
   for he is clean all over;
   so you are clean, but not all."
For he knew who would betray him;
   for this reason, he said, "Not all of you are clean."

So when he had washed their feet
and put his garments back on and reclined at table
again,
he said to them, "Do you realize what I have done
for you?
You call me 'teacher' and 'master,' and rightly so,
for indeed I am.
If I, therefore, the master and teacher, have washed
your feet,
you ought to wash one another's feet.
I have given you a model to follow,
so that as I have done for you, you should also do."

The Gospel of the Lord. All: **Praise to you, Lord Jesus Christ.**

WASHING OF FEET
Antiphons or other appropriate songs are sung.

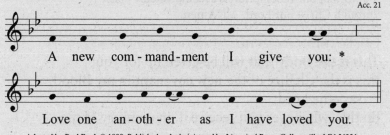

A new com-mand-ment I give you: *
Love one an-oth-er as I have loved you.

or:

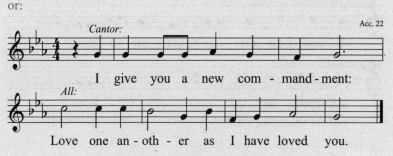

Cantor:
I give you a new com-mand-ment:
All:
Love one an-oth-er as I have loved you.

or:

Acc. 23

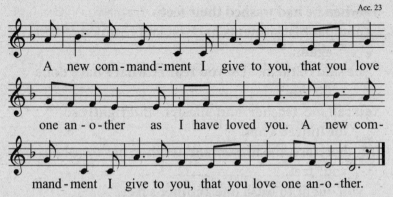

A new com-mand-ment I give to you, that you love one an-o-ther as I have loved you. A new com-mand-ment I give to you, that you love one an-o-ther.

PRAYER OVER THE OFFERINGS

Grant us, O Lord, we pray,
that we may participate worthily in these mysteries,
for whenever the memorial of this sacrifice is celebrated
the work of our redemption is accomplished.
Through Christ our Lord. All: **Amen.**

COMMUNION ANTIPHON (1 Corinthians 11:24-25)

This is the Body that will be given up for you;
this is the Chalice of the new covenant in my Blood,
    says the Lord;
do this, whenever you receive it, in memory of me.

Acc. 24

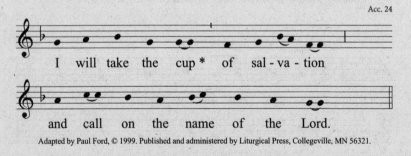

I will take the cup * of sal-va-tion and call on the name of the Lord.

or:

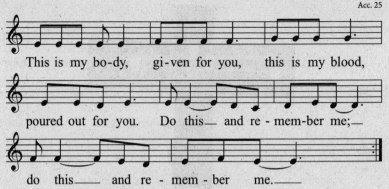

This is my bo-dy, gi-ven for you, this is my blood,

poured out for you. Do this— and re - mem-ber me;—

do this—— and re - mem - ber me.——

PRAYER AFTER COMMUNION
Grant, almighty God,
that, just as we are renewed
by the Supper of your Son in this present age,
so we may enjoy his banquet for all eternity.
Who lives and reigns for ever and ever. All: **Amen.**

THE TRANSFER OF THE MOST BLESSED SACRAMENT

Friday of the Passion of the Lord (Good Friday)

MORNING PRAYER

All stand and make the sign of the cross as the leader begins:

Leader: God, ✛ come to my assistance.

All: **Lord, make haste to help me.**

Leader: Glory to the Father, and to the Son, and to the Holy Spirit.

All: **As it was in the beginning, is now, and will be for ever. Amen.**

HYMN (See no. 174, p. 274, verses 3–4.)

PSALMODY (All are seated. The recitation or chanting of the psalm stanzas may be alternated between two people or groups of people. The flex measure is only sung on lines beginning with the † symbol.)

Antiphon 1 (*Leader*) God did not spare his own Son, but gave him up to suffer for our sake.

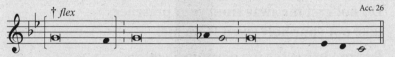

Music: Bartholomew Sayles, O.S.B., and Cecile Gertken, O.S.B., adapt., © 1977, 1989, Order of Saint Benedict.

Psalm 51

Have mercy on me, O God,
according to your merciful love;
according to your great compassion,
blot out my transgressions.
Wash me completely from my iniquity,
and cleanse me from my sin.

My transgressions, truly I know them;
my sin is always before me.
Against you, you alone, have I sinned;
what is evil in your sight I have done.
So you are just in your sentence,
without reproach in your judgment.

O see, in guilt I was born,
a sinner when my mother conceived me.
Yes, you delight in sincerity of heart;
in secret you teach me wisdom.
Cleanse me with hyssop, and I shall be pure;
wash me, and I shall be whiter than snow.

Let me hear rejoicing and gladness,
that the bones you have crushed may exult.
Turn away your face from my sins,
and blot out all my guilt.

Create a pure heart for me, <u>O</u> God;
renew a steadfast sp<u>ir</u>it within me.
Do not cast me away from <u>your</u> presence;
take not your holy sp<u>irit</u> from me.

Restore in me the joy of your <u>sal</u>vation;
sustain in me a <u>will</u>ing spirit.
I will teach transgressors <u>your</u> ways,
that sinners may re<u>turn</u> to you.

† Rescue me from bloodshed, O <u>God</u>,
God of my <u>sal</u>vation,
and then my tongue shall ring <u>out</u> your justice.
O Lord, open <u>my</u> lips
and my mouth shall pro<u>claim</u> your praise.

For in sacrifice you take no <u>de</u>light;
burnt offering from me <u>would</u> not please you.
† My sacrifice to God, a broken <u>spir</u>it:
a broken and hum<u>bled</u> heart,
O God, you <u>will</u> not spurn.

In your good pleasure, show favor <u>to</u> Sion;
rebuild the walls of Je<u>ru</u>salem.
† Then you will delight in right <u>sac</u>rifice,
burnt offerings wholly <u>con</u>sumed.
Then you will be offered young bulls <u>on</u> your altar.

Antiphon 1 (*All*) **God did not spare his own Son, but
gave him up to suffer for our sake.**

Silence

Antiphon 2 (*Leader*) Jesus Christ loved us, and poured out his own blood for us to wash away our sins.

Canticle   Habakkuk 3:2-4, 13a, a5-19

O Lord, I have heard your renown,
and feared, O Lord, your work.
In the course of the years revive it,
in the course of the years make it known;
in your wrath remember compassion!

God comes from Teman
the Holy One from Mount Paran.
Covered are the heavens with his glory,
and with his praise the earth is filled.

His splendor spreads like the light;
rays shine forth from beside him,
where his power is concealed.
You come forth to save your people,
to save your anointed one.

You tread the sea with your steeds
amid the churning of the deep waters.
I hear, and my body trembles;
at the sound, my lips quiver.

Decay invades my bones,
my legs tremble beneath me.
I await the day of distress
that will come upon the people who attack us.

For though the fig tree blossom not
nor fruit be on the vines,
though the yield of the olive fail
and the terraces produce no nourishment,

Though the flocks disappear from the fold
and there be no herd in the stalls,
yet will I rejoice in the Lord
and exult in my saving God.

God, my Lord, is my strength;
he makes my feet swift as those of hinds
and enables me to go upon the heights.

Antiphon 2 (*All*) **Jesus Christ loved us, and poured out**
his own blood for us to wash away our sins.

Silence

Antiphon 3 (*Leader*) We worship your cross, O Lord, and
we praise and glorify your holy resurrection, for the wood
of the cross has brought joy to the world.

Acc. 27

Music: Bartholomew Sayles, O.S.B., and Cecile Gertken, O.S.B., adapt., © 1977, 1989, Order of Saint Benedict.

Psalm 147:12-20

O Jerusalem, glorify <u>the</u> L<small>ORD</small>!
O Sion, <u>praise</u> your God!
He has strengthened the bars of <u>your</u> gates;
he has blessed your chil<u>dren</u> within you.
He established peace on <u>your</u> borders;
he gives you your fill of <u>fin</u>est wheat.

He sends out his word to <u>the</u> earth,
and swiftly runs <u>his</u> command.
He showers down snow <u>like</u> wool;
he scatters hoar<u>frost</u> like ashes.

He hurls down hailstones <u>like</u> crumbs;
before such cold, <u>who</u> can stand?
He sends forth his word and <u>it</u> melts them;
at the blowing of his breath the <u>wa</u>ters flow.

He reveals his word <u>to</u> Jacob;
to Israel, his de<u>crees</u> and judgments.
He has not dealt thus with oth<u>er</u> nations;
he has not taught <u>them</u> his judgments.

All stand.

Glory to the Father, and to <u>the</u> Son,
  and to the <u>Ho</u>ly Spirit.

As it was in the beginning, <u>is</u> now,
  and will be for <u>ev</u>er. Amen.

Antiphon 3 (*All*) **We worship your cross, O Lord, and we praise and glorify your holy resurrection, for the wood of the cross has brought joy to the world.**

All are seated.

Reading   Isaiah 52:13-15

See, my servant shall prosper,
  he shall be raised high and greatly exalted.
Even as many were amazed at him—
  so marred was his look beyond that of man,
  and his appearance beyond that of mortals—
So shall he startle many nations,
  because of him kings shall stand speechless;
For those who have not been told shall see,
  those who have not heard shall ponder it.

Responsory

Leader: For our sake Christ was obedient, accepting even
    death, death on a cross.

Canticle of Zechariah

All stand.

Leader: Over his head they hung their accusation:
    Jesus of Nazareth, King of the Jews.

The text for the Canticle is found on page 96 or see no. 176 or 177 for sung settings.

Intercessions

Leader: For our sake our Redeemer suffered death and
    was buried, and rose again. With heartfelt love let
    us adore him, and pray:
All: **Lord, have mercy on us.**

Leader: Christ our teacher, for our sake you were obedient
even to accepting death,

All: **teach us to obey the Father's will in all things.**

Leader: Christ our life, by your death on the cross you
destroyed the power of evil and death,

All: **may we die with you, to rise with you in glory.**

Leader: Christ our King, you became an outcast among us,
a worm and no man,

All: **teach us the humility by which you saved the
world.**

Leader: Christ our salvation, you gave yourself up to death
out of love for us,

All: **help us to show your love to one another.**

Leader: Christ our Savior, on the cross you embraced all
time with your outstretched arms,

All: **unite God's scattered children in your kingdom
of salvation.**

Our Father . . .

PRAYER

Leader: Father, look with love upon your people,
the love which our Lord Jesus Christ showed us
when he delivered himself to evil men
and suffered the agony of the cross,
for he lives and reigns with you and the Holy
Spirit,
one God, for ever and ever. All: **Amen.**

DISMISSAL

Leader: May the Lord ✢ bless us, protect us from all evil
and bring us to everlasting life. All: **Amen.**

THE CELEBRATION OF
THE PASSION OF THE LORD

PRAYER

Remember your mercies, O Lord,
and with your eternal protection sanctify your servants,
for whom Christ your Son,
by the shedding of his Blood,
established the Paschal Mystery.
Who lives and reigns for ever and ever. All: **Amen.**

Or:

O God, who by the Passion of Christ your Son, our Lord,
abolished the death inherited from ancient sin
by every succeeding generation,
grant that just as, being conformed to him,
we have borne by the law of nature
the image of the man of earth,
so by the sanctification of grace
we may bear the image of the Man of heaven.
Through Christ our Lord. All: **Amen.**

FIRST PART: LITURGY OF THE WORD

READING I (L 40-ABC)   Isaiah 52:13—53:12

A reading from the Book of the Prophet Isaiah

See, my servant shall prosper,
he shall be raised high and greatly exalted.
Even as many were amazed at him—
so marred was his look beyond human semblance
and his appearance beyond that of the sons of man—
so shall he startle many nations,
because of him kings shall stand speechless;
for those who have not been told shall see,
those who have not heard shall ponder it.

Who would believe what we have heard?
To whom has the arm of the LORD been revealed?
He grew up like a sapling before him,
like a shoot from the parched earth;

there was in him no stately bearing to make us look
 at him,
 nor appearance that would attract us to him.
He was spurned and avoided by people,
 a man of suffering, accustomed to infirmity,
one of those from whom people hide their faces,
 spurned, and we held him in no esteem.

Yet it was our infirmities that he bore,
 our sufferings that he endured,
while we thought of him as stricken,
 as one smitten by God and afflicted.
But he was pierced for our offenses,
 crushed for our sins;
upon him was the chastisement that makes us whole,
 by his stripes we were healed.
We had all gone astray like sheep,
 each following his own way;
but the LORD laid upon him
 the guilt of us all.

Though he was harshly treated, he submitted
 and opened not his mouth;
like a lamb led to the slaughter
 or a sheep before the shearers,
 he was silent and opened not his mouth.
Oppressed and condemned, he was taken away,
 and who would have thought any more of his destiny?
When he was cut off from the land of the living,
 and smitten for the sin of his people,
a grave was assigned him among the wicked
 and a burial place with evildoers,
though he had done no wrong
 nor spoken any falsehood.
But the LORD was pleased
 to crush him in infirmity.

If he gives his life as an offering for sin,
>he shall see his descendants in a long life,
>and the will of the LORD shall be accomplished
>>through him.

Because of his affliction
>he shall see the light in fullness of days;
through his suffering, my servant shall justify many,
>and their guilt he shall bear.
Therefore I will give him his portion among the great,
>and he shall divide the spoils with the mighty,
because he surrendered himself to death
>and was counted among the wicked;
and he shall take away the sins of many,
>and win pardon for their offenses.

The word of the Lord. All: Thanks be to God.

RESPONSORIAL PSALM 31

Fa - ther, in - to your hands, in - to your hands I com - mend my spi - rit.

or:

Fath - er, into your hands I com - mend my spir - it.

or:

Acc. 30

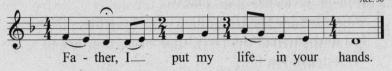

Fa - ther, I — put my   life— in your   hands.

Psalm 31:2, 6, 12-13, 15-16, 17, 25

℟. (Luke 23:46) **Father, into your hands I commend my spirit.**

In you, O LORD, I take refuge;
   let me never be put to shame.
In your justice rescue me.
Into your hands I commend my spirit;
   you will redeem me, O LORD, O faithful God. ℟.

For all my foes I am an object of reproach,
   a laughingstock to my neighbors, and a dread to my
      friends;
   they who see me abroad flee from me.
I am forgotten like the unremembered dead;
   I am like a dish that is broken. ℟.

But my trust is in you, O LORD;
   I say, "You are my God.
In your hands is my destiny; rescue me
   from the clutches of my enemies and my persecutors." ℟.

Let your face shine upon your servant;
   save me in your kindness.
Take courage and be stouthearted,
   all you who hope in the LORD. ℟.

READING II   Hebrews 4:14-16; 5:7-9

A reading from the Letter to the Hebrews

Brothers and sisters:
Since we have a great high priest who has passed through
   the heavens,
   Jesus, the Son of God,
   let us hold fast to our confession.

For we do not have a high priest
   who is unable to sympathize with our weaknesses,
   but one who has similarly been tested in every way,
   yet without sin.
So let us confidently approach the throne of grace
   to receive mercy and to find grace for timely help.

In the days when Christ was in the flesh,
   he offered prayers and supplications with loud cries
      and tears
   to the one who was able to save him from death,
   and he was heard because of his reverence.
Son though he was, he learned obedience from what he
      suffered;
   and when he was made perfect,
   he became the source of eternal salvation for all who
      obey him.

The word of the Lord. All: Thanks be to God.

Verse before the Gospel (Philippians 2:8-9)
Christ became obedient to the point of death,
even death on a cross.
Because of this, God greatly exalted him
and bestowed on him the name which is above every other
   name.

Gospel   John 18:1—19:42

The symbols in the following passion narrative represent:

   C.   Narrator;
   ☩   Christ;
   S.   speakers other than Christ;
   SS.   groups of speakers.

The Passion of our Lord Jesus Christ according to John

C.   Jesus went out with his disciples across the Kidron
         valley
         to where there was a garden,
         into which he and his disciples entered.

Judas his betrayer also knew the place,
    because Jesus had often met there with his disciples.
So Judas got a band of soldiers and guards
    from the chief priests and the Pharisees
    and went there with lanterns, torches, and weapons.
Jesus, knowing everything that was going to happen
      to him,
    went out and said to them,

✠   "Whom are you looking for?"

C.   They answered him,

SS.   "Jesus the Nazorean."

C.   He said to them,

✠   "I AM."

C.   Judas his betrayer was also with them.
    When he said to them, "I AM,"
      they turned away and fell to the ground.
    So he again asked them,

✠   "Whom are you looking for?"

C.   They said,

SS.   "Jesus the Nazorean."

C.   Jesus answered,

✠   "I told you that I AM.
    So if you are looking for me, let these men go."

C.   This was to fulfill what he had said,
     "I have not lost any of those you gave me."

    Then Simon Peter, who had a sword, drew it,
      struck the high priest's slave, and cut off his right ear.
    The slave's name was Malchus.
    Jesus said to Peter,

✠   "Put your sword into its scabbard.
    Shall I not drink the cup that the Father gave me?"

C.   So the band of soldiers, the tribune, and the Jewish
      guards seized Jesus,
    bound him, and brought him to Annas first.
    He was the father-in-law of Caiaphas,
    who was high priest that year.

It was Caiaphas who had counseled the Jews
> that it was better that one man should die rather
> > than the people.

Simon Peter and another disciple followed Jesus.
Now the other disciple was known to the high priest,
> and he entered the courtyard of the high priest
> > with Jesus.
But Peter stood at the gate outside.
So the other disciple, the acquaintance of the high
> > priest,
> went out and spoke to the gatekeeper and brought
> > Peter in.
Then the maid who was the gatekeeper said to Peter,

S.   "You are not one of this man's disciples, are you?"

C. He said,

S.   "I am not."

C. Now the slaves and the guards were standing around
> a charcoal fire
> > that they had made, because it was cold,
> > and were warming themselves.
Peter was also standing there keeping warm.

The high priest questioned Jesus
> about his disciples and about his doctrine.
Jesus answered him,

✝   "I have spoken publicly to the world.
I have always taught in a synagogue
> or in the temple area where all the Jews gather,
> and in secret I have said nothing. Why ask me?
Ask those who heard me what I said to them.
They know what I said."

C. When he had said this,
> one of the temple guards standing there struck
> > Jesus and said,

S.   "Is this the way you answer the high priest?"

C. Jesus answered him,

✠   "If I have spoken wrongly, testify to the wrong;
      but if I have spoken rightly, why do you strike me?"

C.   Then Annas sent him bound to Caiaphas the high
      priest.

Now Simon Peter was standing there keeping warm.
And they said to him,

S.   "You are not one of his disciples, are you?"

C.   He denied it and said,

S.   "I am not."

C.   One of the slaves of the high priest,
      a relative of the one whose ear Peter had cut off,
      said,

S.   "Didn't I see you in the garden with him?"

C.   Again Peter denied it.
And immediately the cock crowed.

Then they brought Jesus from Caiaphas to the
      praetorium.
It was morning.
And they themselves did not enter the praetorium,
      in order not to be defiled so that they could eat
        the Passover.
So Pilate came out to them and said,

S.   "What charge do you bring against this man?"

C.   They answered and said to him,

SS.   "If he were not a criminal,
      we would not have handed him over to you."

C.   At this, Pilate said to them,

S.   "Take him yourselves, and judge him according
      to your law."

C.   The Jews answered him,

SS.   "We do not have the right to execute anyone,"

C.   in order that the word of Jesus might be fulfilled
      that he said indicating the kind of death he would
        die.

So Pilate went back into the praetorium
and summoned Jesus and said to him,

S. "Are you the King of the Jews?"

C. Jesus answered,

✠ "Do you say this on your own
or have others told you about me?"

C. Pilate answered,

S. "I am not a Jew, am I?
Your own nation and the chief priests handed you
over to me.
What have you done?"

C. Jesus answered,

✠ "My kingdom does not belong to this world.
If my kingdom did belong to this world,
my attendants would be fighting
to keep me from being handed over to the Jews.
But as it is, my kingdom is not here."

C. So Pilate said to him,

S. "Then you are a king?"

C. Jesus answered,

✠ "You say I am a king.
For this I was born and for this I came into the world,
to testify to the truth.
Everyone who belongs to the truth listens to my voice."

C. Pilate said to him,

S. "What is truth?"

C. When he had said this,
he again went out to the Jews and said to them,

S. "I find no guilt in him.
But you have a custom that I release one prisoner to
you at Passover.
Do you want me to release to you the King of the Jews?"

C. They cried out again,

SS. "Not this one but Barabbas!"

C. Now Barabbas was a revolutionary.

Then Pilate took Jesus and had him scourged.
And the soldiers wove a crown out of thorns and
    placed it on his head,
  and clothed him in a purple cloak,
  and they came to him and said,

SS.   "Hail, King of the Jews!"

C. And they struck him repeatedly.
Once more Pilate went out and said to them,

S.   "Look, I am bringing him out to you,
  so that you may know that I find no guilt in him."

C. So Jesus came out,
  wearing the crown of thorns and the purple cloak.
And Pilate said to them,

S.   "Behold, the man!"

C. When the chief priests and the guards saw him they
    cried out,

SS.   "Crucify him, crucify him!"

C. Pilate said to them,

S.   "Take him yourselves and crucify him.
I find no guilt in him."

C. The Jews answered,

SS.   "We have a law, and according to that law he ought
    to die,
  because he made himself the Son of God."

C. Now when Pilate heard this statement,
  he became even more afraid,
  and went back into the praetorium and said to Jesus,

S.   "Where are you from?"

C. Jesus did not answer him.
So Pilate said to him,

S.   "Do you not speak to me?
Do you not know that I have power to release you
  and I have power to crucify you?"

C. Jesus answered him,

✠   "You would have no power over me
  if it had not been given to you from above.

For this reason the one who handed me over to you
　　has the greater sin."

C.　Consequently, Pilate tried to release him; but the
　　　Jews cried out,

SS.　"If you release him, you are not a Friend of Caesar.
　　Everyone who makes himself a king opposes Caesar."

C.　When Pilate heard these words he brought Jesus out
　　　and seated him on the judge's bench
　　　in the place called Stone Pavement, in Hebrew,
　　　　Gabbatha.
　　It was preparation day for Passover, and it was
　　　about noon.
　　And he said to the Jews,

S.　"Behold, your king!"

C.　They cried out,

SS.　"Take him away, take him away! Crucify him!"

C.　Pilate said to them,

S.　"Shall I crucify your king?"

C.　The chief priests answered,

SS.　"We have no king but Caesar."

C.　Then he handed him over to them to be crucified.

So they took Jesus, and, carrying the cross himself,
　　he went out to what is called the Place of the Skull,
　　in Hebrew, Golgotha.
There they crucified him, and with him two others,
　　one on either side, with Jesus in the middle.
Pilate also had an inscription written and put on the
　　cross.
It read,
　　"Jesus the Nazorean, the King of the Jews."
Now many of the Jews read this inscription,
　　because the place where Jesus was crucified was
　　　near the city;
　　and it was written in Hebrew, Latin, and Greek.
So the chief priests of the Jews said to Pilate,

SS.   "Do not write 'The King of the Jews,'
    but that he said, 'I am the King of the Jews.'"

C.   Pilate answered,

S.   "What I have written, I have written."

C.   When the soldiers had crucified Jesus,
    they took his clothes and divided them into four
        shares,
    a share for each soldier.
    They also took his tunic, but the tunic was seamless,
    woven in one piece from the top down.
    So they said to one another,

SS.   "Let's not tear it, but cast lots for it to see whose it
    will be,"

C.   in order that the passage of Scripture might be
    fulfilled that says:
      They divided my garments among them,
      and for my vesture they cast lots.
    This is what the soldiers did.
    Standing by the cross of Jesus were his mother
    and his mother's sister, Mary the wife of Clopas,
    and Mary of Magdala.
    When Jesus saw his mother and the disciple there
    whom he loved he said to his mother,

✝   "Woman, behold, your son."

C.   Then he said to the disciple,

✝   "Behold, your mother."

C.   And from that hour the disciple took her into his home.

    After this, aware that everything was now finished,
    in order that the Scripture might be fulfilled,
    Jesus said,

✝   "I thirst."

C.   There was a vessel filled with common wine.
    So they put a sponge soaked in wine on a sprig of
        hyssop
    and put it up to his mouth.

When Jesus had taken the wine, he said,

✠   "It is finished."

C. And bowing his head, he handed over the spirit.

Here all kneel and pause for a short time.

Now since it was preparation day,
    in order that the bodies might not remain
        on the cross on the sabbath,
    for the sabbath day of that week was a solemn one,
    the Jews asked Pilate that their legs be broken
    and that they be taken down.
So the soldiers came and broke the legs of the first
    and then of the other one who was crucified with
        Jesus.
But when they came to Jesus and saw that he was
      already dead,
    they did not break his legs,
    but one soldier thrust his lance into his side,
    and immediately blood and water flowed out.
An eyewitness has testified, and his testimony is true;
    he knows that he is speaking the truth,
    so that you also may come to believe.
For this happened so that the Scripture passage
      might be fulfilled:
    Not a bone of it will be broken.
And again another passage says:
    They will look upon him whom they have pierced.

After this, Joseph of Arimathea,
    secretly a disciple of Jesus for fear of the Jews,
    asked Pilate if he could remove the body of Jesus.
And Pilate permitted it.
So he came and took his body.
Nicodemus, the one who had first come to him at
      night,
    also came bringing a mixture of myrrh and aloes
    weighing about one hundred pounds.

They took the body of Jesus
>   and bound it with burial cloths along with the
>   spices,
>   according to the Jewish burial custom.
> Now in the place where he had been crucified there
>   was a garden,
>   and in the garden a new tomb, in which no one
>   had yet been buried.
> So they laid Jesus there because of the Jewish
>   preparation day;
>   for the tomb was close by.

The Gospel of the Lord. All: **Praise to you, Lord Jesus Christ.**

THE SOLEMN INTERCESSIONS

I. FOR HOLY CHURCH
Let us pray, dearly beloved, for the holy Church of God,
that our God and Lord be pleased to give her peace,
to guard her and to unite her throughout the whole world
and grant that, leading our life in tranquility and quiet,
we may glorify God the Father almighty.

Prayer in silence. Then the Priest sings or says:

Almighty ever-living God,
who in Christ revealed your glory to all the nations,
watch over the works of your mercy,
that your Church, spread throughout all the world,
may persevere with steadfast faith in confessing your name.
Through Christ our Lord. All: **Amen.**

II. FOR THE POPE
Let us pray also for our most Holy Father Pope N.,
that our God and Lord,
who chose him for the Order of Bishops,
may keep him safe and unharmed for the Lord's holy Church,
to govern the holy People of God.

Prayer in silence. Then the Priest sings or says:

Almighty ever-living God,
by whose decree all things are founded,
look with favor on our prayers
and in your kindness protect the Pope chosen for us,
that, under him, the Christian people,
governed by you their maker,

may grow in merit by reason of their faith.
Through Christ our Lord. All: **Amen.**

III. For All Orders and Degrees of the Faithful

Let us pray also for our Bishop N.,*
for all Bishops, Priests, and Deacons of the Church
and for the whole of the faithful people.

Prayer in silence. Then the Priest sings or says:

Almighty ever-living God,
by whose Spirit the whole body of the Church
is sanctified and governed,
hear our humble prayer for your ministers,
that, by the gift of your grace,
all may serve you faithfully.
Through Christ our Lord. All: **Amen.**

IV. For Catechumens

Let us pray also for (our) catechumens,
that our God and Lord
may open wide the ears of their inmost hearts
and unlock the gates of his mercy,
that, having received forgiveness of all their sins
through the waters of rebirth,
they, too, may be one with Christ Jesus our Lord.

Prayer in silence. Then the Priest sings or says:

Almighty ever-living God,
who make your Church ever fruitful with new offspring,
increase the faith and understanding of (our) catechumens,
that, reborn in the font of Baptism,
they may be added to the number of your adopted children.
Through Christ our Lord. All: **Amen.**

V. For the Unity of Christians

Let us pray also for all our brothers and sisters who believe in Christ,
that our God and Lord may be pleased,
as they live the truth,
to gather them together and keep them in his one Church.

Prayer in silence. Then the Priest sings or says:

Almighty ever-living God,
who gather what is scattered
and keep together what you have gathered,

---

* Mention may be made here of the Coadjutor Bishop, or Auxiliary Bishops,
  as noted in the *General Instruction of the Roman Missal*, no. 149.

look kindly on the flock of your Son,
that those whom one Baptism has consecrated
may be joined together by integrity of faith
and united in the bond of charity.
Through Christ our Lord. All: **Amen.**

VI. For the Jewish People

Let us pray also for the Jewish people,
to whom the Lord our God spoke first,
that he may grant them to advance in love of his name
and in faithfulness to his covenant.

Prayer in silence. Then the Priest sings or says:

Almighty ever-living God,
who bestowed your promises on Abraham and his descendants,
graciously hear the prayers of your Church,
that the people you first made your own
may attain the fullness of redemption.
Through Christ our Lord. All: **Amen.**

VII. For Those Who Do Not Believe in Christ

Let us pray also for those who do not believe in Christ,
that, enlightened by the Holy Spirit,
they, too, may enter on the way of salvation.

Prayer in silence. Then the Priest sings or says:

Almighty ever-living God,
grant to those who do not confess Christ
that, by walking before you with a sincere heart,
they may find the truth
and that we ourselves, being constant in mutual love
and striving to understand more fully the mystery of your life,
may be made more perfect witnesses to your love in the world.
Through Christ our Lord. All: **Amen.**

VIII. For Those Who Do Not Believe in God

Let us pray also for those who do not acknowledge God,
that, following what is right in sincerity of heart,
they may find the way to God himself.

Prayer in silence. Then the Priest sings or says:

Almighty ever-living God,
who created all people
to seek you always by desiring you
and, by finding you, come to rest,
grant, we pray,
that, despite every harmful obstacle,

all may recognize the signs of your fatherly love
and the witness of the good works
done by those who believe in you,
and so in gladness confess you,
the one true God and Father of our human race.
Through Christ our Lord. All: **Amen.**

IX. FOR THOSE IN PUBLIC OFFICE

Let us pray also for those in public office,
that our God and Lord
may direct their minds and hearts according to his will
for the true peace and freedom of all.

Prayer in silence. Then the Priest sings or says:

Almighty ever-living God,
in whose hand lies every human heart
and the rights of peoples,
look with favor, we pray,
on those who govern with authority over us,
that throughout the whole world,
the prosperity of peoples,
the assurance of peace,
and freedom of religion
may through your gift be made secure.
Through Christ our Lord. All: **Amen.**

X. FOR THOSE IN TRIBULATION

Let us pray, dearly beloved,
to God the Father almighty,
that he may cleanse the world of all errors,
banish disease, drive out hunger,
unlock prisons, loosen fetters,
granting to travelers safety, to pilgrims return,
health to the sick, and salvation to the dying.

Prayer in silence. Then the Priest sings or says:

Almighty ever-living God,
comfort of mourners, strength of all who toil,
may the prayers of those who cry out in any tribulation
come before you,
that all may rejoice,
because in their hour of need
your mercy was at hand.
Through Christ our Lord. All: **Amen.**

SECOND PART: THE ADORATION OF THE HOLY CROSS

℣. Ecce lignum Crucis.
All respond: **Venite, adoremus.**

Ve - ní - te,   ad - o - ré   mus.

or:

℣. Behold the wood of the Cross,
on which hung the salvation of the world.
All respond: **Come, let us adore.**

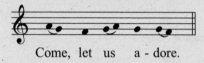

Come, let us a - dore.

THE ADORATION OF THE HOLY CROSS

All approach to venerate the Cross, showing reverence to it by a simple genuflection or some other appropriate sign.

CHANTS TO BE SUNG DURING THE ADORATION OF THE HOLY CROSS

Ant. We adore your Cross, O Lord,
we praise and glorify your holy Resurrection,
for behold, because of the wood of a tree
joy has come to the whole world.

May God have mercy on us and bless us;   Cf. Psalm 67[66]:2
may he let his face shed its light upon us
and have mercy on us.

And the antiphon is repeated: We adore . . .

Acc. 31

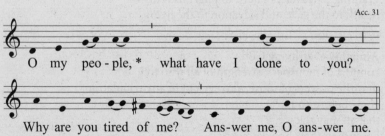

O my peo - ple, * what have I done to you?

Why are you tired of me?   Ans-wer me, O ans-wer me.

Adapted by Paul Ford, © 1999. Published and administered by Liturgical Press, Collegeville, MN 56321.

THE REPROACHES

I

1 and 2   My people, what have I done to you?
       Or how have I grieved you? Answer me!

1   Because I led you out of the land of Egypt,
       you have prepared a Cross for your Savior.

1   Hagios o Theos,
2   Holy is God,
1   Hagios Ischyros,
2   Holy and Mighty,
1   Hagios Athanatos, eleison himas.
2   Holy and Immortal One, have mercy on us.

1 and 2   Because I led you out through the desert forty years
       and fed you with manna and brought you into a land of plenty,
       you have prepared a Cross for your Savior.

1   Hagios o Theos,
2   Holy is God,
1   Hagios Ischyros,
2   Holy and Mighty,
1   Hagios Athanatos, eleison himas.
2   Holy and Immortal One, have mercy on us.

1 and 2   What more should I have done for you and have not done?
       Indeed, I planted you as my most beautiful chosen vine
       and you have turned very bitter for me,
       for in my thirst you gave me vinegar to drink
       and with a lance you pierced your Savior's side.

1   Hagios o Theos,
2   Holy is God,
1   Hagios Ischyros,
2   Holy and Mighty,
1   Hagios Athanatos, eleison himas.
2   Holy and Immortal One, have mercy on us.

II

Cantors: I scourged Egypt for your sake with its firstborn sons,
       and you scourged me and handed me over.

1 and 2 repeat: My people, what have I done to you?
       Or how have I grieved you? Answer me!

Cantors: I led you out from Egypt as Pharoah lay sunk in the Red Sea,
       and you handed me over to the chief priests.

1 and 2 repeat: My people . . .

Cantors: I opened up the sea before you,
and you opened my side with a lance.

1 and 2 repeat: My people . . .

Cantors: I went before you in a pillar of cloud,
and you led me into Pilate's palace.

1 and 2 repeat: My people . . .

Cantors: I fed you with manna in the desert,
and on me you rained blows and lashes.

1 and 2 repeat: My people . . .

Cantors: I gave you saving water from the rock to drink,
and for drink you gave me gall and vinegar.

1 and 2 repeat: My people . . .

Cantors: I struck down for you the kings of the Canaanites,
and you struck my head with a reed.

1 and 2 repeat: My people . . .

Cantors: I put in your hand a royal scepter,
and you put on my head a crown of thorns.

1 and 2 repeat: My people . . .

Cantors: I exalted you with great power,
and you hung me on the scaffold of the Cross.

1 and 2 repeat: My people . . .

The hymn Crux fidelis (Faithful Cross) or other suitable chants are sung.

THIRD PART: HOLY COMMUNION

At the Savior's command
and formed by divine teaching,
we dare to say:

The Priest, with hands extended says, and all present continue:
Our Father, who art in heaven,
hallowed be thy name;
thy kingdom come,
thy will be done
on earth as it is in heaven.
Give us this day our daily bread,
and forgive us our trespasses,
as we forgive those who trespass against us;
and lead us not into temptation,
but deliver us from evil.

With hands extended, the Priest continues alone:

Deliver us, Lord, we pray, from every evil,
graciously grant peace in our days,
that, by the help of your mercy,
we may be always free from sin
and safe from all distress,
as we await the blessed hope
and the coming of our Savior, Jesus Christ.

He joins his hands. The people conclude the prayer, acclaiming:

**For the kingdom, the power and the glory are yours
now and for ever.**

The Priest then genuflects, takes a particle, and, holding it slightly raised over the ciborium, while facing the people, says aloud:

Behold the Lamb of God,
behold him who takes away the sins of the world.
Blessed are those called to the supper of the Lamb.

And together with the people he adds once:

**Lord, I am not worthy
that you should enter under my roof,
but only say the word
and my soul shall be healed.**

PRAYER AFTER COMMUNION

Almighty ever-living God,
who have restored us to life
by the blessed Death and Resurrection of your Christ,
preserve in us the work of your mercy,
that, by partaking of this mystery,
we may have a life unceasingly devoted to you.
Through Christ our Lord. All: **Amen.**

PRAYER OVER THE PEOPLE

May abundant blessing, O Lord, we pray,
descend upon your people,
who have honored the Death of your Son
in the hope of their resurrection:
may pardon come,
comfort be given,
holy faith increase,
and everlasting redemption be made secure.
Through Christ our Lord. All: **Amen.**

After genuflecting to the Cross, all depart in silence.

Holy Saturday

MORNING PRAYER

All stand and make the sign of the cross as the leader begins:

Leader: God, ✟ come to my assistance.

All: **Lord, make haste to help me.**

Leader: Glory to the Father, and to the Son, and to the Holy Spirit.

All: **As it was in the beginning, is now, and will be for ever. Amen.**

HYMN (See no. 174, p. 274, verses 5–6.)

PSALMODY (All are seated. The recitation or chanting of the psalm stanzas may be alternated between two people or groups of people. The flex measure is only sung on lines beginning with the † symbol.)

Antiphon 1 (*Leader*) Though sinless, the Lord has been put to death. The world is in mourning as for an only son.

Music: Bartholomew Sayles, O.S.B., and Cecile Gertken, O.S.B., adapt., © 1977, 1989, Order of Saint Benedict.

Psalm 64

Hear, O God, the voice of my com_plaint_**;**
guard my life from dread _of_ **the foe.**
From the assembly of the wick_ed_**, hide me,**
from the throng of those _who_ **do evil.**

They sharpen their tongues _like_ **swords.**
They aim bitter _words_ **like arrows,**
to shoot at the innocent _from_ **ambush,**
shooting suddenly and _fear_**lessly.**

Holding firm in their e_vil_ **course,**
they conspire to lay _secret_ **snares.**
They say, "Who _will_ **see us?**
Who can search _out_ **our crimes?"**

†They have hatched their wicked _plots_**,**
and brought them to _per_**fection.**
How profound the depths _of_ **the heart!**

God will shoot them with _his_ **arrow,**
and deal them _sud_**den wounds.**
Their own tongue brings them _to_ **ruin;**
all who see them _shake_ **their heads.**

†Then will all be a_fraid_**;**
they will tell what God _has_ **done.**
They will pon_der_ **God's deeds.**
†The just one will rejoice in the _Lord_**;**
and fly to him _for_ **refuge.**
All upright _hearts_ **will glory.**

Antiphon 1 (*All*) **Though sinless, the Lord has been put to death. The world is in mourning as for an only son.**

Silence

Antiphon 2 (*Leader*) From the jaws of hell, Lord, rescue my soul.

Canticle   Isaiah 38:10-14, 17-20

Once I said,
"In the noontime of life I must depart!
To the gates of the nether world I shall be consigned
for the rest of my years."

I said, "I shall see the Lord no more
in the land of the living.
No longer shall I behold my fellow men
among those who dwell in the world."

My dwelling, like a shepherd's tent,
is struck down and borne away from me;
you have folded up my life, like a weaver
who severs the last thread.

Day and night you give me over to torment;
I cry out until the dawn.
Like a lion he breaks all my bones;
day and night you give me over to torment.

Like a swallow I utter shrill cries;
I moan like a dove.
My eyes grow weak, gazing heaven-ward:
O Lord, I am in straits; be my surety!

You have preserved my life
from the pit of destruction,
when you cast behind your back
all my sins.

For it is not the nether world that gives you thanks,
nor death that praises you;
neither do those who go down into the pit
await your kindness.

The living, the living give you thanks,
as I do today.
Fathers declare to their sons,
O God, your faithfulness.

The Lord is our savior;
we shall sing to stringed instruments
in the house of the Lord
all the days of our life.

Antiphon 2 (*All*) **From the jaws of hell, Lord, rescue my soul.**

Silence

Antiphon 3 (*Leader*) I was dead, but now I live for ever, and I hold the keys of death and of hell.

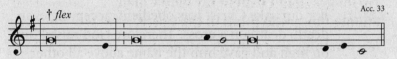

Music: Bartholomew Sayles, O.S.B., and Cecile Gertken, O.S.B., adapt., © 1977, 1989, Order of Saint Benedict.

Psalm 150

**Praise God in his holy place;
praise him in his mighty firmament.
Praise him for his powerful deeds;
praise him for his boundless grandeur.**

**O praise him with sound of trumpet;
praise him with lute and harp.
Praise him with timbrel and dance;
praise him with strings and pipes.**

**†O praise him with resounding cymbals;
praise him with clashing of cymbals.
Let everything that breathes praise the Lord!**

All stand.

**Glory to the Father, and to the Son,
     and to the Holy Spirit.**

**As it was in the beginning, is now,
     and will be for ever. Amen.**

Antiphon 3 (*All*) I was dead, but now I live for ever, and I hold the keys of death and of hell.

All are seated.

READING   Hosea 5:15b—16:2

Thus says the Lord
In their affliction, they shall look for me:
 "Come, let us return to the Lord,
For it is he who has rent, but he will heal us;
 he has struck us, but he will bind our wounds.
He will revive us after two days;
 on the third day he will raise us up,
 to live in his presence."

RESPONSORY

Leader: For our sake Christ was obedient, accepting even
         death, death on a cross. Therefore God raised him
         on high and gave him the name above all other
         names.

CANTICLE OF ZECHARIAH
All stand.

Leader: Save us, O Savior of the world. On the cross you
         redeemed us by the shedding of your blood;
         we cry out for your help, O God.

*The text for the Canticle is found on page 96 or see no. 176 or 177 for
sung settings.*

INTERCESSIONS

Leader: Our Redeemer suffered and was buried for us in
         order to rise again. With sincere love we adore
         him, and aware of our needs we cry out:
  All: **Lord, have mercy on us.**

Leader: Christ our Savior, your sorrowing Mother stood
         by you at your death and burial,
  All: **in our sorrow may we share your suffering.**

Leader: Christ our Lord, like the seed buried in the ground,
         you brought forth for us the harvest of grace,
  All: **may we die to sin and live for God.**

Leader: Christ, the Good Shepherd, in death you lay hidden from the world,

All: **teach us to love a life hidden with you in the Father.**

Leader: Christ, the new Adam, you entered the kingdom of death to release all the just since the beginning of the world,

All: **may all who lie dead in sin hear your voice and rise to life.**

Leader: Christ, Son of the living God, through baptism we were buried with you,

All: **risen also with you in baptism, may we walk in newness of life.**

Our Father . . .

PRAYER

Leader: All-powerful and ever-living God,
your only Son went down among the dead
and rose again in glory.
In your goodness
raise up your faithful people
buried with him in baptism,
to be one with him
in the eternal life of heaven,
where he lives and reigns with you and the Holy
  Spirit,
one God, for ever and ever. All: **Amen.**

DISMISSAL

Leader: May the Lord ✝ bless us, protect us from all evil and bring us to everlasting life. All: **Amen.**

THE EASTER VIGIL IN THE HOLY NIGHT

FIRST PART: THE SOLEMN BEGINNING OF THE VIGIL OR LUCERNARIUM

THE BLESSING OF THE FIRE AND PREPARATION OF THE CANDLE

Priest: In the name of the Father, and of the Son, and of the Holy Spirit.
All: **Amen.**

Dear brethren (brothers and sisters),
on this most sacred night,
in which our Lord Jesus Christ
passed over from death to life,
the Church calls upon her sons and daughters,
scattered throughout the world,
to come together to watch and pray.
If we keep the memorial
of the Lord's paschal solemnity in this way,
listening to his word and celebrating his mysteries,
then we shall have the sure hope
of sharing his triumph over death
and living with him in God.

Let us pray.
O God, who through your Son
bestowed upon the faithful the fire of your glory,
sanctify ✠ this new fire, we pray,
and grant that,
by these paschal celebrations,
we may be so inflamed with heavenly desires,
that with minds made pure
we may attain festivities of unending splendor.
Through Christ our Lord. All: **Amen.**

PREPARATION OF THE CANDLE

Christ yesterday and today
the Beginning and the End
the Alpha
and the Omega
All time belongs to him
and all the ages
To him be glory and power
through every age and for ever. Amen.

By his holy
and glorious wounds,
may Christ the Lord
guard us
and protect us. Amen.

May the light of Christ rising in glory
dispel the darkness of our hearts and minds.

PROCESSION

℣. The Light of Christ.   *or*   ℣. Lumen Christi.
℟. **Thanks be to God.**   ℟. **Deo Gratias.**

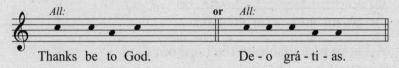

All: Thanks be to God.   **or**   *All:* De - o grá - ti - as.

THE EASTER PROCLAMATION (EXSULTET)
Longer Form of the Easter Proclamation
[Shorter Form]
(Omitted by a lay cantor)

[Exult, let them exult, the hosts of heaven,
exult, let Angel ministers of God exult,
let the trumpet of salvation
sound aloud our mighty King's triumph!
Be glad, let earth be glad, as glory floods her,
ablaze with light from her eternal King,
let all corners of the earth be glad,
knowing an end to gloom and darkness.
Rejoice, let Mother Church also rejoice,
arrayed with the lightning of his glory,
let this holy building shake with joy,
filled with the mighty voices of the peoples.]

(Therefore, dearest friends,
standing in the awesome glory of this holy light,
invoke with me, I ask you,
the mercy of God almighty,
that he, who has been pleased to number me,
though unworthy, among the Levites,
may pour into me his light unshadowed,
that I may sing this candle's perfect praises).

[(℣. The Lord be with you.
℟. **And with your spirit.**)

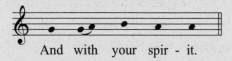

And with your spir - it.

℣. Lift up your hearts.
℟. **We lift them up to the Lord.**

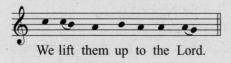

We lift them up to the Lord.

℣. Let us give thanks to the Lord our God.
℟. **It is right and just.**

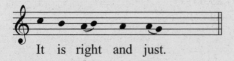

It is right and just.

It is truly right and just,
with ardent love of mind and heart
and with devoted service of our voice,
to acclaim our God invisible, the almighty Father,
and Jesus Christ, our Lord, his Son, his Only Begotten.

Who for our sake paid Adam's debt to the eternal Father,
and, pouring out his own dear Blood,
wiped clean the record of our ancient sinfulness.

These then are the feasts of Passover,
in which is slain the Lamb, the one true Lamb,
whose Blood anoints the doorposts of believers.

This is the night,
when once you led our forebears, Israel's children,
from slavery in Egypt
and made them pass dry-shod through the Red Sea.

This is the night
that with a pillar of fire
banished the darkness of sin.

This is the night
that even now, throughout the world,
sets Christian believers apart from worldly vices
and from the gloom of sin,
leading them to grace
and joining them to his holy ones.

This is the night,
when Christ broke the prison-bars of death
and rose victorious from the underworld.]

Our birth would have been no gain,
had we not been redeemed.
[O wonder of your humble care for us!
O love, O charity beyond all telling,
to ransom a slave you gave away your Son!

O truly necessary sin of Adam,
destroyed completely by the Death of Christ!

O happy fault
that earned so great, so glorious a Redeemer!]

O truly blessed night,
worthy alone to know the time and hour
when Christ rose from the underworld!

This is the night
of which it is written:
The night shall be as bright as day,
dazzling is the night for me,
and full of gladness.

[The sanctifying power of this night
dispels wickedness, washes faults away,
restores innocence to the fallen, and joy to mourners,]
drives out hatred, fosters concord, and brings down the
    mighty.

[**On this, your night of grace, O holy Father,
accept this candle, a solemn offering,
the work of bees and of your servants' hands,
an evening sacrifice of praise,
this gift from your most holy Church.]

But now we know the praises of this pillar,
which glowing fire ignites for God's honor,
a fire into many flames divided,
yet never dimmed by sharing of its light,
for it is fed by melting wax,
drawn out by mother bees
to build a torch so precious.

[O truly blessed night,
when things of heaven are wed to those of earth,
and divine to the human.] [**]

[Therefore, O Lord,
we pray you that this candle,
hallowed to the honor of your name,
may persevere undimmed,
to overcome the darkness of this night.
Receive it as a pleasing fragrance,
and let it mingle with the lights of heaven.
May this flame be found still burning
by the Morning Star:
the one Morning Star who never sets,
Christ your Son,
who, coming back from death's domain,
has shed his peaceful light on humanity,
and lives and reigns for ever and ever. All: **Amen.**

SECOND PART: THE LITURGY OF THE WORD

Dear brethren (brothers and sisters),
now that we have begun our solemn Vigil,
let us listen with quiet hearts to the Word of God.
Let us meditate on how God in times past saved his people
and in these, the last days, has sent us his Son as our Redeemer.
Let us pray that our God may complete this paschal work of salvation
by the fullness of redemption.

READING I (L 41-ABC)   Genesis 1:1—2:2 *or* Shorter Form [ ]
Genesis 1:1, 26-31a

A reading from the Book of Genesis

**[In the beginning, when God created the heavens and
    the earth,]**
    **the earth was a formless wasteland, and darkness
        covered the abyss,**
    while a mighty wind swept over the waters.

Then God said,
    "Let there be light," and there was light.
God saw how good the light was.
God then separated the light from the darkness.
**God called the light "day," and the darkness he called
    "night."**
Thus evening came, and morning followed—the first day.

Then God said,
    "Let there be a dome in the middle of the waters,
    to separate one body of water from the other."
And so it happened:
    God made the dome,
    **and it separated the water above the dome from the
        water below it.**
God called the dome "the sky."
Evening came, and morning followed—the second day.

Then God said,
    **"Let the water under the sky be gathered into a single
        basin,**
    so that the dry land may appear."

And so it happened:

the water under the sky was gathered into its basin,
and the dry land appeared.

God called the dry land "the earth,"

and the basin of the water he called "the sea."

God saw how good it was.

Then God said,

"Let the earth bring forth vegetation:
every kind of plant that bears seed
and every kind of fruit tree on earth
that bears fruit with its seed in it."

And so it happened:

the earth brought forth every kind of plant that
  bears seed
and every kind of fruit tree on earth
that bears fruit with its seed in it.

God saw how good it was.

Evening came, and morning followed—the third day.

Then God said:

"Let there be lights in the dome of the sky,
to separate day from night.

Let them mark the fixed times, the days and the years,
and serve as luminaries in the dome of the sky,
to shed light upon the earth."

And so it happened:

God made the two great lights,
the greater one to govern the day,
and the lesser one to govern the night;
and he made the stars.

God set them in the dome of the sky,
to shed light upon the earth,
to govern the day and the night,
and to separate the light from the darkness.

God saw how good it was.

Evening came, and morning followed—the fourth day.

Then God said,
  "Let the water teem with an abundance of living
      creatures,
  and on the earth let birds fly beneath the dome of
      the sky."
And so it happened:
  God created the great sea monsters
  and all kinds of swimming creatures with which the
      water teems,
  and all kinds of winged birds.
God saw how good it was, and God blessed them, saying,
  "Be fertile, multiply, and fill the water of the seas;
  and let the birds multiply on the earth."
Evening came, and morning followed—the fifth day.

Then God said,
  "Let the earth bring forth all kinds of living creatures:
  cattle, creeping things, and wild animals of all kinds."
And so it happened:
  God made all kinds of wild animals, all kinds of cattle,
  and all kinds of creeping things of the earth.
God saw how good it was.
Then [God said:
  "Let us make man in our image, after our likeness.
Let them have dominion over the fish of the sea,
  the birds of the air, and the cattle,
  and over all the wild animals
  and all the creatures that crawl on the ground."
God created man in his image;
  in the image of God he created him;
  male and female he created them.
God blessed them, saying:
  "Be fertile and multiply;
  fill the earth and subdue it.
Have dominion over the fish of the sea, the birds of the air,
  and all the living things that move on the earth."

God also said:

"See, I give you every seed-bearing plant all over the
earth

and every tree that has seed-bearing fruit on it to be
your food;

and to all the animals of the land, all the birds of the air,

and all the living creatures that crawl on the ground,

I give all the green plants for food."

And so it happened.

**God looked at everything he had made, and he found it
very good.]**

Evening came, and morning followed—the sixth day.

**Thus the heavens and the earth and all their array were
completed.**

Since on the seventh day God was finished

with the work he had been doing,

he rested on the seventh day from all the work he had
undertaken.

The word of the Lord. All: **Thanks be to God.**

RESPONSORIAL PSALM 104 or 33

Acc. 34

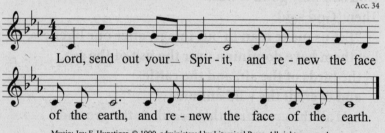

Lord, send out your Spir-it, and re-new the face
of the earth, and re-new the face of the earth.

Music: Jay F. Hunstiger, © 1990, administered by Liturgical Press. All rights reserved.

or:

Acc. 35

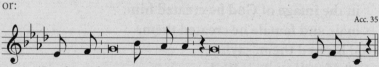

Lord, send out your Spir-it, and renew the face of the earth.

Music: Bartholomew Sayles, O.S.B., and Cecile Gertken, O.S.B., adapt., © 1977, 1989, Order of Saint Benedict.

or:

Acc. 36

Send out your Spi - rit   o - ver the wa - ters:

you will re - new   the   face of the earth.

A Psalm 104:1-2, 5-6, 10, 12, 13-14, 24, 35

℟. (30) **Lord, send out your Spirit, and renew the face of the earth.**

Bless the LORD, O my soul!
    O LORD, my God, you are great indeed!
You are clothed with majesty and glory,
    robed in light as with a cloak. ℟.

You fixed the earth upon its foundation,
    not to be moved forever;
with the ocean, as with a garment, you covered it;
    above the mountains the waters stood. ℟.

You send forth springs into the watercourses
    that wind among the mountains.
Beside them the birds of heaven dwell;
    from among the branches they send forth their song. ℟.

You water the mountains from your palace;
    the earth is replete with the fruit of your works.
You raise grass for the cattle,
    and vegetation for man's use,
producing bread from the earth. ℟.

How manifold are your works, O LORD!
    In wisdom you have wrought them all—
the earth is full of your creatures.
    Bless the LORD, O my soul! ℟.

or:

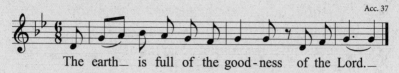

The earth — is full of the good-ness of the Lord. —

or:

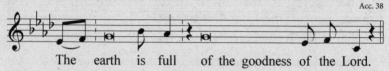

The earth is full of the goodness of the Lord.

or:

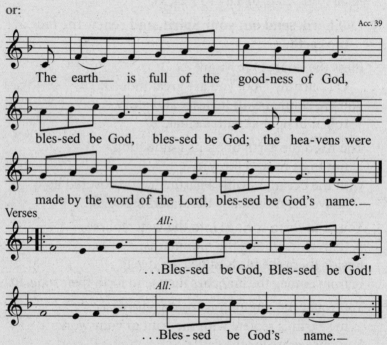

The earth — is full of the good-ness of God,

bles-sed be God, bles-sed be God; the hea-vens were

made by the word of the Lord, bles-sed be God's name. —

Verses

All:

...Bles-sed be God, Bles-sed be God!

All:

...Bles-sed be God's name. —

B Psalm 33:4-5, 6-7, 12-13, 20-22

℟. (5b) **The earth is full of the goodness of the Lord.**

Upright is the word of the LORD,
  and all his works are trustworthy.
He loves justice and right;
  of the kindness of the LORD the earth is full. ℟.

By the word of the Lord the heavens were made;
  by the breath of his mouth all their host.
He gathers the waters of the sea as in a flask;
  in cellars he confines the deep. ℟.

Blessed the nation whose God is the Lord,
  the people he has chosen for his own inheritance.
From heaven the Lord looks down;
  he sees all mankind. ℟.

Our soul waits for the Lord,
  who is our help and our shield.
May your kindness, O Lord, be upon us
  who have put our hope in you. ℟.

PRAYER
Let us pray.

Almighty ever-living God,
who are wonderful in the ordering of all your works,
may those you have redeemed understand
that there exists nothing more marvelous
than the world's creation in the beginning
except that, at the end of the ages,
Christ our Passover has been sacrificed.
Who lives and reigns for ever and ever. All: **Amen.**

Or:

On the creation of man:
O God, who wonderfully created human nature
and still more wonderfully redeemed it,
grant us, we pray,
to set our minds against the enticements of sin,
that we may merit to attain eternal joys.
Through Christ our Lord. All: **Amen.**

READING II   Genesis 22:1-18 *or* Shorter Form [ ]
Genesis 22:1-2, 9a, 10-13, 15-18
A reading from the Book of Genesis

[God put Abraham to the test.
He called to him, "Abraham!"
"Here I am," he replied.
Then God said:

"Take your son Isaac, your only one, whom you love,
   and go to the land of Moriah.
There you shall offer him up as a holocaust
   on a height that I will point out to you."]
Early the next morning Abraham saddled his donkey,
   took with him his son Isaac and two of his servants
         as well,
   and with the wood that he had cut for the holocaust,
   set out for the place of which God had told him.

On the third day Abraham got sight of the place from afar.
Then he said to his servants:
   "Both of you stay here with the donkey,
   while the boy and I go on over yonder.
We will worship and then come back to you."
Thereupon Abraham took the wood for the holocaust
   and laid it on his son Isaac's shoulders,
   while he himself carried the fire and the knife.
As the two walked on together, Isaac spoke to his father
         Abraham:
   "Father!" Isaac said.
"Yes, son," he replied.
Isaac continued, "Here are the fire and the wood,
   but where is the sheep for the holocaust?"
"Son," Abraham answered,
   "God himself will provide the sheep for the holocaust."
Then the two continued going forward.

[When they came to the place of which God had told him,
   Abraham built an altar there and arranged the wood
         on it.]
Next he tied up his son Isaac,
   and put him on top of the wood on the altar.
[Then he reached out and took the knife to slaughter
         his son.
But the LORD's messenger called to him from heaven,
   "Abraham, Abraham!"

"Here I am!" he answered.

"Do not lay your hand on the boy," said the messenger.
"Do not do the least thing to him.
I know now how devoted you are to God,
    since you did not withhold from me your own
        beloved son."
As Abraham looked about,
    he spied a ram caught by its horns in the thicket.
So he went and took the ram
    and offered it up as a holocaust in place of his son.]
Abraham named the site Yahweh-yireh;
    hence people now say, "On the mountain the Lord
        will see."

[Again the Lord's messenger called to Abraham from
        heaven and said:
    "I swear by myself, declares the Lord,
    that because you acted as you did
    in not withholding from me your beloved son,
    I will bless you abundantly
    and make your descendants as countless
    as the stars of the sky and the sands of the seashore;
    your descendants shall take possession
    of the gates of their enemies,
    and in your descendants all the nations of the earth
        shall find blessing—
    all this because you obeyed my command."]

The word of the Lord. All: Thanks be to God.

RESPONSORIAL PSALM 16

Acc. 40

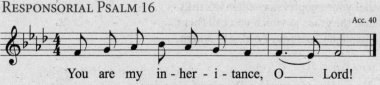

You are my in - her - i - tance, O____ Lord!

or:

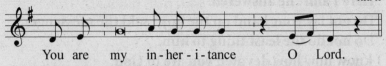

You are my in-her-i-tance O Lord.

Music: Bartholomew Sayles, O.S.B., and Cecile Gertken, O.S.B., adapt., © 1977, 1989, Order of Saint Benedict.

Psalm 16:5, 8, 9-10, 11

℟. (1) **You are my inheritance, O Lord.**

O LORD, my allotted portion and my cup,
　　you it is who hold fast my lot.
I set the LORD ever before me;
　　with him at my right hand I shall not be disturbed. ℟.

Therefore my heart is glad and my soul rejoices,
　　my body, too, abides in confidence;
because you will not abandon my soul to the netherworld,
　　nor will you suffer your faithful one to undergo
　　　　corruption. ℟.

You will show me the path to life,
　　fullness of joys in your presence,
　　the delights at your right hand forever. ℟.

PRAYER
Let us pray.

O God, supreme Father of the faithful,
who increase the children of your promise
by pouring out the grace of adoption
throughout the whole world
and who through the Paschal Mystery
make your servant Abraham father of nations,
as once you swore,
grant, we pray,
that your peoples may enter worthily
into the grace to which you call them.
Through Christ our Lord. All: **Amen.**

READING III   Exodus 14:15—15:1
A reading from the Book of Exodus

**The LORD said to Moses, "Why are you crying out to me?
Tell the Israelites to go forward.**

And you, lift up your staff and, with hand outstretched
    over the sea,
  split the sea in two,
  that the Israelites may pass through it on dry land.
But I will make the Egyptians so obstinate
  that they will go in after them.
Then I will receive glory through Pharaoh and all his army,
  his chariots and charioteers.
The Egyptians shall know that I am the LORD,
  when I receive glory through Pharaoh
  and his chariots and charioteers."

The angel of God, who had been leading Israel's camp,
  now moved and went around behind them.
The column of cloud also, leaving the front,
  took up its place behind them,
  so that it came between the camp of the Egyptians
  and that of Israel.
But the cloud now became dark, and thus the night passed
  without the rival camps coming any closer together
    all night long.
Then Moses stretched out his hand over the sea,
  and the LORD swept the sea
  with a strong east wind throughout the night
  and so turned it into dry land.
When the water was thus divided,
  the Israelites marched into the midst of the sea on
    dry land,
  with the water like a wall to their right and to their left.

The Egyptians followed in pursuit;
  all Pharaoh's horses and chariots and charioteers went
    after them
  right into the midst of the sea.
In the night watch just before dawn
  the LORD cast through the column of the fiery cloud

upon the Egyptian force a glance that threw it into a
      panic;
and he so clogged their chariot wheels
that they could hardly drive.
With that the Egyptians sounded the retreat before Israel,
   because the LORD was fighting for them against the
      Egyptians.

Then the LORD told Moses, "Stretch out your hand over
      the sea,
   that the water may flow back upon the Egyptians,
   upon their chariots and their charioteers."
So Moses stretched out his hand over the sea,
   and at dawn the sea flowed back to its normal depth.
The Egyptians were fleeing head on toward the sea,
   when the LORD hurled them into its midst.
As the water flowed back,
   it covered the chariots and the charioteers of Pharaoh's
      whole army
   which had followed the Israelites into the sea.
Not a single one of them escaped.
But the Israelites had marched on dry land
   through the midst of the sea,
   with the water like a wall to their right and to their left.
Thus the LORD saved Israel on that day
   from the power of the Egyptians.
When Israel saw the Egyptians lying dead on the seashore
   and beheld the great power that the LORD
   had shown against the Egyptians,
   they feared the LORD and believed in him and in his
      servant Moses.

Then Moses and the Israelites sang this song to the LORD:
   I will sing to the LORD, for he is gloriously triumphant;
   horse and chariot he has cast into the sea.

The word of the Lord. All: Thanks be to God.

RESPONSORIAL PSALM (Exodus 15)

Acc. 42

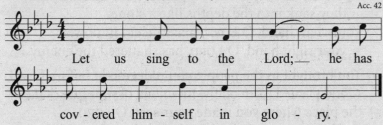

Let us sing to the Lord;— he has cov-ered him-self in glo-ry.

or:

Acc. 43

Let us sing to the Lord; he has covered him-self in glo-ry.

or:

Acc. 44

Sing to the Lord, sing to the Lord, co-vered in glo-ry: O sing to the Lord.

Exodus 15:1-2, 3-4, 5-6, 17-18

℟. (1b) **Let us sing to the Lord; he has covered himself in glory.**

I will sing to the LORD, for he is gloriously triumphant;
    horse and chariot he has cast into the sea.
My strength and my courage is the LORD,
    and he has been my savior.
He is my God, I praise him;
    the God of my father, I extol him. ℟.

The LORD is a warrior,
    LORD is his name!
Pharaoh's chariots and army he hurled into the sea;
    the elite of his officers were submerged in the Red Sea. ℟.

(continued)

The flood waters covered them,
　　they sank into the depths like a stone.
Your right hand, O Lord, magnificent in power,
　　your right hand, O Lord, has shattered the enemy. R̷.

You brought in the people you redeemed
　　and planted them on the mountain of your inheritance—
the place where you made your seat, O Lord,
　　the sanctuary, Lord, which your hands established.
The Lord shall reign forever and ever. R̷.

PRAYER
Let us pray.

O God, whose ancient wonders
remain undimmed in splendor even in our day,
for what you once bestowed on a single people,
freeing them from Pharaoh's persecution
by the power of your right hand,
now you bring about as the salvation of the nations
through the waters of rebirth,
grant, we pray, that the whole world
may become children of Abraham
and inherit the dignity of Israel's birthright.
Through Christ our Lord. All: **Amen.**

Or:

O God, who by the light of the New Testament
have unlocked the meaning
of wonders worked in former times,
so that the Red Sea prefigures the sacred font
and the nation delivered from slavery
foreshadows the Christian people,
grant, we pray, that all nations,
obtaining the privilege of Israel by merit of faith,
may be reborn by partaking of your Spirit.
Through Christ our Lord. All: **Amen.**

READING IV   Isaiah 54:5-14

A reading from the Book of the Prophet Isaiah

The One who has become your husband is your Maker;
　　his name is the Lord of hosts;
your redeemer is the Holy One of Israel,
　　called God of all the earth.

The LORD calls you back,
   like a wife forsaken and grieved in spirit,
   a wife married in youth and then cast off,
   says your God.
For a brief moment I abandoned you,
   but with great tenderness I will take you back.
In an outburst of wrath, for a moment
   I hid my face from you;
but with enduring love I take pity on you,
   says the LORD, your redeemer.
This is for me like the days of Noah,
   when I swore that the waters of Noah
   should never again deluge the earth;
so I have sworn not to be angry with you,
   or to rebuke you.
Though the mountains leave their place
   and the hills be shaken,
my love shall never leave you
   nor my covenant of peace be shaken,
   says the LORD, who has mercy on you.
O afflicted one, storm-battered and unconsoled,
   I lay your pavements in carnelians,
   and your foundations in sapphires;
I will make your battlements of rubies,
   your gates of carbuncles,
   and all your walls of precious stones.
All your children shall be taught by the LORD,
   and great shall be the peace of your children.
In justice shall you be established,
   far from the fear of oppression,
   where destruction cannot come near you.

The word of the Lord. All: Thanks be to God.

RESPONSORIAL PSALM 30

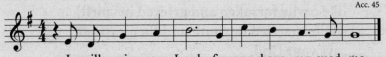

I will praise you, Lord, for you have res-cued me.

or:

I will praise you, Lord,　for you have res-cued me.

or:

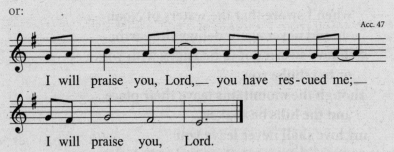

I will praise you, Lord,— you have res-cued me;—

I will praise you, Lord.

Psalm 30:2, 4, 5-6, 11-12, 13

℞. (2a) **I will praise you, Lord, for you have rescued me.**

I will extol you, O LORD, for you drew me clear
　　and did not let my enemies rejoice over me.
O LORD, you brought me up from the netherworld;
　　you preserved me from among those going down into
　　　　the pit. ℞.

Sing praise to the LORD, you his faithful ones,
　　and give thanks to his holy name.
For his anger lasts but a moment;
　　a lifetime, his good will.
At nightfall, weeping enters in,
　　but with the dawn, rejoicing. ℞.

Hear, O LORD, and have pity on me;
　　O LORD, be my helper.

You changed my mourning into dancing;
   O LORD, my God, forever will I give you thanks. R̊.

PRAYER
Let us pray.

Almighty ever-living God,
surpass, for the honor of your name,
what you pledged to the Patriarchs by reason of their faith,
and through sacred adoption increase the children of your promise,
so that what the Saints of old never doubted would come to pass
your Church may now see in great part fulfilled.
Through Christ our Lord. All: **Amen.**

READING V   Isaiah 55:1-11

A reading from the Book of the Prophet Isaiah

Thus says the LORD:
All you who are thirsty,
   come to the water!
You who have no money,
   come, receive grain and eat;
come, without paying and without cost,
   drink wine and milk!
Why spend your money for what is not bread,
   your wages for what fails to satisfy?
Heed me, and you shall eat well,
   you shall delight in rich fare.
Come to me heedfully,
   listen, that you may have life.
I will renew with you the everlasting covenant,
   the benefits assured to David.
As I made him a witness to the peoples,
   a leader and commander of nations,
so shall you summon a nation you knew not,
   and nations that knew you not shall run to you,
because of the LORD, your God,
   the Holy One of Israel, who has glorified you.

Seek the LORD while he may be found,
   call him while he is near.

Let the scoundrel forsake his way,
  and the wicked man his thoughts;
let him turn to the L ORD for mercy;
  to our God, who is generous in forgiving.
For my thoughts are not your thoughts,
  nor are your ways my ways, says the L ORD.
As high as the heavens are above the earth,
  so high are my ways above your ways
  and my thoughts above your thoughts.

For just as from the heavens
  the rain and snow come down
and do not return there
  till they have watered the earth,
  making it fertile and fruitful,
giving seed to the one who sows
  and bread to the one who eats,
so shall my word be
  that goes forth from my mouth;
my word shall not return to me void,
  but shall do my will,
  achieving the end for which I sent it.

The word of the Lord. All: **Thanks be to God.**

R ESPONSORIAL P SALM (Isaiah 12)

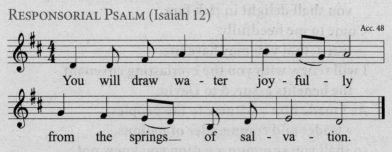

Music: Jay F. Hunstiger, © 1990, administered by Liturgical Press. All rights reserved.

or:

You will draw water joy-ful-ly   from the springs of sal-va-tion.

Music: Bartholomew Sayles, O.S.B., and Cecile Gertken, O.S.B., adapt., © 1977, 1989, Order of Saint Benedict.

or:

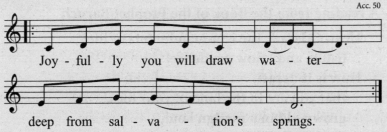

Acc. 50

Joy - ful - ly you will draw wa - ter___
deep from sal - va - tion's springs.

Isaiah 12:2-3, 4, 5-6

℟. (3) **You will draw water joyfully from the springs of salvation.**

God indeed is my savior;
 I am confident and unafraid.
My strength and my courage is the LORD,
 and he has been my savior.
With joy you will draw water
 at the fountain of salvation. ℟.

Give thanks to the LORD, acclaim his name;
 among the nations make known his deeds,
 proclaim how exalted is his name. ℟.

Sing praise to the LORD for his glorious achievement;
 let this be known throughout all the earth.
Shout with exultation, O city of Zion,
 for great in your midst
 is the Holy One of Israel! ℟.

PRAYER
Let us pray.

Almighty ever-living God,
sole hope of the world,
who by the preaching of your Prophets
unveiled the mysteries of this present age,
graciously increase the longing of your people,
for only at the prompting of your grace
do the faithful progress in any kind of virtue.
Through Christ our Lord. All: **Amen.**

READING VI   Baruch 3:9-15, 32—4:4

A reading from the Book of the Prophet Baruch

Hear, O Israel, the commandments of life:
  listen, and know prudence!
How is it, Israel,
  that you are in the land of your foes,
  grown old in a foreign land,
defiled with the dead,
  accounted with those destined for the netherworld?
You have forsaken the fountain of wisdom!
  Had you walked in the way of God,
  you would have dwelt in enduring peace.
Learn where prudence is,
  where strength, where understanding;
that you may know also
  where are length of days, and life,
  where light of the eyes, and peace.
Who has found the place of wisdom,
  who has entered into her treasuries?

The One who knows all things knows her;
  he has probed her by his knowledge—
the One who established the earth for all time,
  and filled it with four-footed beasts;
he who dismisses the light, and it departs,
  calls it, and it obeys him trembling;
before whom the stars at their posts
  shine and rejoice;
when he calls them, they answer, "Here we are!"
  shining with joy for their Maker.
Such is our God;
  no other is to be compared to him:
he has traced out the whole way of understanding,
  and has given her to Jacob, his servant,
  to Israel, his beloved son.

Since then she has appeared on earth,
   and moved among people.
She is the book of the precepts of God,
   the law that endures forever;
all who cling to her will live,
   but those will die who forsake her.
Turn, O Jacob, and receive her:
   walk by her light toward splendor.
Give not your glory to another,
   your privileges to an alien race.
Blessed are we, O Israel;
   for what pleases God is known to us!

The word of the Lord. All: **Thanks be to God.**

RESPONSORIAL PSALM 19

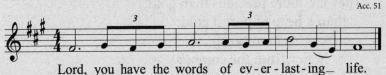

Lord, you have the words of ev‑er‑last‑ing life.

or:

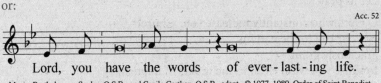

Lord, you have the words of ever‑last‑ing life.

or:

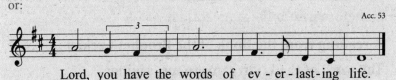

Lord, you have the words of ev‑er‑last‑ing life.

or:

Lord, you have the words of ev‑er‑last‑ing life.

Psalm 19:8, 9, 10, 11

℟. (John 6:68c) **Lord, you have the words of everlasting life.**

> The law of the LORD is perfect,
> > refreshing the soul;
> the decree of the LORD is trustworthy,
> > giving wisdom to the simple. ℟.
>
> The precepts of the LORD are right,   ·
> > rejoicing the heart;
> the command of the LORD is clear,
> > enlightening the eye. ℟.
>
> The fear of the LORD is pure,
> > enduring forever;
> the ordinances of the LORD are true,
> > all of them just. ℟.
>
> They are more precious than gold,
> > than a heap of purest gold;
> sweeter also than syrup
> > or honey from the comb. ℟.

PRAYER
Let us pray.

O God, who constantly increase your Church
by your call to the nations,
graciously grant
to those you wash clean in the waters of Baptism
the assurance of your unfailing protection.
Through Christ our Lord. All: **Amen.**

READING VII   Ezekiel 36:16-17a, 18-28

A reading from the Book of the Prophet Ezekiel

The word of the LORD came to me, saying:
> **Son of man, when the house of Israel lived in their land,**
> **they defiled it by their conduct and deeds.**
Therefore I poured out my fury upon them
> **because of the blood that they poured out on the**
> > **ground,**
> **and because they defiled it with idols.**

I scattered them among the nations,
   dispersing them over foreign lands;
   according to their conduct and deeds I judged them.
But when they came among the nations wherever
     they came,
   they served to profane my holy name,
   because it was said of them: "These are the people of
     the LORD,
   yet they had to leave their land."
So I have relented because of my holy name
   which the house of Israel profaned
   among the nations where they came.
Therefore say to the house of Israel: Thus says the
     Lord GOD:
   Not for your sakes do I act, house of Israel,
   but for the sake of my holy name,
   which you profaned among the nations to which
     you came.
I will prove the holiness of my great name, profaned
     among the nations,
   in whose midst you have profaned it.
Thus the nations shall know that I am the LORD, says the
     Lord GOD,
   when in their sight I prove my holiness through you.
For I will take you away from among the nations,
   gather you from all the foreign lands,
   and bring you back to your own land.
I will sprinkle clean water upon you
   to cleanse you from all your impurities,
   and from all your idols I will cleanse you.
I will give you a new heart and place a new spirit within
     you,
   taking from your bodies your stony hearts
   and giving you natural hearts.

I will put my spirit within you and make you live by my
**　　statutes,**
**　careful to observe my decrees.**
You shall live in the land I gave your fathers;
**　you shall be my people, and I will be your God.**

The word of the Lord. All: **Thanks be to God.**

RESPONSORIAL PSALM

A　*When baptism is celebrated*

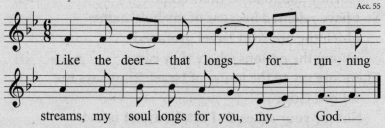

Like the deer— that longs— for— run - ning

streams, my soul longs for you, my— God.—

or:

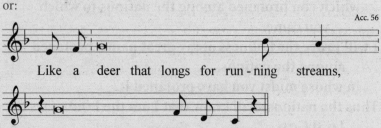

Like a deer that longs for run - ning streams,

my soul longs for you, my God.

or:

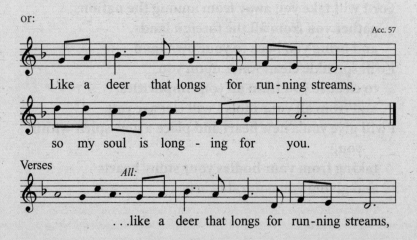

Like a deer that longs for run - ning streams,

so my soul is long - ing for you.

Verses

All:

...like a deer that longs for run - ning streams,

...so my soul is long-ing for you.

Psalm 42:3, 5; 43:3, 4

℟. (42:2) **Like a deer that longs for running streams,
my soul longs for you, my God.**

Athirst is my soul for God, the living God.
   When shall I go and behold the face of God? ℟.

I went with the throng
   and led them in procession to the house of God,
amid loud cries of joy and thanksgiving,
   with the multitude keeping festival. ℟.

Send forth your light and your fidelity;
   they shall lead me on
and bring me to your holy mountain,
   to your dwelling-place. ℟.

Then will I go in to the altar of God,
   the God of my gladness and joy;
then will I give you thanks upon the harp,
   O God, my God! ℟.

B *When baptism is not celebrated*

Acc. 58

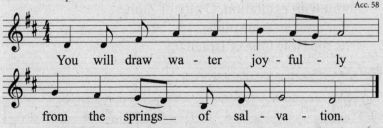

You will draw wa-ter joy-ful-ly

from the springs of sal-va-tion.

or:

Acc. 59

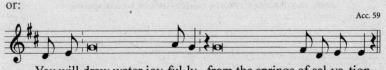

You will draw water joy-ful-ly from the springs of sal-va-tion.

or:

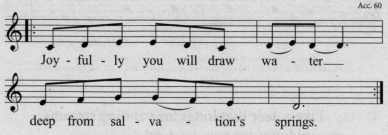

Joy - ful - ly you will draw wa - ter___
deep from sal - va - tion's springs.

Isaiah 12:2-3, 4bcd, 5-6

℟. (3) **You will draw water joyfully from the springs of
    salvation.**

God indeed is my savior;
    I am confident and unafraid.
My strength and my courage is the LORD,
    and he has been my savior.
With joy you will draw water
    at the fountain of salvation. ℟.

Give thanks to the LORD, acclaim his name;
    among the nations make known his deeds,
    proclaim how exalted is his name. ℟.

Sing praise to the LORD for his glorious achievement;
    let this be known throughout all the earth.
Shout with exultation, O city of Zion,
    for great in your midst
    is the Holy One of Israel! ℟.

C *When baptism is not celebrated*

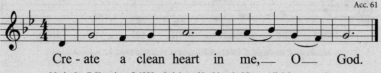

Cre - ate a clean heart in me,___ O___ God.

or:

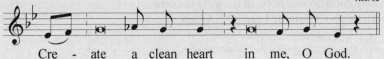

Cre - ate   a clean heart   in me, O God.

Music: Bartholomew Sayles, O.S.B., and Cecile Gertken, O.S.B., adapt., © 1977, 1989, Order of Saint Benedict.

Psalm 51:12-13, 14-15, 18-19

℟. (12a) **Create a clean heart in me, O God.**

A clean heart create for me, O God,
  and a steadfast spirit renew within me.
Cast me not out from your presence,
  and your Holy Spirit take not from me. ℟.

Give me back the joy of your salvation,
  and a willing spirit sustain in me.
I will teach transgressors your ways,
  and sinners shall return to you. ℟.

For you are not pleased with sacrifices;
  should I offer a holocaust, you would not accept it.
My sacrifice, O God, is a contrite spirit;
  a heart contrite and humbled, O God, you will not
    spurn. ℟.

PRAYER
Let us pray.

O God of unchanging power and eternal light,
look with favor on the wondrous mystery of the whole Church
and serenely accomplish the work of human salvation,
which you planned from all eternity;
may the whole world know and see
that what was cast down is raised up,
what had become old is made new,
and all things are restored to integrity through Christ,
just as by him they came into being.
Who lives and reigns for ever and ever. All: **Amen.**

Or:

O God, who by the pages of both Testaments
instruct and prepare us to celebrate the Paschal Mystery,
grant that we may comprehend your mercy,
so that the gifts we receive from you this night

may confirm our hope of the gifts to come.
Through Christ our Lord. All: **Amen.**

GLORIA (*See* pages 6–7, 217, 220, or 224.)

COLLECT
O God, who make this most sacred night radiant
with the glory of the Lord's Resurrection,
stir up in your Church a spirit of adoption,
so that, renewed in body and mind,
we may render you undivided service.
Through our Lord Jesus Christ, your Son,
who lives and reigns with you in the unity of the Holy Spirit,
one God, for ever and ever. All: **Amen.**

EPISTLE   Romans 6:3-11

A reading from the Letter of Saint Paul to the Romans

Brothers and sisters:

Are you unaware that we who were baptized into
    Christ Jesus
    were baptized into his death?
We were indeed buried with him through baptism into
    death,
    so that, just as Christ was raised from the dead
    by the glory of the Father,
    we too might live in newness of life.

For if we have grown into union with him through a
    death like his,
    we shall also be united with him in the resurrection.
We know that our old self was crucified with him,
    so that our sinful body might be done away with,
    that we might no longer be in slavery to sin.
For a dead person has been absolved from sin.
If, then, we have died with Christ,
    we believe that we shall also live with him.
We know that Christ, raised from the dead, dies no more;
    death no longer has power over him.
As to his death, he died to sin once and for all;
    as to his life, he lives for God.

Consequently, you too must think of yourselves as being
dead to sin
and living for God in Christ Jesus.

The word of the Lord. All: **Thanks be to God.**

The Priest solemnly intones the Alleluia three times, raising his voice by a step each time, with all repeating it. If necessary, the psalmist intones the Alleluia.

RESPONSORIAL PSALM 118

or:

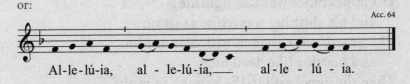

or:

Psalm 118:1-2, 16-17, 22-23

℟. **Alleluia, alleluia, alleluia.**

Give thanks to the LORD, for he is good,
for his mercy endures forever.
Let the house of Israel say,
"His mercy endures forever." ℟.

"The right hand of the LORD has struck with power;
the right hand of the LORD is exalted.
I shall not die, but live,
and declare the works of the LORD." ℟.

The stone which the builders rejected
has become the cornerstone.
By the LORD has this been done;
it is wonderful in our eyes. ℟.

GOSPEL   Matthew 28:1-10

✠ A reading from the holy Gospel according to Matthew

All: **Glory to you, O Lord.**

After the sabbath, as the first day of the week was dawning,
    Mary Magdalene and the other Mary came to see the
        tomb.
And behold, there was a great earthquake;
    for an angel of the Lord descended from heaven,
    approached, rolled back the stone, and sat upon it.
His appearance was like lightning
    and his clothing was white as snow.
The guards were shaken with fear of him
    and became like dead men.
Then the angel said to the women in reply,
    "Do not be afraid!
I know that you are seeking Jesus the crucified.
He is not here, for he has been raised just as he said.
Come and see the place where he lay.
Then go quickly and tell his disciples,
    'He has been raised from the dead,
    and he is going before you to Galilee;
    there you will see him.'
    Behold, I have told you."
Then they went away quickly from the tomb,
    fearful yet overjoyed,
    and ran to announce this to his disciples.
And behold, Jesus met them on their way and greeted them.
They approached, embraced his feet, and did him homage.
Then Jesus said to them, "Do not be afraid.
Go tell my brothers to go to Galilee,
    and there they will see me."

The Gospel of the Lord. All: **Praise to you, Lord Jesus Christ.**

Year B (L 41-B): 2012, 2015, 2018, etc.

GOSPEL   Mark 16:1-7

☩ A reading from the holy Gospel according to Mark

All: **Glory to you, O Lord.**

When the sabbath was over,
  Mary Magdalene, Mary, the mother of James, and
      Salome
  bought spices so that they might go and anoint him.
Very early when the sun had risen,
  on the first day of the week, they came to the tomb.
They were saying to one another,
  "Who will roll back the stone for us
  from the entrance to the tomb?"
When they looked up,
  they saw that the stone had been rolled back;
  it was very large.
On entering the tomb they saw a young man
  sitting on the right side, clothed in a white robe,
  and they were utterly amazed.
He said to them, "Do not be amazed!
You seek Jesus of Nazareth, the crucified.
He has been raised; he is not here.
Behold the place where they laid him.
But go and tell his disciples and Peter,
  'He is going before you to Galilee;
  there you will see him, as he told you.'"

The Gospel of the Lord. All: **Praise to you, Lord Jesus Christ.**

Year C (L 41-C): 2013, 2016, 2019, etc.

GOSPEL   Luke 24:1-12

✝ **A reading from the holy Gospel according to Luke**

All: **Glory to you, O Lord.**

At daybreak on the first day of the week
   the women who had come from Galilee with Jesus
   took the spices they had prepared
   and went to the tomb.
They found the stone rolled away from the tomb;
   but when they entered,
   they did not find the body of the Lord Jesus.
While they were puzzling over this, behold,
   two men in dazzling garments appeared to them.
They were terrified and bowed their faces to the ground.
They said to them,
   "Why do you seek the living one among the dead?
He is not here, but he has been raised.
Remember what he said to you while he was still in Galilee,
   that the Son of Man must be handed over to sinners
   and be crucified, and rise on the third day."
And they remembered his words.
Then they returned from the tomb
   and announced all these things to the eleven
   and to all the others.
The women were Mary Magdalene, Joanna, and Mary the
      mother of James;
   the others who accompanied them also told this to
      the apostles,
   but their story seemed like nonsense
   and they did not believe them.
But Peter got up and ran to the tomb,
   bent down, and saw the burial cloths alone;
   then he went home amazed at what had happened.

The Gospel of the Lord. All: **Praise to you, Lord Jesus Christ.**

THIRD PART: THE BAPTISMAL LITURGY

If there are candidates to be baptized:

Dearly beloved,
with one heart and one soul, let us by our prayers
come to the aid of these our brothers and sisters in their blessed hope,
so that, as they approach the font of rebirth,
the almighty Father may bestow on them
all his merciful help.

If the font is to be blessed, but no one to be baptized:

Dearly beloved,
let us humbly invoke upon this font
the grace of God the almighty Father,
that those who from it are born anew
may be numbered among the children of adoption in Christ.

If no one is to be baptized and the font is not to be blessed, the Litany is
omitted and the Blessing of Water (page 183) takes place at once.

The Litany is sung by two cantors, with all standing (because it is Easter Time)
and responding. In the Litany, the names of some saints may be added,
especially the Titular Saint of the church and the Patron Saints of the place
and of those to be baptized.

LITANY OF THE SAINTS

Acc. 66

Cantor: Lord, have mer-cy. / All: Lord, have mer-cy.
Christ, have mer-cy. / Christ, have mer-cy.
Lord, have mer-cy. / Lord, have mer-cy.

Cantor: Holy Mary, Mother of God, / All: pray for us.
Saint Mich-ael,
Invocation . . .

Cantor: Lord, be mer-ci-ful, / All: Lord, de-liv-er us, we pray.
Invocation . . .

Cantor: Be merciful to us sin-ners, / All: Lord, we ask you, hear our prayer.
Invocation . . .

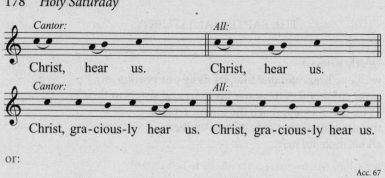

Cantor: Christ, hear us. All: Christ, hear us.

Cantor: Christ, gra-cious-ly hear us. All: Christ, gra-cious-ly hear us.

or:

Acc. 67

Cantor: Lord, have mer - cy. All: Lord, have mer - cy.

Cantor: Christ, have mer - cy. All: Christ, have mer - cy.

Cantor: Lord, have mer - cy. All: Lord, have mer - cy.

Cantor: All:

Holy Mary, Mother of God: pray for us, be with us.
Saint Mi - chael:
Invocation . . .

Cantor: All:

Lord, be merciful: Save us, Lord; hear us, Lord.
Invocation . . .

Cantor: All:

Be merciful to us sinners: {Hear us, Lord; hear our prayer.
Invocation . . . *or:* {Save us, Lord; hear us, Lord.

Jesus, Son of the living God: Save us, Lord; hear us, Lord.
Invocation . . .

If there are candidates to be baptized, the Priest says the following prayer:

Almighty ever-living God,
be present by the mysteries of your great love
and send forth the spirit of adoption
to create the new peoples
brought to birth for you in the font of Baptism,
so that what is to be carried out by our humble service
may be brought to fulfillment by your mighty power.
Through Christ our Lord. All: **Amen.**

BLESSING OF BAPTISMAL WATER

The Priest then blesses the baptismal water.

O God, who by invisible power
accomplish a wondrous effect
through sacramental signs
and who in many ways have prepared water, your creation,
to show forth the grace of Baptism;

O God, whose Spirit
in the first moments of the world's creation
hovered over the waters,
so that the very substance of water
would even then take to itself the power to sanctify;

O God, who by the outpouring of the flood
foreshadowed regeneration,
so that from the mystery of one and the same element of water
would come an end to vice and a beginning of virtue;

O God, who caused the children of Abraham
to pass dry-shod through the Red Sea,
so that the chosen people,
set free from slavery to Pharaoh,
would prefigure the people of the baptized;

O God, whose Son,
baptized by John in the waters of the Jordan,
was anointed with the Holy Spirit,

and, as he hung upon the Cross,
gave forth water from his side along with blood,
and after his Resurrection, commanded his disciples:
"Go forth, teach all nations, baptizing them
in the name of the Father and of the Son and of the Holy Spirit,"
look now, we pray, upon the face of your Church
and graciously unseal for her the fountain of Baptism.

May this water receive by the Holy Spirit
the grace of your Only Begotten Son,
so that human nature, created in your image
and washed clean through the Sacrament of Baptism
from all the squalor of the life of old,
may be found worthy to rise to the life of newborn children
through water and the Holy Spirit.

If appropriate, the Priest lowers the Paschal Candle into the water either once
or three times, continuing:

May the power of the Holy Spirit,
O Lord, we pray,
come down through your Son
into the fullness of this font,

Holding the candle in the water, he continues:

so that all who have been buried with Christ
by Baptism into death
may rise again to life with him.
Who lives and reigns with you in the unity of the Holy Spirit,
one God, for ever and ever. All: **Amen.**

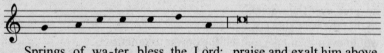

Springs of wa-ter, bless the Lord; praise and exalt him above

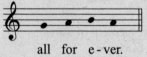

all for e-ver.

Renunciation of Sin and Profession of Faith

If there are candidates to be baptized, the Priest, through a sequence of
questions, asks them (or the parents or godparents of infant children) to
renounce sin and profess their faith.

BAPTISM

Each candidate is baptized immediately after his or her profession of faith. The Priest baptizes each candidate either by immersion or by the pouring of water.

N., I baptize you in the name of the Father,

He immerses the candidate or pours water the first time.

and of the Son,

He immerses the candidate or pours water the second time.

and of the Holy Spirit.

He immerses the candidate or pours water the third time.
After each baptism, one of the following acclamations may be sung:

Acc. 68

Clothed in Christ, one in Christ, we have been bap-tized in Christ. tized in Christ.

or:

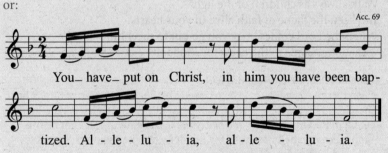

Acc. 69

You have put on Christ, in him you have been bap-tized. Al-le-lu - ia, al-le - lu - ia.

ANOINTING AFTER BAPTISM (optional)

If the confirmation of those baptized is separated from their baptism, the Priest anoints them with chrism immediately after baptism. The Priest says the following over the newly baptized before the anointing:

**The God of power and Father of our Lord Jesus Christ
has freed you from sin
and brought you to new life
through water and the Holy Spirit.**

He now anoints you with the chrism of salvation,
so that, united with his people,
you may remain for ever a member of Christ
who is Priest, Prophet, and King. Newly baptized: **Amen.**

Clothing with a Baptismal Garment (optional)

The newly baptized are clothed with their baptismal garment. At the words
"Receive this baptismal garment" the godparents place the garment on the
newly baptized.

N. and N., you have become a new creation
and have clothed yourselves in Christ.
Receive this baptismal garment
and bring it unstained to the judgment seat of our Lord Jesus Christ,
so that you may have everlasting life. Newly baptized: **Amen.**

Presentation of a Lighted Candle

The Priest takes the Easter candle in his hands or touches it, saying to the
godparents:

Godparents, please come forward to give to the newly baptized the
light of Christ.

A godparent of each of the newly baptized goes to the Priest, lights a candle
from the Easter candle, then presents it to the newly baptized. Then the Priest
says to the newly baptized:

You have been enlightened by Christ.
Walk always as children of the light
and keep the flame of faith alive in your hearts.
When the Lord comes, may you go out to meet him
with all the saints in the heavenly kingdom. Newly baptized: **Amen.**

Celebration of Confirmation

When there are candidates to be received into full communion of the Catholic
Church and if they are also to be confirmed, the Rite of Confirmation follows
the Act of Reception. If not, the newly baptized adults are now confirmed.
Standing before the Priest, with their godparents, the Priest first speaks to
them and then invites all to pray in silence.

Laying on of Hands

The Priest, with outstretched hands, prays these words over the newly
baptized:

All-powerful God, Father of our Lord Jesus Christ,
by water and the Holy Spirit
you freed your sons and daughters from sin
and gave them new life.
Send your Holy Spirit upon them to be their helper and guide.
Give them the spirit of wisdom and understanding,

the spirit of right judgment and courage,
the spirit of knowledge and reverence.
Fill them with the spirit of wonder and awe in your presence.
We ask this through Christ our Lord. All: **Amen.**

ANOINTING WITH CHRISM

N., be sealed with the Gift of the Holy Spirit.
Newly confirmed: **Amen.**

The minister of the sacrament adds: **Peace be with you.**
Newly confirmed: **And with your spirit.**

BLESSING OF WATER

If no one present is to be baptized and the font is not to be blessed, the Priest
introduces the faithful to the blessing of water, saying:

Dear brothers and sisters,
let us humbly beseech the Lord our God
to bless this water he has created,
which will be sprinkled upon us
as a memorial of our Baptism.
May he graciously renew us,
that we may remain faithful to the Spirit
whom we have received.

And after a brief pause in silence, he proclaims the following prayer:

Lord our God,
in your mercy be present to your people
who keep vigil on this most sacred night,
and, for us who recall the wondrous work of our creation
and the still greater work of our redemption,
graciously bless this water.
For you created water to make the fields fruitful
and to refresh and cleanse our bodies.
You also made water the instrument of your mercy:
for through water you freed your people from slavery
and quenched their thirst in the desert;
through water the Prophets proclaimed the new covenant
you were to enter upon with the human race;
and last of all,
through water, which Christ made holy in the Jordan,
you have renewed our corrupted nature
in the bath of regeneration.
Therefore, may this water be for us
a memorial of the Baptism we have received,
and grant that we may share

in the gladness of our brothers and sisters,
who at Easter have received their Baptism.
Through Christ our Lord. All: **Amen.**

RENEWAL OF BAPTISMAL PROMISES

Holding lighted candles, all stand and renew the promise of baptismal faith,
unless this has already been done together with those to be baptized. The
Priest addresses the people in these or similar words:

Dear brethren (brothers and sisters), through the Paschal Mystery
we have been buried with Christ in Baptism,
so that we may walk with him in newness of life.
And so, now that our Lenten observance is concluded,
let us renew the promises of Holy Baptism,
by which we once renounced Satan and his works
and promised to serve God in the holy Catholic Church.

And so I ask you:

A Priest: Do you renounce Satan?   All: **I do.**
  Priest: And all his works?   All: **I do.**
  Priest: And all his empty show?   All: **I do.**

Or:

B Priest: Do you renounce sin, so as to live in the freedom of the
    children of God?
  All: **I do.**

  Priest: Do you renounce the lure of evil, so that sin may have no
    mastery over you?
  All: **I do.**

  Priest: Do you renounce Satan, the author and prince of sin?
  All: **I do.**

Then the Priest continues:

Priest: Do you believe in God, the Father almighty, Creator of heaven
    and earth?
All: **I do.**

Priest: Do you believe in Jesus Christ, his only Son, our Lord, who
    was born of the Virgin Mary, suffered death and was buried,
    rose again from the dead and is seated at the right hand of the
    Father?
All: **I do.**

Priest: Do you believe in the Holy Spirit, the holy Catholic Church,
    the communion of saints, the forgiveness of sins, the resurrec-
    tion of the body, and life everlasting?
All: **I do.**

And may almighty God, the Father of our Lord Jesus Christ,
who has given us new birth by water and the Holy Spirit
and bestowed on us forgiveness of our sins,
keep us by his grace,
in Christ Jesus our Lord,
for eternal life. All: **Amen.**

Acc. 70

> We do be-lieve! This is our faith, this is the faith of the
> Church. We are proud to pro-fess it, in Christ Je - sus.

SPRINKLING WITH BAPTISMAL WATER

The Priest sprinkles the people with the blessed water, while all sing the
following song or another that is baptismal in character.

Ant. I saw water flowing from the Temple,
from its right-hand side, alleluia;
and all to whom this water came were saved
and shall say: Alleluia, alleluia.

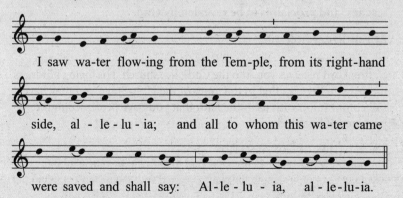

> I saw wa-ter flow-ing from the Tem-ple, from its right-hand
> side, al - le - lu - ia; and all to whom this wa-ter came
> were saved and shall say: Al-le - lu - ia, al - le-lu-ia.

or:

Acc. 71

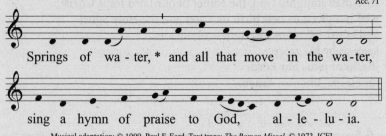

Springs of wa - ter, * and all that move in the wa - ter,
sing a hymn of praise to God, al - le - lu - ia.

CELEBRATION OF RECEPTION

The Priest invites the candidates for reception into full communion of the Catholic Church to make a profession of faith.

N. and N., of your own free will you have asked to be received into the full communion of the Catholic Church. You have made your decision after careful thought under the guidance of the Holy Spirit. I now invite you to come forward with your sponsors and in the presence of this community to profess the Catholic faith. In this faith you will be one with us for the first time at the eucharistic table of the Lord Jesus, the sign of the Church's unity.

PROFESSION BY THE CANDIDATES

The candidates make their profession, saying:

I believe and profess all that the holy Catholic Church believes, teaches, and proclaims to be revealed by God.

ACT OF RECEPTION

The Priest receives each of the candidates, saying:

N., the Lord receives you into the Catholic Church. His loving kindness has led you here, so that in the unity of the Holy Spirit you may have full communion with us in the faith that you have professed in the presence of his family.

CELEBRATION OF CONFIRMATION

The newly baptized with their godparents and, if they are to receive the Sacrament of Confirmation, the newly received with their sponsors, stand before the Priest who speaks to them first and then invites all to pray in silence.

LAYING ON OF HANDS

The Priest, with outstretched hands, prays the following prayer over those who will receive the Sacrament of Confirmation:

**All-powerful God, Father of our Lord Jesus Christ,
by water and the Holy Spirit**

you freed your sons and daughters from sin
and gave them new life.
Send your Holy Spirit upon them to be their helper and guide.
Give them the spirit of wisdom and understanding,
the spirit of right judgment and courage,
the spirit of knowledge and reverence.
Fill them with the spirit of wonder and awe in your presence.
We ask this through Christ our Lord. All: **Amen.**

ANOINTING WITH CHRISM
N., be sealed with the Gift of the Holy Spirit.
Newly confirmed: **Amen.**

The minister of the sacrament adds: **Peace be with you.**
Newly confirmed: **And with your spirit.**

PRAYER OF THE FAITHFUL

FOURTH PART: THE LITURGY OF THE EUCHARIST

PRAYER OVER THE OFFERINGS
Accept, we ask, O Lord,
the prayers of your people
with the sacrificial offerings,
that what has begun in the paschal mysteries
may, by the working of your power,
bring us to the healing of eternity.
Through Christ our Lord. All: **Amen.**

COMMUNION ANTIPHON (1 Corinthians 5:7-8)
Christ our Passover has been sacrificed;
therefore let us keep the feast
with the unleavened bread of purity and truth, alleluia.

Acc. 72

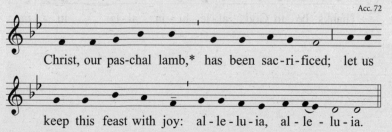

Christ, our pas-chal lamb,* has been sac-ri-ficed; let us keep this feast with joy: al-le-lu-ia, al-le-lu-ia.

Adapted by Paul Ford, © 1999. Published and administered by Liturgical Press, Collegeville, MN 56321.

PRAYER AFTER COMMUNION
Pour out on us, O Lord, the Spirit of your love,
and in your kindness make those you have nourished
by this paschal Sacrament
one in mind and heart.
Through Christ our Lord. All: **Amen.**

SOLEMN BLESSING
May almighty God bless you
through today's Easter Solemnity
and, in his compassion,
defend you from every assault of sin. All: **Amen.**

And may he, who restores you to eternal life
in the Resurrection of his Only Begotten,
endow you with the prize of immortality. All: **Amen.**

Now that the days of the Lord's Passion have drawn to a close,
may you who celebrate the gladness of the Paschal Feast
come with Christ's help, and exulting in spirit,
to those feasts that are celebrated in eternal joy. All: **Amen.**

And may the blessing of almighty God,
the Father, and the Son, ✠ and the Holy Spirit,
come down on you and remain with you for ever. All: **Amen.**

DISMISSAL
To dismiss the people the Deacon or, if there is no Deacon, the Priest himself
sings or says:

Go forth, the Mass is ended, alleluia, alleluia.

Or:

Go in peace, alleluia, alleluia.
All reply: **Thanks be to God, alleluia, alleluia.**

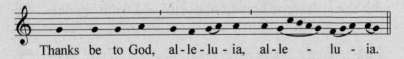

Thanks be to God, al-le-lu-ia, al-le-lu-ia.

Easter Sunday

THE RESURRECTION OF THE LORD

MORNING PRAYER

All stand and trace the cross over their lips as the leader begins:

Invitatory

Leader: Lord, ✚ open my lips.

All: **And my mouth will proclaim your praise.**

Leader: Glory to the Father, and to the Son, and to the Holy Spirit.

All: **As it was in the beginning, is now, and will be for ever. Amen. Alleluia.**

Hymn (See no. 175, p. 275, or another Easter hymn.)

PSALMODY (All are seated. The recitation or chanting of the psalm stanzas may be alternated between two people or groups of people.)

Antiphon 1 (*Leader*) The splendor of Christ risen from the dead has shone on the people redeemed by his blood, alleluia.

Acc. 73

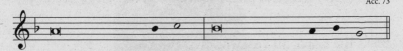

Music: The Collegeville Composers Group,
published and administered by the Liturgical Press, Collegeville, MN 56321. All rights reserved.

Psalm 63:2-9

O God, you are my God; at dawn <u>I</u> seek you;
for you my <u>soul</u> is thirsting.
For you my flesh <u>is</u> pining,
like a dry, weary land <u>with</u>out water.
I have come before you in <u>the</u> sanctuary,
to behold your strength <u>and</u> your glory.

Your loving mercy is better <u>than</u> life;
my lips will <u>speak</u> your praise.
I will bless you all <u>my</u> life;
in your name I will lift <u>up</u> my hands.
My soul shall be filled as with <u>a</u> banquet;
with joyful lips, my <u>mouth</u> shall praise you.

When I remember you upon <u>my</u> bed,
I muse on you through the watches <u>of</u> the night.
For you have been <u>my</u> strength;
in the shadow of your wings <u>I</u> rejoice.
My soul clings fast <u>to</u> you;
your right <u>hand</u> upholds me.

Psalm-prayer (*Leader*) Father, creator of unfailing light, give that same light to those who call to you. May our lips praise you; our lives proclaim your goodness; our work give you honor, and our voices celebrate you for ever.

Antiphon 1 (*All*) **The splendor of Christ risen from the dead has shone on the people redeemed by his blood, alleluia.**

Silence

Antiphon 2 (*Leader*) Our Redeemer has risen from the tomb; let us sing a hymn of praise to the Lord our God, alleluia.

Canticle   Daniel 3:57-88, 56

Bless the Lord, all you works of the Lord.
Praise and exalt him above all for ever.
Angels of the Lord, bless the Lord.
You heavens, bless the Lord.
All you waters above the heavens, bless the Lord.
All you hosts of the Lord, bless the Lord.
Sun and moon, bless the Lord.
Stars of heaven, bless the Lord.

Every shower and dew, bless the Lord.
All you winds, bless the Lord.
Fire and heat, bless the Lord.
Cold and chill, bless the Lord.
Dew and rain, bless the Lord.
Frost and chill, bless the Lord.
Ice and snow, bless the Lord.
Nights and days, bless the Lord.
Light and darkness, bless the Lord.
Lightnings and clouds, bless the Lord.

Let the earth bless the Lord.
Praise and exalt him above all for ever.
Mountains and hills, bless the Lord.
Everything growing from the earth, bless the Lord.
You springs, bless the Lord.
Seas and rivers, bless the Lord.
You dolphins and all water creatures, bless the Lord.
All you birds of the air, bless the Lord.
All you beasts, wild and tame, bless the Lord.
You sons of men, bless the Lord.

O Israel, bless the Lord.
Praise and exalt him above all for ever.
Priests of the Lord, bless the Lord.
Servants of the Lord, bless the Lord.
Spirits and souls of the just, bless the Lord.
Holy men of humble heart, bless the Lord.
Hananiah, Azariah, Mishael, bless the Lord.
Praise and exalt him above all for ever.

Let us bless the Father, and the Son, and the Holy Spirit.
Let us praise and exalt him above all for ever.
Blessed are you, Lord, in the firmament of heaven.
Praiseworthy and glorious and exalted above all for ever.

Antiphon 2 (*All*) **Our Redeemer has risen from the tomb;**
let us sing a hymn of praise to the Lord our God, alleluia.

Silence

Antiphon 3 (*Leader*) Alleluia, the Lord is risen as he
promised, alleluia.

Acc. 74

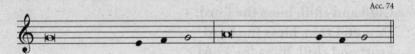

Psalm 149

Sing a new song <u>to</u> the L<small>ORD</small>,
his praise in the assembly <u>of</u> the faithful.
Let Israel rejoice <u>in</u> its Maker;
let Sion's children exult <u>in</u> their king.
Let them praise his <u>name</u> with dancing,
and make music with tim<u>brel</u> and harp.

For the L<small>ORD</small> takes delight <u>in</u> his people;
he crowns the poor <u>with</u> salvation.
Let the faithful ex<u>ult</u> in glory,
and rejoice as they <u>take</u> their rest.

Let the praise of God be <u>in</u> their mouths
and a two-edged sword <u>in</u> their hand,

To deal out vengeance <u>to</u> the nations
and punishment up<u>on</u> the peoples;
to bind their <u>kings</u> in chains
and their nobles in fet<u>ters</u> of iron;
to carry out the judg<u>ment</u> decreed.
This is an honor for <u>all</u> his faithful.

All stand.

Glory to the Father, and <u>to</u> the Son,
   and to the <u>Ho</u>ly Spirit.

As it was in the beginn<u>ing</u>, is now,
   and will be for ever. Amen. <u>Alle</u>luia.

Psalm-prayer (*Leader*) Let Israel rejoice in you, Lord, and
acknowledge you as creator and redeemer. We put our
trust in your faithfulness and proclaim the wonderful
truths of salvation. May your loving kindness embrace us
now and for ever.

Antiphon 3 (*All*) **Alleluia, the Lord is risen as he promised,
alleluia.**

All are seated.

READING   Acts 10:40-43

God raised up Jesus on the third day and granted that he
be seen, not by all, but only by such witnesses as had been
chosen beforehand by God—by us who ate and drank
with him after he rose from the dead. He commissioned us
to preach to the people and to bear witness that he is the
one set apart by God as judge of the living and the dead.
To him all the prophets testify, saying that everyone who
believes in him has forgiveness of sins through his name.

RESPONSORY

Leader: This is the day the Lord has made; let us rejoice
             and be glad, alleluia.

CANTICLE OF ZECHARIAH

All stand.

Leader: Very early on the morning after the Sabbath, when the sun had just risen, they came to the tomb, alleluia.

The text for the Canticle is found on page 96 or see no. 176 or 177 for sung settings.

INTERCESSIONS

Leader: Christ is the Lord of life, raised up by the Father; in his turn he will raise us up by his power. Let us pray to him, saying:

All: **Christ our life, save us.**

Leader: Lord Jesus, light shining in the darkness, you lead your people into life, and give our mortal nature the gift of holiness,

All: **may we spend this day in praise of your glory.**

Leader: Lord, you walked the way of suffering and crucifixion,

All: **may we suffer and die with you, and rise again to share your glory.**

Leader: Son of the Father, our master and our brother, you have made us a kingdom of priests for our God,

All: **may we offer you our joyful sacrifice of praise.**

Leader: King of glory, we look forward to the great day of your coming in splendor,

All: **that we may see you face to face, and be transformed in your likeness.**

Our Father . . .

PRAYER

Leader: God our Father,
by raising Christ your Son
you conquered the power of death
and opened for us the way to eternal life.
Let our celebration today

raise us up and renew our lives
by the Spirit that is within us.
Grant this through our Lord Jesus Christ, your Son,
who lives and reigns with you and the Holy Spirit,
one God, for ever and ever. All: **Amen.**

DISMISSAL

Leader: Go in peace, alleluia, alleluia.
All: **Thanks be to God, alleluia, alleluia.**

CELEBRATION OF THE EUCHARIST

ENTRANCE ANTIPHON (Cf. Psalm 139[138]:18, 5-6)
I have risen, and I am with you still, alleluia.
You have laid your hand upon me, alleluia.
Too wonderful for me, this knowledge, alleluia, alleluia.

Or:

(Luke 24:34; cf. Revelation 1:6)
The Lord is truly risen, alleluia.
To him be glory and power
for all the ages of eternity, alleluia, alleluia.

Adapted by Paul Ford, © 1999. Published and administered by Liturgical Press, Collegeville, MN 56321.

COLLECT

O God, who on this day,
through your Only Begotten Son,
have conquered death
and unlocked for us the path to eternity,
grant, we pray, that we who keep
the solemnity of the Lord's Resurrection

may, through the renewal brought by your Spirit,
rise up in the light of life.
Through our Lord Jesus Christ, your Son,
who lives and reigns with you in the unity of the Holy Spirit,
one God, for ever and ever. All: **Amen.**

READING I (L 42)   Acts of the Apostles 10:34a, 37-43

A reading from the Acts of the Apostles

Peter proceeded to speak and said:
　"You know what has happened all over Judea,
　　beginning in Galilee after the baptism
　　that John preached,
　　how God anointed Jesus of Nazareth
　　with the Holy Spirit and power.
He went about doing good
　　and healing all those oppressed by the devil,
　　for God was with him.
We are witnesses of all that he did
　　both in the country of the Jews and in Jerusalem.
They put him to death by hanging him on a tree.
This man God raised on the third day and granted that
　　　he be visible,
　　not to all the people, but to us,
　　the witnesses chosen by God in advance,
　　who ate and drank with him after he rose from the dead.
He commissioned us to preach to the people
　　and testify that he is the one appointed by God
　　as judge of the living and the dead.
To him all the prophets bear witness,
　　that everyone who believes in him
　　will receive forgiveness of sins through his name."
The word of the Lord. All: **Thanks be to God.**

RESPONSORIAL PSALM 118

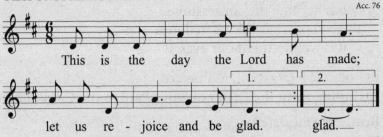

This is the day the Lord has made;
let us re - joice and be glad. glad.

or:

This is the day the Lord has made; let us re-joice and be glad.

or:

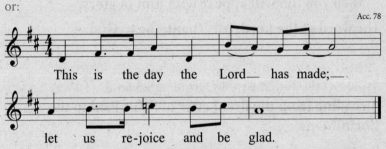

This is the day the Lord__ has made;__
let us re-joice and be glad.

Psalm 118:1-2, 16-17, 22-23

℟. (24) **This is the day the Lord has made; let us rejoice and be glad.** *or:* ℟. **Alleluia.**

Give thanks to the LORD, for he is good,
    for his mercy endures forever.
Let the house of Israel say,
    "His mercy endures forever." ℟.

"The right hand of the LORD has struck with power;
    the right hand of the LORD is exalted.
I shall not die, but live,
    and declare the works of the LORD." ℟.

(continued)

The stone which the builders rejected
　　has become the cornerstone.
By the Lord has this been done;
　　it is wonderful in our eyes. ℟.

Reading II (Option A)　Colossians 3:1-4

A reading from the Letter of Saint Paul to the Colossians

Brothers and sisters:

If then you were raised with Christ, seek what is above,
　　where Christ is seated at the right hand of God.
Think of what is above, not of what is on earth.
For you have died, and your life is hidden with Christ
　　in God.
When Christ your life appears,
　　then you too will appear with him in glory.

The word of the Lord. All: **Thanks be to God.**

Or:

Reading II (Option B)　1 Corinthians 5:6b-8

A reading from the first Letter of Saint Paul to the Corinthians

Brothers and sisters:

Do you not know that a little yeast leavens all the dough?
Clear out the old yeast,
　　so that you may become a fresh batch of dough,
　　inasmuch as you are unleavened.
For our paschal lamb, Christ, has been sacrificed.
Therefore, let us celebrate the feast,
　　not with the old yeast, the yeast of malice and
　　　　wickedness,
　　but with the unleavened bread of sincerity and truth.

The word of the Lord. All: **Thanks be to God.**

SEQUENCE
Victimae paschali laudes

Acc. 79

Al - le - lu - ia, Christ is ri - sen, al - le - lu - ia.

Christians, to the Paschal Victim
   Offer your thankful praises!
A Lamb the sheep redeems;
   Christ, who only is sinless,
   Reconciles sinners to the Father.
Death and life have contended in that combat stupendous:
   The Prince of life, who died, reigns immortal.
Speak, Mary, declaring
   What you saw, wayfaring.
"The tomb of Christ, who is living,
   The glory of Jesus' resurrection;
Bright angels attesting,
   The shroud and napkin resting.
Yes, Christ my hope is arisen;
   To Galilee he goes before you."
Christ indeed from death is risen, our new life obtaining.
   Have mercy, victor King, ever reigning!
   Amen. Alleluia.

VERSE BEFORE THE GOSPEL (*See* 1 Corinthians 5:7b-8a)
Christ, our paschal lamb, has been sacrificed;
let us then feast with joy in the Lord.

Acc. 80

Christ is ri-sen, al-le-lu-ia. Tru-ly ri-sen, al-le-lu-ia. Ri-sen from the dead, al-le-lu-ia, al-le-lu-ia, al-le-lu-ia.

GOSPEL   John 20:1-9

The Gospel from the Easter Vigil, Matthew 28:1-10 (p. 174) or Luke 24:13-35, may be read in place of the following Gospel.

✠ **A reading from the holy Gospel according to John**

All: **Glory to you, O Lord.**

On the first day of the week,
Mary of Magdala came to the tomb early in the
morning,
while it was still dark,
and saw the stone removed from the tomb.
So she ran and went to Simon Peter
and to the other disciple whom Jesus loved, and
told them,
"They have taken the Lord from the tomb,
and we don't know where they put him."
So Peter and the other disciple went out and came to
the tomb.
They both ran, but the other disciple ran faster than Peter
and arrived at the tomb first;
he bent down and saw the burial cloths there, but did
not go in.
When Simon Peter arrived after him,
he went into the tomb and saw the burial cloths there,
and the cloth that had covered his head,

not with the burial cloths but rolled up in a separate
place.

Then the other disciple also went in,
the one who had arrived at the tomb first,
and he saw and believed.

For they did not yet understand the Scripture
that he had to rise from the dead.

The Gospel of the Lord. All: **Praise to you, Lord Jesus Christ.**

RENEWAL OF BAPTISMAL PROMISES

The renewal of baptismal promises may take place at all Masses today,
according to the text used at the Easter Vigil (page 184).

PRAYER OVER THE OFFERINGS

Exultant with paschal gladness, O Lord,
we offer the sacrifice
by which your Church
is wondrously reborn and nourished.
Through Christ our Lord. All: **Amen.**

COMMUNION ANTIPHON (1 Corinthians 5:7-8)

Christ our Passover has been sacrificed, alleluia;
therefore let us keep the feast with the unleavened bread
of purity and truth, alleluia, alleluia.

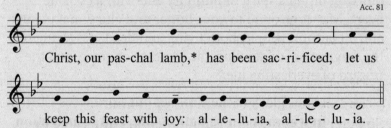

Acc. 81

Christ, our pas-chal lamb,* has been sac-ri-ficed; let us
keep this feast with joy: al-le-lu-ia, al-le-lu-ia.

Adapted by Paul Ford, © 1999. Published and administered by Liturgical Press, Collegeville, MN 56321.

PRAYER AFTER COMMUNION

Look upon your Church, O God,
with unfailing love and favor,
so that, renewed by the paschal mysteries,
she may come to the glory of the resurrection.
Through Christ our Lord. All: **Amen.**

DISMISSAL (*See* p. 188)

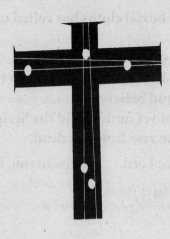

Stations of the Cross

INTRODUCTION

Leader: In the name of the Father, and of the Son, and of the Holy Spirit.

All: **Amen.**

Leader: To you, eternal Father, we now offer this tribute of our worship in a spirit of humility and with a contrite heart. May it resound to your honor and glory, making us and all faithful people, both living and dead, deserving of the forgiveness of our sins, the increase of grace, and the reward of everlasting life.

Leader: Let us glory in the Cross of our Lord Jesus Christ;

All: **In whom is our salvation, life, and resurrection.**

Leader: Let us pray: O God, through the passion, death, and resurrection of your Son, you showed us the path to eternal glory by the way of the Cross. As we now follow him by our prayers to the place of Calvary, may we also share in his victory over sin and death, and be received into his kingdom for all eternity, where he lives and reigns with you and the Holy Spirit for ever. All: **Amen.**

Verse

Were you there when they crucified my Lord?
Were you there when they crucified my Lord?
Oh! Sometimes it causes me to tremble, tremble, tremble!
Were you there when they crucified my Lord?

FIRST STATION: Jesus Is Condemned to Death

Acclamation

Leader: We adore you, O Christ, and we praise you.

All: **By your holy Cross you have redeemed the world.**

or:

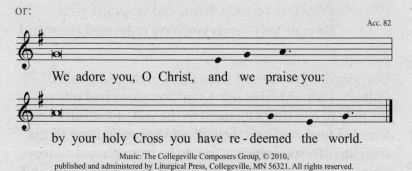

We adore you, O Christ, and we praise you:

by your holy Cross you have re-deemed the world.

Reflection

In the morning, the chief priests, elders, scribes, and the whole council, binding Jesus, led him away and took him to Pilate. And they all condemned him, saying: He is guilty of death; we have found this man saying that he is Christ the King. And Pilate, sitting in the place of judgment, handed Jesus over to them to be crucified.

Response

Leader: God spared not his only Son.

All: **But delivered him up for all of us.**

Leader: Let us pray: Lord Jesus Christ, you came down upon earth from the glory of the Father in heaven, and shed your precious Blood for the remission of our sins. We humbly pray that, on the Day of Judgment, you may find us worthy to be placed at your right hand, and to hear your words: Come, you blessed of my Father! This we ask of you, now living and reigning for ever. All: **Amen.**

Verse

Were you there when they sentenced him to death?
Were you there when they sentenced him to death?
Oh! Sometimes it causes me to tremble, tremble, tremble!
Were you there when they sentenced him to death?

SECOND STATION: Jesus Takes Up His Cross

Acclamation

Leader:　We adore you, O Christ, and we praise you.
All:　　　**By your holy Cross you have redeemed the world.**

Reflection

Carrying his cross, Jesus went forth to the place called Calvary. Hail, O Christ our King! You alone had pity on the folly of our sins. Obedient to the will of the Father, you were led forth and crucified, like an innocent lamb to the slaughter. To you be glory; to you be triumph and victory over sin and death; to you the crown of highest honor and acclaim.

Response

Leader:　The Lord has laid on him the iniquity of us all.
All:　　　**For the wickedness of his people he has stricken him.**

Leader:　Let us pray: Lord, you once said: Take my yoke upon you, and learn from me, for I am gentle and lowly of heart, and you will find rest for your souls; for my yoke is easy and my burden is light. Grant that we may be able so to carry it as to obtain your saving grace. This we ask of you, now living and reigning for ever. All: **Amen.**

Verse

Were you there when he bore the wooden cross?
Were you there when he bore the wooden cross?
Oh! Sometimes it causes me to tremble, tremble, tremble!
Were you there when he bore the wooden cross?

THIRD STATION: Jesus Falls the First Time

Acclamation

Leader: We adore you, O Christ, and we praise you.

All: **By your holy Cross you have redeemed the world.**

Reflection

Our Lord Jesus Christ humbled himself to the point of death, even to death on the cross. That is why God exalted him above every creature, and gave him a name that is above all other names. Come, let us adore and bow down in worship before God; let us weep in the presence of the Lord who made us, who is indeed the Lord our God.

Response

Leader: Surely he has borne our infirmities.

All: **And he has carried our sorrows.**

Leader: Let us pray: Almighty God and Father, we confess that we are weak and that we often fail in the midst of trials and sufferings. Through the merits of the passion, death, and resurrection of Christ, your only begotten Son, you give us new courage and hope. This we ask in Jesus' Name, who lives and reigns for ever. All: **Amen.**

Verse

Were you there when he stumbled to the ground? . . .

FOURTH STATION: Jesus Meets His Mother

Acclamation

Leader: We adore you, O Christ, and we praise you.

All: **By your holy Cross you have redeemed the world.**

Reflection

To what shall I compare you? Or to what shall I liken you, virgin daughter of Jerusalem? For great as the sea is your distress. O Mother of mercy, grant that we may always realize in ourselves the death of Jesus, and share with him in his saving passion.

Response

Leader: A sword of sorrow has pierced your soul.

All: **And has filled your heart with bitter pain.**

Leader: Let us pray: Lord Jesus Christ, at the hour of your cruel death on the cross, a sword of sorrow pierced the grieving soul of the Virgin Mary, your Mother. May she plead for clemency in our behalf, now and at the hour of our death. This we ask of you, now living and reigning for ever. All: **Amen.**

Verse

Were you there when he met his mother's gaze? . . .

FIFTH STATION: Simon of Cyrene Helps Jesus Carry His Cross

Acclamation

Leader: We adore you, O Christ, and we praise you.

All: **By your holy Cross you have redeemed the world.**

Reflection

As the soldiers were leading Jesus away on the road to Calvary, they laid hold of a certain Simon, of Cyrene, a passerby, who was coming in from the country, and forced him to take up the cross of Jesus. If anyone would come after me, let them deny themselves, and take up their cross daily, and follow me.

Response

Leader: Whoever does not carry their cross and come after me.

All: **Cannot be my disciple.**

Leader: Let us pray: O God of grace and might, accept our prayers and sacrifices, and be moved to have mercy on us. Strengthen us in our weakness so that our rebellious wills may yield to your divine will in all things. This we ask of you, through Christ our Lord. All: **Amen.**

Verse

Were you there when they beckoned Simon's help? . . .

SIXTH STATION: Veronica Wipes the Face of Jesus

Acclamation

Leader: We adore you, O Christ, and we praise you.

All: **By your holy Cross you have redeemed the world.**

Reflection

Lo, we have seen him, and there is no beauty in him. He is despised and rejected, a man of sorrows, his face full of grief. He is worn out by suffering, like one in whose presence the people hide their faces. He is scorned and disdained. His appearance is that of one tortured beyond human endurance. Yet, he is fairer than any human, and by his wounds, we are healed.

Response

Leader: Turn not your face away from us.

All: **And withdraw not from your servants in your anger.**

Leader: Let us pray: O God, renew us according to your own image and likeness by the precious Blood of Jesus Christ your Son. Guide our footsteps in your paths, that we may truly experience the gift of your divine charity. This we ask through the same Christ our Lord. All: **Amen.**

Verse

Were you there when she offered him her veil? . . .

SEVENTH STATION: Jesus Falls a Second Time

Acclamation

Leader: We adore you, O Christ, and we praise you.

All: **By your holy Cross you have redeemed the world.**

Reflection

They delivered me into the hands of the impious, they cast me out among the wicked, and they spared not my life. The powerful gathered together against me, and like giants they stood against me. Afflicting me with cruel wounds, they mocked me.

Response

Leader: But I am a worm and no man.

All: **The reproach of many and the outcast of the people.**

Leader: Let us pray: O God, by the humiliation of your Son, you lifted up our fallen world. Grant your faithful people abiding peace and joy. Deliver us from the perils of eternal death, and guide us to eternal happiness in heaven. This we ask through the same Christ our Lord. All: **Amen.**

Verse

Were you there when he fell a second time? . . .

EIGHTH STATION: Jesus Meets the Women of Jerusalem

Acclamation

Leader: We adore you, O Christ, and we praise you.

All: **By your holy Cross you have redeemed the world.**

Reflection

Following Jesus on the road to Calvary was a great multitude of people and of women who bewailed and lamented him. Jesus turned to them and said: Daughters of Jerusalem, weep not for me, but weep for yourselves and for your children. Remember that the days are coming when they will say to the mountains, 'Fall on us,' and to the hills, 'Cover us.' If they do this when the wood is green, what will happen when it is dry?

Response

Leader: They who sow in tears.

All: **Shall reap in joy.**

Leader: Let us pray: O God, you choose rather to have mercy than to be angry with those who place their hope in you. Grant us your grace that we may truly grieve and make amends for the evil we have done, and thus obtain the gift of your heavenly consolation. This we ask through Christ our Lord. All: **Amen.**

Verse

Were you there when the women wept for him? . . .

NINTH STATION: Jesus Falls a Third Time

Acclamation

Leader: We adore you, O Christ, and we praise you.

All: **By your holy Cross you have redeemed the world.**

Reflection

My people, what have I done to you, or in what have I grieved you? Answer me. I brought you out of the land of Egypt, and you have led me to the gibbet of the cross. Forty years I fed you with manna in the desert, and you have beaten me with blows and scourges. What more should I have done for you that I have not done?

Response

Leader: He was led as a sheep to the slaughter.

All: **He was mute as a lamb before the shearer.**

Leader: Let us pray: Guard us, O God on High, by your ever present mercy and goodness. Without your help, we cannot overcome the evil that beckons us, because of our weak human nature. Without you we shall surely fall. Help us to avoid all that is sinful, and guide our steps in the way of all that is profitable for our salvation. This we ask of you through Christ our Lord. All: **Amen.**

Verse

Were you there when he struck the ground again? . . .

TENTH STATION: Jesus Is Stripped of His Garments

Acclamation

Leader: We adore you, O Christ, and we praise you.

All: **By your holy Cross you have redeemed the world.**

Reflection

They came to the place that is called Golgotha, or Calvary, the Place of the Skull. There they gave him wine to drink, mingled with gall. He tasted it, but would not drink. They divided his garments among them by drawing lots, and thus fulfilled what the prophet had said: They divided my garments among them, and for my vesture they cast lots.

Response

Leader: They gave me gall for my food.

All: **And in my thirst they gave me vinegar to drink.**

Leader: Let us pray: Strip us, Lord Jesus, of our former self, with its evil deeds and ways. And clothe us with that newness of nature, which you have created in justice, holiness, and truth. This we ask of you, now living and reigning for ever. All: **Amen.**

Verse

Were you there when the soldiers stripped his clothes? . . .

ELEVENTH STATION: Jesus Is Nailed to the Cross

Acclamation

Leader: We adore you, O Christ, and we praise you.

All: **By your holy Cross you have redeemed the world.**

Reflection

Having arrived at the place called Calvary, they crucified him there, and with him two thieves, one on the right, the other on the left, and Jesus in the midst. My people, what have I done to you? I exalted you with great power, and you have hanged me on the gibbet of the cross.

Response

Leader: They have pierced my hands and feet.

All: **They have numbered all my bones.**

Leader: Let us pray: O God, by the sacred passion of your only begotten Son, and by the five wounds from which his Blood was poured, you repaired the evil wrought by sin in our human nature. As we on earth revere the wounds that he received, we pray that in heaven we may experience the fruit of his most precious Blood. This we ask through Christ our Lord. All: **Amen.**

Verse

Were you there when they nailed him to the tree? . . .

TWELFTH STATION: Jesus Dies on the Cross

Acclamation

Leader: We adore you, O Christ, and we praise you.

All: **By your holy Cross you have redeemed the world.**

Reflection

When Jesus saw his mother at the foot of the cross and, standing near her, the disciple whom he loved, he said to his mother: woman, behold your son. After that he said to the disciple: behold your mother. Having tasted the vinegar, Jesus said: It is finished. Then, crying in a loud voice, he said: Father, into your hands I commend my spirit. And, bowing his head, he gave up his spirit.

Silent Prayer

Response

Leader: Christ for our sake became obedient unto death.

All: **Even to death on the Cross.**

Leader: Let us pray: Lord Jesus Christ, Son of the living God, at the sixth hour you mounted the gibbet of the cross for the redemption of the world, and shed your precious Blood for the remission of our sins. We humbly beg that, after our death, we may enter with joy the gates of paradise. This we ask of you, now living and reigning for ever. All: **Amen.**

Verse

Were you there when he bowed his head and died? . . .

Thirteenth Station: The Body of Jesus is Placed in the
Arms of His Mother

Acclamation

Leader: We adore you, O Christ, and we praise you.

All: **By your holy Cross you have redeemed the world.**

Reflection

All you who pass by the way, look, and see if there be any
sorrow like my sorrow. My eyes are spent with weeping,
my whole being is troubled, and my strength is poured
out upon the earth, as I behold the cruel death of my Son,
for the enemy has prevailed against him. Call me not
Naomi (that is, beautiful), but call me Mara (that is, bitter),
for the Almighty has afflicted me and has dealt quite
bitterly with me.

Response

Leader: Tears are on her cheeks.

All: **And there is none to comfort her.**

Leader: Let us pray: At your passion, Lord Jesus, as Simeon
had foretold, a sword of sorrow pierced the sweet soul of
Mary, your glorious Virgin Mother. As we now reverently
recall her bitter anguish and suffering, grant that we may
obtain the blessed fruits of your redemption. This we ask
of you, now living and reigning for ever. All: **Amen.**

Verse

Were you there when she held him in her arms? . . .

Fourteenth Station: The Body of Jesus Is Laid in the Tomb

Acclamation

Leader: We adore you, O Christ, and we praise you.

All: **By your holy Cross you have redeemed the world.**

Reflection

Joseph of Arimathea, who was a disciple of Jesus, went to
Pilate and asked for the body of Jesus, and Pilate ordered it
to be given to him. Having taken the body down from the

cross, Joseph wrapped it in a clean linen shroud, and laid it in his own new tomb, which he had hewn out in a rock. And he rolled a great stone over the door of the tomb.

Response

Leader: You will not leave my soul in the netherworld.
All: **Nor will you let your holy one see corruption.**

Leader: Let us pray: Lord Jesus Christ, you left us a record of your passion in the holy shroud wherein Joseph wrapped your sacred body when it was taken down from the cross. In your mercy, grant that through your death and burial we may experience the glory of your resurrection. This we ask of you, now living and reigning for ever. All: **Amen.**

Verse

Were you there when they laid him in the tomb? . . .

Conclusion

Leader: Let us pray: O God, you willed that your only begotten Son should suffer and die on the cross for us, in order to rescue us from the power of the enemy. As we now glory in honoring that same holy cross, grant that we may everywhere rejoice in your loving care and obtain the grace of rising with him. This we ask of you through the same Christ our Lord. All: **Amen.**

Dismissal

Leader: May the Lord ✠ bless us, protect us from all evil and bring us to everlasting life. All: **Amen.**

Verse

Were you there when he rose and conquered death? . . .

AT THE CROSS HER STATION KEEPING

Acc. 83

1. At the cross her sta-tion keep-ing,
2. Through her heart, his sor-row shar-ing,
3. Oh, how sad and sore dis-tressed___
4. Christ a-bove in tor-ment hangs;___

1. Stood the mourn-ful moth-er weep-ing,
2. All his bit-ter an-guish bear-ing,
3. Was that Moth-er high-ly blest___
4. She be-neath be-holds the pangs___

1. Close to Je-sus to the last.
2. Now at length the sword has passed.
3. Of the sole be-got-ten One!
4. Of her dy-ing, glo-rious Son.

5. Is there one who would not weep, 'Whelmed in miseries so deep,
   Christ's dear Mother to behold?

6. Can the human heart refrain From partaking in her pain,
   In that Mother's pain untold?

7. Bruised, derided, cursed, defiled, She beheld her tender Child,
   All with bloody scourges rent.

8. For the sins of his own nation, Saw him hang in desolation
   Till his spirit forth he sent.

9. O sweet Mother! fount of love, Touch my spirit from above,
   Make my heart with yours accord.

10. Make me feel as you have felt; Make my soul to glow and melt
    With the love of Christ, my Lord.

11. Holy Mother, pierce me through, In my heart each wound renew
    Of my Savior crucified.

12. Let me share with you his pain, Who for all our sins was slain,
    Who for me in torment died.

13. Let me mingle tears with thee, Mourning him who mourned for me,
    All the days that I may live:

14. By the cross with you to stay, There with you to weep and pray,
    This I ask of you to give.

Text: Ascr. to Jacopone da Todi, c. 1230–1306; tr. by Edward Caswall, 1814–1878, alt.
Music: STABAT MATER, 887; *Maintzisch Gesangbuch*, 1661.

PERSONAL PRAYERS

ANIMA CHRISTI

Soul of Christ, sanctify me.
Body of Christ, save me.
Blood of Christ, inebriate me.
Water from the side of Christ, wash me.
Passion of Christ, strengthen me.
O good Jesus, hear me.
Within your wounds conceal me.
Do not permit me to be parted from you.
From the evil foe protect me.
At the hour of my death call me.
And bid me come to you,
to praise you with all your saints
for ever and ever. Amen.

ACT OF CONTRITION

My God, I am sorry for my sins with all my heart.
In choosing to do wrong and failing to do good,
I have sinned against you
    whom I should love above all things.
I firmly intend, with your help, to do penance,
to sin no more, and to avoid whatever leads me to sin.
Our Savior Jesus Christ suffered and died for us.
In his name, my God, have mercy. Amen.

— from the *Rite of Penance*, © 1974, International Commission on English in
  the Liturgy. All rights reserved.

A PRAYER BEFORE A CRUCIFIX

Look down upon me, good and gentle Jesus, while before
you I humbly kneel and with burning soul pray and beseech
you to fix deep in my heart lively sentiments of faith, hope,
and charity, true contrition for my sins, and a firm purpose
of amendment; while I contemplate with great love and
tender pity your five wounds, pondering over them within
me and calling to mind the words which David, your
prophet, said of you, my Jesus: "They have pierced my
hands and my feet; they have numbered all my bones."

MEMORARE

Remember, O most gracious Virgin Mary, that never was it known that anyone who fled to your protection, implored your help, or sought your intercession was left unaided.

Inspired with this confidence, we fly unto you, O Virgin of virgins, our Mother. To you we come, before you we stand, sinful and sorrowful. O Mother of the Word Incarnate, despise not our petitions, but in your mercy hear and answer us. Amen.

A PRAYER FOR LIFE

Father and maker of all, you adorn all creation with splendor and beauty, and fashion human lives in your image and likeness. Awaken in every heart reverence for the work of your hands, and renew among your people a readiness to nurture and sustain your precious gift of life.

Grant this through our Lord Jesus Christ, your Son, who lives and reigns with you in the unity of the Holy Spirit, God, for ever and ever. Amen.

— Copyright © 2001, United States Conference of Catholic Bishops, Inc., Washington, DC. All rights reserved. Used with permission.

A PRAYER FOR CHARITY IN TRUTH

Father, your truth is made known in your Word. Guide us to seek the truth of the human person. Teach us the way to love because you are Love.

Jesus, you embody Love and Truth. Help us to recognize your face in the poor. Enable us to live out our vocation to bring love and justice to your people.

Holy Spirit, you inspire us to transform our world. Empower us to seek the common good for all persons. Give us a spirit of solidarity and make us one human family.

We ask this through Christ our Lord. Amen.

— This prayer is based on Pope Benedict XVI's 2009 encyclical, *Caritas in Veritate (Charity in Truth).*

THE PSALLITE MASS: AT THE TABLE OF THE LORD

84. KYRIE

Cantor: Ký - ri - e, e - lé - i - son.   *All:* Ký - ri - e, e - lé - i - son.
Chri - ste, e - lé - i - son.   Chri - ste, e - lé - i - son.
Ký - ri - e, e - lé - i - son.   Ký - ri - e, e - lé - i - son.

Ký - ri - e, Ký - ri - e,   Ký - ri - e, e - lé - i - son.
Chri - ste, Chri - ste,   Chri - ste, e - lé - i - son.
Ký - ri - e, Ký - ri - e,   Ký - ri - e, e - lé - i - son.

85. GLORIA

1. Glory to   God in the   highest,
2. We praise you, we   bless you, we a - dore you,
3. Lord God,   heavenly   King,

1. and on earth peace to people   of   good   will.
2. we glorify you, we give you thanks for   your   great   glory,
3. O God, al -   might - y   Father.

4. Lord Jesus Christ, Only Be - got - ten   Son,
5. you take away the sins   of   the   world,
6. you take away the sins   of   the   world,
7. you are seated at the right hand   of   the   Father,

4. Lord God, Lamb of God, Son of   the   Father,
5. have mercy   on   us;
6. receive   our   prayer;
7. have mercy   on   us.

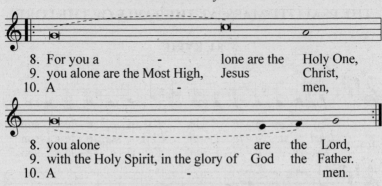

8. For you a - lone are the Holy One,
9. you alone are the Most High, Jesus Christ,
10. A - men,

8. you alone are the Lord,
9. with the Holy Spirit, in the glory of God the Father.
10. A - men.

86. SANCTUS

Holy, Holy, Holy Lord God of hosts.

Heaven and earth are full of your glory.

Ho - san - na in the highest.

Blessed is he who comes in the name of the Lord.

Ho - san - na in the highest.

87–89. MYSTERIUM FIDEI

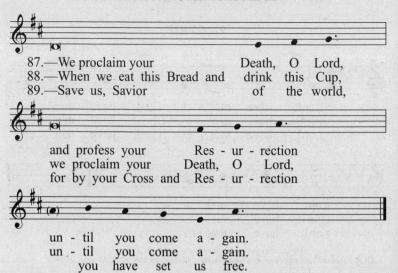

87.—We proclaim your Death, O Lord,
88.—When we eat this Bread and drink this Cup,
89.—Save us, Savior of the world,

and profess your Res - ur - rection
we proclaim your Death, O Lord,
for by your Cross and Res - ur - rection

un - til you come a - gain.
un - til you come a - gain.
you have set us free.

Text: *The Roman Missal,* © 2010, ICEL. All rights reserved.
Music: *Psallite Mass,* The Collegeville Composers Group, © 2010.
Published and administered by Liturgical Press, Collegeville, MN 56321. All rights reserved.

90. AMEN

A - men, A - men, A - men.

Music: *Psallite Mass: At the Table of the Lord,* The Collegeville Composers Group, © 2010.
Published and administered by Liturgical Press, Collegeville, MN 56321. All rights reserved.

91. AGNUS DEI

Cantor: Choir (or all):

A - gnus Dei, qui tollis peccáta mundi:
Lamb of God, you take away the sins of the world:
Cordero de Dios, que quitas el pecado del mundo:
A - gnus Dei, qui tollis peccáta mundi:

All: (To repeat)   All: (Last time)

mi - se - ré - re no - bis.   do - na no - bis pa - cem.

Spanish text: *Misal Romano,* © 1999, 2002, Obra Nacional de la Buena Prensa, A.C. All rights reserved.
Music: *Psallite Mass,* The Collegeville Composers Group, © 2010.
Published and administered by Liturgical Press, Collegeville, MN 56321. All rights reserved.

MASS IN HONOR OF SAINT BENEDICT

92. KYRIE

Cantor: All:

Lord, have mer - cy. Lord, have mer - cy.
Christ, have mer - cy. Christ, have mer - cy.
Lord, have mer - cy. Lord, have mer - cy.

To repeat Last time

Lord, have mer - cy.
Christ, have mer - cy.
Lord, have mer - cy.

93. GLORIA

All:

Glo-ry to God in the high - est, and on earth peace to

peo-ple of good will. We praise you, we bless you, we a-

dore you, we glo-ri-fy you, we give you thanks for your

great glo-ry, Lord God, heav-en-ly King, O God, al-might-y

Cantor/Choir or All:

Fa - ther. Lord Je-sus Christ, On-ly Be-got-ten Son,

Lord God, Lamb of God, Son of the Fa-ther, you take a-

way the sins of the world, have mer-cy on us; you take a-way the sins of the world, re-ceive our prayer; you are__ seat-ed at the right hand of the Fa-ther, have mer-cy on us. *All:* For you a-lone are the Ho-ly One, you a-lone are the Lord, you a-lone are the Most__ High, Je-sus Christ, with the Ho-ly Spir-it, in the glo-ry of God the Fa-ther. A-men, a-men, a-__ men.

94. GOSPEL ACCLAMATION

Al-le-lu-ia, al-le-lu-ia, al-le-lu-ia.

95. GOSPEL ACCLAMATION (LENT)

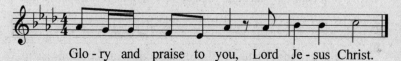

Glo-ry and praise to you, Lord Je-sus Christ.

96. SANCTUS

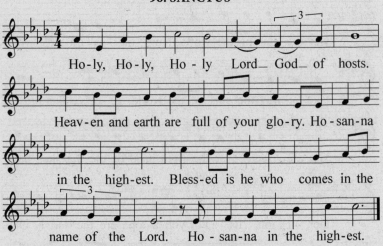

Ho-ly, Ho-ly, Ho-ly Lord God of hosts.

Heav-en and earth are full of your glo-ry. Ho-san-na

in the high-est. Bless-ed is he who comes in the

name of the Lord. Ho-san-na in the high-est.

97. MYSTERIUM FIDEI A

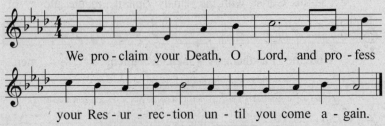

We pro-claim your Death, O Lord, and pro-fess

your Res-ur-rec-tion un-til you come a-gain.

98. MYSTERIUM FIDEI B

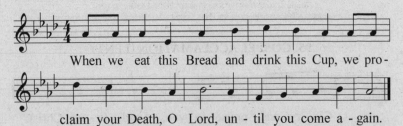

When we eat this Bread and drink this Cup, we pro-

claim your Death, O Lord, un-til you come a-gain.

99. MYSTERIUM FIDEI C

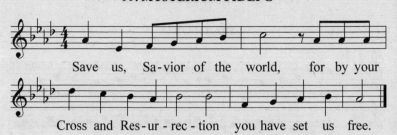

Save us, Sa-vior of the world, for by your

Cross and Res-ur-rec-tion you have set us free.

Text: *The Roman Missal*, © 2010, ICEL. All rights reserved.
Music: *Mass in Honor of Saint Benedict*, Robert LeBlanc, © 2010.
Published and administered by Liturgical Press, Collegeville, MN 56321. All rights reserved.

100. AMEN

A - men, a - men, a - men.

Music: *Mass in Honor of Saint Benedict*, Robert LeBlanc, © 1991.
Published and administered by Liturgical Press, Collegeville, MN 56321. All rights reserved.

101. AGNUS DEI

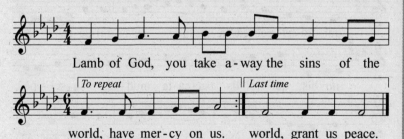

Lamb of God, you take a-way the sins of the

To repeat   Last time

world, have mer-cy on us.   world, grant us peace.

Music: *Mass in Honor of Saint Benedict*, Robert LeBlanc, © 1991.
Published and administered by Liturgical Press, Collegeville, MN 56321. All rights reserved.

CANTUS MISSÆ: IUBILATE DEO

102. GLORIA

Gló-ri-a in ex-cél-sis De-o et in ter-ra pax ho-mí-ni-bus

bo-næ vo-lun-tá-tis. Lau-dá-mus te, be-ne-dí-ci-mus te,

a-do-rá-mus te, glo-ri-fi-cá-mus te, grá-ti-as á-gi-mus

ti-bi pro-pter ma-gnam gló-ri-am tu-am, Dó-mi-ne

De-us, Rex cæ-lé-stis, De-us Pa-ter o-mní-po-tens.

Dó-mi-ne Fi-li U-ni-gé-ni-te, Ie-su Chri-ste,

Dó-mi-ne De-us, A-gnus De-i, Fí-li-us Pa-tris,

qui tol-lis pec-cá-ta mun-di, mi-se-ré-re

no-bis; qui tol-lis pec-cá-ta mun-di, sú-sci-pe

de-pre-ca-ti-ó-nem no-stram. Qui se-des ad

déx-te-ram Pa-tris, mi-se-ré-re no-bis. Quó-ni-am

tu so-lus San-ctus, tu so-lus Dó-mi-nus, tu so-lus

Al - tís - si - mus, Ie - su Chri - ste, cum San - cto
Spí - ri - tu: in gló - ri - a De - i Pa - tris.
A - men.

Text and music: Mass VIII, Mode V, from *Cantus Missae,* Vatican ed., 1974.

103. SANCTUS

San - ctus, San - ctus, San - ctus Dó - mi - nus De - us
Sá - ba - oth. Ple - ni sunt cæ - li et ter - ra gló - ri - a tu - a.
Ho - sán - na in ex - cél - sis. Be - ne - dí - ctus qui ve - nit
in nó - mi - ne Dó - mi - ni. Ho - sán - na in ex - cél - sis.

Text and music: Mass XVIII from *Cantus Missae,* Vatican ed., 1974.

104. MYSTERIUM FIDEI

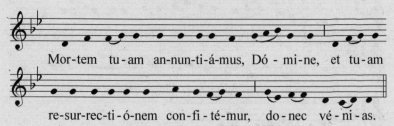

Mor-tem tu-am an-nun-ti-á-mus, Dó - mi-ne, et tu-am
re-sur-rec-ti-ó-nem con-fi - té-mur, do-nec vé - ni - as.

Text and music: *Cantus Missae,* Vatican ed., 1974.

105. AGNUS DEI

A-gnus De - i, qui tol-lis pec-cá-ta mun-di,
mi - se - ré - re no - bis.

A-gnus De - i, qui tol-lis pec-cá-ta mun-di,
mi - se - ré - re no - bis.

A-gnus De - i, qui tol-lis pec-cá-ta mun-di,
do - na no-bis pa - cem.

Text and music: *Cantus Missae,* Vatican ed., 1974.

106. ALL GLORY, LAUD, AND HONOR

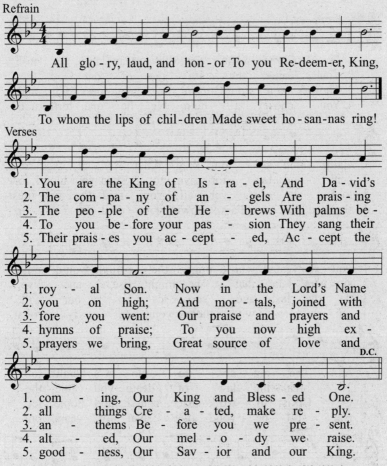

Refrain

All glo - ry, laud, and hon - or To you Re-deem-er, King,

To whom the lips of chil - dren Made sweet ho - san - nas ring!

Verses

1. You are the King of Is - ra - el, And Da - vid's
2. The com - pa - ny of an - gels Are prais - ing
3. The peo - ple of the He - brews With palms be -
4. To you be - fore your pas - sion They sang their
5. Their prais - es you ac - cept - ed, Ac - cept the

1. roy - al Son. Now in the Lord's Name
2. you on high; And mor - tals, joined with
3. fore you went: Our praise and prayers and
4. hymns of praise; To you now high ex -
5. prayers we bring, Great source of love and

1. com - ing, Our King and Bless - ed One.
2. all things Cre - a - ted, make re - ply.
3. an - thems Be - fore you we pre - sent.
4. alt - ed, Our mel - o - dy we raise.
5. good - ness, Our Sav - ior and our King.

Text: *Gloria, laus et honor;* Theodulph of Orleans, c. 760–821; tr. John M. Neale, 1818–1866, alt.
Music: ST. THEODULPH, 76 76 D, Melchior Teschner, 1584–1635.

107. HOSANNA

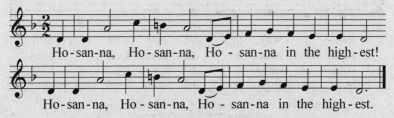

Ho - san - na, Ho - san - na, Ho - san - na in the high - est!

Ho - san - na, Ho - san - na, Ho - san - na in the high - est.

228

108. O CHRIST, WHAT CAN IT MEAN FOR US

1. O Christ, what can it mean for us to
2. You came, the im - age of our God, to
3. Though some would make their great - ness felt and
4. You chose a hum - ble hu - man form and

1. claim you as our king? What roy - al face have
2. heal and to for - give, to shed your blood for
3. lord it o - ver all, you said the first must
4. shunned the world's re - nown; you died for us up -

1. you re - vealed whose praise the church would sing?
2. sin - ners' sake that we might rise and live.
3. be the last and serv - ice be our call.
4. on a cross with thorns your on - ly crown.

1. As - pir - ing not to glo - ry's height, to
2. To break the law of death you came, the
3. O Christ in work - place, church, and home, let
4. But still, be - yond the span of years, our

1. pow - er, wealth, and fame, you walked a dif - ferent,
2. law of love to bring: a dif - ferent rule of
3. none to pow - er cling; for still, through us, you
4. glad ho - san - nas ring, for now at God's right

1. low - ly way, an - oth - er's will your aim.
2. right - eous - ness, a dif - ferent kind of king.
3. come to serve, a dif - ferent kind of king.
4. hand you reign, a dif - ferent kind of king!

Text: Delores Dufner, O.S.B., b. 1939, © 2001, 2003, GIA Publications, Inc.
All rights reserved. Used with permission.
Music: KINGSFOLD, English folk melody; Ralph Vaughan Williams, 1872–1958.

109. REJOICE, O ZION'S DAUGHTER

1. Re - joice, O Zi - on's daugh - ter, and
2. O Christ, though king they hailed you, they
3. But still you come a - mong us in
4. We shout a - gain, "Ho - san - na!" We

1. greet your prom - ised king. Spread branch - es in
2. sent you out do die, for soon the songs
3. cit - ies built with pride. You walk the streets
4. hail you as our king! Christ, stir our wills

1. his path - way and loud Ho - san - nas sing!
2. of prais - es were drowned by, "Cru - ci - fy!"
3. of sor - row where hate and greed di - vide.
4. to ac - tion to match the praise we sing.

1. He comes a - stride a don - key in deep
2. They stripped a - way your gar - ments. They made
3. Re - deem us from our mad - ness, the clash
4. Send us where truth is threat - ened, where jus -

1. hu - mil - i - ty to claim God's com - ing
2. a cross your throne, and there you died in
3. of class and race. Es - tab - lish soon your
4. tice is de - nied, and move our hearts to

1. king - dom, of truth and eq - ui - ty.
2. dark - ness, a - ban - doned and a - lone.
3. king - dom of jus - tice, truth and grace.
4. of - fer the love for which you died.

Text: Herman G. Stuempfle, 1923–2007, © 1997, GIA Publications, Inc. All rights reserved. Used with permission.
Music: ST. THEODULPH, 76 76 D, Melchior Teschner, 1584–1635.

110. O KING OF MIGHT AND SPLENDOR

1. O King of might and splen - dor, Cre - a - tor
2. Thy bod - y thou hast giv - en, Thy blood thou

1. most a - dored, This sac - ri - fice we ren - der To
2. hast out - poured That sin might be for - giv - en, O

1. thee as sov - 'reign Lord. May these our gifts be
2. Je - sus, lov - ing Lord. As now with love most

1. pleas - ing Un - to thy maj - es - ty. Sin - ners from
2. ten - der Thy death we cel - e - brate. Our lives in

1. guilt re - leas - ing Who have of - fend - ed thee.
2. self - sur - ren - der To thee we con - se - crate.

111. TO JESUS CHRIST, OUR SOV'REIGN KING

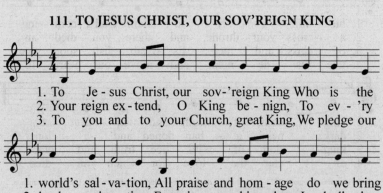

1. To Je - sus Christ, our sov-'reign King Who is the
2. Your reign ex - tend, O King be - nign, To ev - 'ry
3. To you and to your Church, great King, We pledge our

1. world's sal - va-tion, All praise and hom - age do we bring
2. land and na-tion; For in your king-dom, Lord di - vine,
3. hearts' ob - la-tion; Un - til be - fore your throne we sing

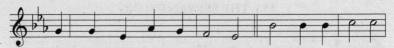

1. And thanks and ad - o - ra - tion.
2. A - lone we find sal - va - tion. Christ Je-sus, Vic-tor!
3. In end - less ju - bi - la - tion.

Christ Je-sus, Rul-er! Christ Je-sus, Lord and Re-deem-er!

112. LIFT HIGH THE CROSS

Lift high the cross, the love of Christ pro - claim

till all the world a - dore his sa - cred name.

1. Come, Chris - tians, fol - low where the Mas - ter trod,
2. Led on their way by this tri - um - phant sign,
3. Each new - born fol-l'wer of the Cru - ci - fied
4. O Lord, once lift - ed on the glo - rious tree,
5. So shall our song of tri - umph ev - er be:

D.C.

1. Our King vic - to - rious, Christ, the Son of God.
2. The hosts of God in con - quering ranks com - bine.
3. Bears on the brow the seal of him who died.
4. Your death has bought us life e - ter - nal - ly.
5. Praise to the Cru - ci - fied for vic - to - ry.

113. THE SERVANT SONG

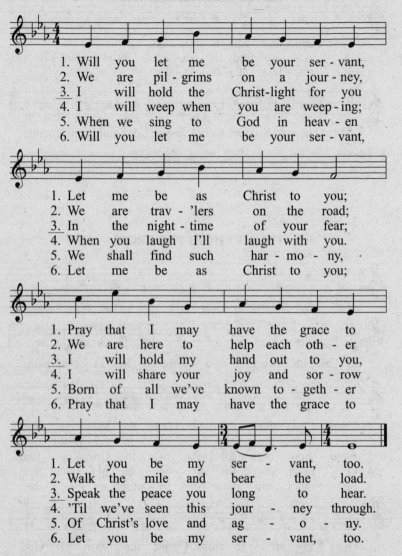

1. Will you let me be your ser - vant,
2. We are pil - grims on a jour - ney,
3. I will hold the Christ-light for you
4. I will weep when you are weep - ing;
5. When we sing to God in heav - en
6. Will you let me be your ser - vant,

1. Let me be as Christ to you;
2. We are trav - 'lers on the road;
3. In the night - time of your fear;
4. When you laugh I'll laugh with you.
5. We shall find such har - mo - ny,
6. Let me be as Christ to you;

1. Pray that I may have the grace to
2. We are here to help each oth - er
3. I will hold my hand out to you,
4. I will share your joy and sor - row
5. Born of all we've known to - geth - er
6. Pray that I may have the grace to

1. Let you be my ser - vant, too.
2. Walk the mile and bear the load.
3. Speak the peace you long to hear.
4. 'Til we've seen this jour - ney through.
5. Of Christ's love and ag - o - ny.
6. Let you be my ser - vant, too.

114. WHERE CHARITY AND LOVE PREVAIL

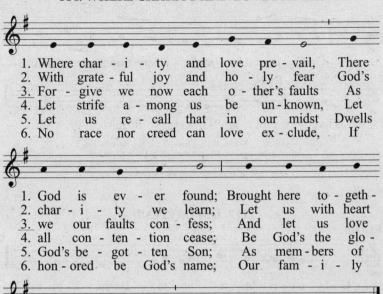

1. Where char - i - ty and love pre - vail, There
2. With grate - ful joy and ho - ly fear God's
3. For - give we now each o - ther's faults As
4. Let strife a - mong us be un - known, Let
5. Let us re - call that in our midst Dwells
6. No race nor creed can love ex - clude, If

1. God is ev - er found; Brought here to - geth -
2. char - i - ty we learn; Let us with heart
3. we our faults con - fess; And let us love
4. all con - ten - tion cease; Be God's the glo -
5. God's be - got - ten Son; As mem - bers of
6. hon - ored be God's name; Our fam - i - ly

1. er by Christ's love By love are we thus bound.
2. and mind and soul Now love God in re - turn.
3. each oth - er well In Chris - tian ho - li - ness.
4. ry that we seek, Be ours God's ho - ly peace.
5. his bod - y joined We are in Christ made one.
6. em - bra - ces all Whose Fa - ther is the same.

Text: Based on *Ubi caritas,* 9th cent., tr. by Omer Westendorf, 1916–1997. Music: CHRISTIAN LOVE, CM, 86 86; Paul Benoit, 1893–1979. Text and music: © 1960, World Library Publications, 3825 N. Willow Rd., Schiller Park, IL 60176. All rights reserved. Used with permission.

115. NO GREATER LOVE

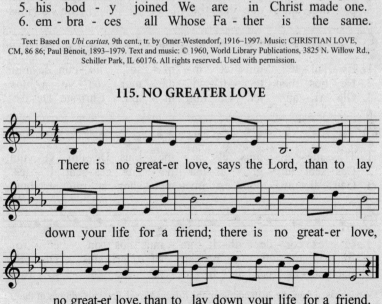

There is no great-er love, says the Lord, than to lay

down your life for a friend; there is no great-er love,

no great-er love, than to lay down your life for a friend.

Text and music: Michael Joncas, b. 1951, © 1988, GIA Publications, Inc. All rights reserved. Used with permission.

116. GOD IS LOVE

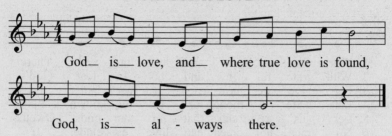

God— is— love, and— where true love is found,

God, is— al - ways there.

117. UBI CARITAS

Refrain

U - bi cá - ri - tas *est ve - ra De - us i - bi est.

Verses

1. Con - gre - gá - vit nos in u - num Chri - sti a - mor.
2. Si - mul er - go cum in u - num con - gre - gá - mur:
3. Si - mul quo - que cum be - á - tis vi - de - á - mus

1. Ex - sul - té - mus et in ip - so iu - cun - dé - mur.
2. Ne nos men - te di - vi - dá - mur, ca - ve - á - mus.
3. Glo - ri - án - ter vul - tum tu - um, Chri - ste De - us:

1. Ti - me - á - mus et a - mé - mus De - um vi - vum.
2. Ces - sent iúr - gi - a ma - lí - gna, ces - sent li - tes.
3. Gáu - di - um, quod est im - mén - sum at - que pro - bum,

D.C.

1. Et ex cor - de di - li - gá - mus nos sin - cé - ro.
2. Et in mé - di - o no - stri sit Chri - stus De - us.
3. Saé - cu - la per in - fi - ní - ta sae - cu - ló - rum.

*Version taken from the 2010 edition of the *Roman Missal*. Previous editions of the
Missal used "et amor."

118. WHERE TRUE CHARITY IS DWELLING

Refrain

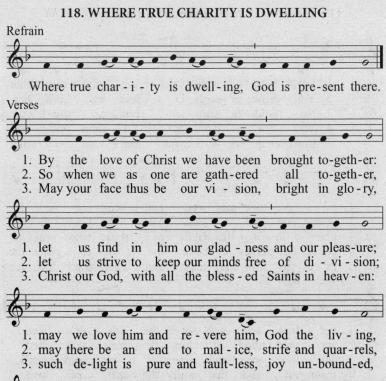

Where true char-i-ty is dwell-ing, God is pre-sent there.

Verses

1. By the love of Christ we have been brought to-geth-er:
2. So when we as one are gath-ered all to-geth-er,
3. May your face thus be our vi-sion, bright in glo-ry,

1. let us find in him our glad-ness and our pleas-ure;
2. let us strive to keep our minds free of di-vi-sion;
3. Christ our God, with all the bless-ed Saints in heav-en:

1. may we love him and re-vere him, God the liv-ing,
2. may there be an end to mal-ice, strife and quar-rels,
3. such de-light is pure and fault-less, joy un-bound-ed,

1. and in love re-spect each oth-er
2. and let Christ our God be dwell-ing
3. which en-dures through count-less ag-es

D.C.

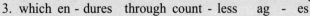
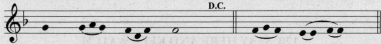

1. with sin-cere hearts.
2. here a-mong us.
3. world with-out end. A-men.

Text: *Ubi Caritas*, tr. International Commission on English in the Liturgy (ICEL), © 2010. All rights reserved.
Music: UBI CARITAS, Plainchant, Mode VI.

236

119. LORD, HELP US WALK YOUR SERVANT WAY

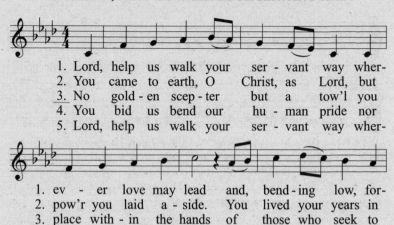

1. Lord, help us walk your ser - vant way wher-
2. You came to earth, O Christ, as Lord, but
3. No gold - en scep - ter but a tow'l you
4. You bid us bend our hu - man pride nor
5. Lord, help us walk your ser - vant way wher-

1. ev - er love may lead and, bend-ing low, for-
2. pow'r you laid a - side. You lived your years in
3. place with - in the hands of those who seek to
4. count our-selves a - bove the low - est place, the
5. ev - er love may lead and, bend-ing low, for-

1. get - ting self, each serve the oth - er's need.
2. ser - vant-hood, in low - li - ness you died.
3. fol - low you and live by your com - mands.
4. mean - est task that waits the gift of love.
5. get - ting self, each serve the oth - er's need.

Text: Herman G. Stuempfle, Jr., 1923–2007, © 1994, 1997, GIA Publications, Inc. All rights reserved.
Used with permission. Music: MORNING SONG, 86 86, *Kentucky Harmony*.

120. STAY HERE AND KEEP WATCH

Ostinato Refrain

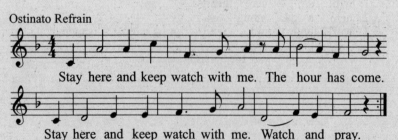

Stay here and keep watch with me. The hour has come.

Stay here and keep watch with me. Watch and pray.

Text: Taizé Community. Music: Jacques Berthier, 1923–1994, © 1984, Les Presses de Taizé,
GIA Publications, Inc., agent. All rights reserved. Used with permission.

121. SO YOU MUST DO

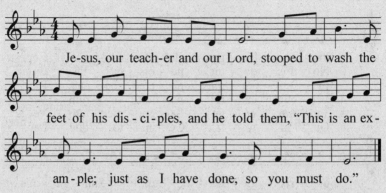

Je-sus, our teach-er and our Lord, stooped to wash the feet of his dis-ci-ples, and he told them, "This is an ex-am-ple; just as I have done, so you must do."

122. UBI CARITAS / LIVE IN CHARITY

U - bi ca - ri - tas et a - mor,
Live in char - i - ty and stead - fast love,

u - bi ca - ri - tas De - us i - bi est.
live in char - i - ty; God will dwell in you.

123. JESUS TOOK A TOWEL

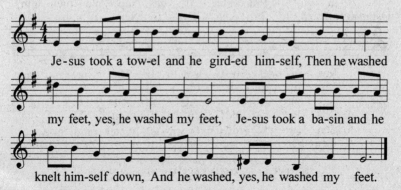

Je-sus took a tow-el and he gird-ed him-self, Then he washed my feet, yes, he washed my feet, Je-sus took a ba-sin and he knelt him-self down, And he washed, yes, he washed my feet.

124. PANGE LINGUA

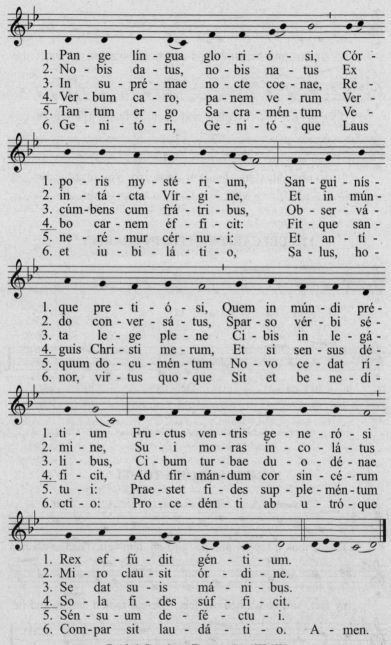

1. Pan - ge lín - gua glo - ri - ó - si, Cór -
2. No - bis da - tus, no - bis na - tus Ex
3. In su - pré - mae no - cte coe - nae, Re -
4. Ver - bum ca - ro, pa - nem ve - rum Ver -
5. Tan - tum er - go Sa - cra - mén - tum Ve -
6. Ge - ni - tó - ri, Ge - ni - tó - que Laus

1. po - ris my - sté - ri - um, San - gui - nís -
2. in - tá - cta Vír - gi - ne, Et in mún -
3. cúm - bens cum frá - tri - bus, Ob - ser - vá -
4. bo car - nem éf - fi - cit: Fit - que san -
5. ne - ré - mur cér - nu - i: Et an - tí -
6. et iu - bi - lá - ti - o, Sa - lus, ho -

1. que pre - ti - ó - si, Quem in mún - di pré -
2. do con - ver - sá - tus, Spar - so vér - bi sé -
3. ta le - ge ple - ne Ci - bis in le - gá -
4. guis Chri - sti me - rum, Et si sen - sus dé -
5. quum do - cu - mén - tum No - vo ce - dat rí -
6. nor, vir - tus quo - que Sit et be - ne - dí -

1. ti - um Fru - ctus ven - tris ge - ne - ró - si
2. mi - ne, Su - i mo - ras in - co - lá - tus
3. li - bus, Ci - bum tur - bae du - o - dé - nae
4. fi - cit, Ad fir - mán - dum cor sin - cé - rum
5. tu - i: Prae - stet fi - des sup - ple - mén - tum
6. cti - o: Pro - ce - dén - ti ab u - tró - que

1. Rex ef - fú - dit gén - ti - um.
2. Mi - ro clau - sit ór - di - ne.
3. Se dat su - is má - ni - bus.
4. So - la fi - des súf - fi - cit.
5. Sén - su - um de - fé - ctu - i.
6. Com - par sit lau - dá - ti - o. A - men.

Text: Latin *Pange lingua,* Thomas Aquinas, 1227–1274.
Music: PANGE LINGUA GLORIOSI, 87 87 87, Plainchant, Mode III.

125. SING, MY TONGUE! ACCLAIM CHRIST PRESENT

1. Sing, my tongue! Ac - claim Christ pres - ent,
2. Heav - en's prom - ised gift to mor - tals,
3. Din - ing with his twelve a - pos - tles
4. Word - made - flesh makes bread his bod - y,
5. Bow - ing low, then, of - fer hom - age
6. Praise and glo - ri - fy the Fa - ther,

1. Veiled with - in this sa - cred sign: Pre - cious blood
2. Born to vir - gin full of grace, Plants the seed
3. On the night be - fore he died, Tak - ing for
4. Con - se - crates it by his word. Wine be - comes
5. To a Sac - ra - ment so great! Here is new
6. Bless his Son's life - giv - ing Name, Sing - ing their

1. and ris - en bod - y Un - der forms of bread
2. of faith se - cure - ly While he dwells with Ad -
3. the pas - chal sup - per Foods the law had spec -
4. the blood of Je - sus: He it is whose voice
5. and per - fect wor - ship; All the old must ter -
6. e - ter - nal God - head, Pow - er, maj - es - ty

1. and wine: Blood once shed for our re - demp - tion
2. am's race. Ends his mis - sion, leaves a sym - bol
3. i - fied. Lo, he sets new bread be - fore them,
4. is heard. Minds in doubt need faith's as - sur - ance;
5. mi - nate. Sens - es can - not grasp this mar - vel;
6. and fame, Of - fer - ing their Ho - ly Spir - it

1. By this king, of Da - vid's line.
2. Of the death he will em - brace.
3. Hand - ing each Christ cru - ci - fied!
4. God who spoke can - not have erred.
5. Faith must serve to com - pen - sate.
6. E - qual wor - ship and ac - claim. A - men.

Text: Latin *Pange lingua*, Thomas Aquinas, 1227–1274; tr. Benedict Avery, 1919–2008.
© 1959, 1977, Order of Saint Benedict.
Published and administered by Liturgical Press, Collegeville, MN 56321. All rights reserved.
Music: PANGE LINGUA GLORIOSI, 87 87 87, Plainchant, Mode III.

126. HAIL OUR SAVIOR'S GLORIOUS BODY

1. Hail our Sav - ior's glo - rious Bod - y, which
2. To the Vir - gin, for our heal - ing, His
3. On that pas - chal eve - ning see him with
4. By his word the Word al - might - y makes
5. Come, a - dore this won-drous pres - ence; bow
6. Glo - ry be to God the Fa - ther, praise

1. his Vir - gin Moth - er bore; hail the Blood
2. own Son the Fa - ther sends; from the Fa -
3. the cho - sen twelve re - cline, to the old
4. of bread his flesh in - deed; wine be-comes
5. to Christ, the source of grace! Here is kept
6. to his co - e - qual Son, ad - o - ra -

1. which, shed for sin - ners, did a bro - ken world
2. ther's love pro - ceed - ing sow - er, seed and word
3. law still o - be - dient in its feast of love
4. his ver - y life-blood; faith God's liv - ing Word
5. the an - cient pro - mise of God's earth - ly dwell-
6. tion to the Spir - it, bond of love, in God-

1. re - store; hail the sac - ra - ment most ho - ly,
2. de - scends; won-drous life of Word in - car - nate
3. di - vine; love di - vine, the new law giv - ing,
4. must heed! Faith a - lone may safe - ly guide us
5. ing place! Sight is blind be - fore God's glo - ry,
6. head one! Blest be God by all cre - a - tion

1. flesh and blood of Christ a - dore!
2. with his great - est won - der ends.
3. gives him - self as bread and wine.
4. where the sens - es can - not lead!
5. faith a - lone may see his face!
6. joy - ous - ly while a - ges run! A - men.

Text: Latin *Pange lingua*, Thomas Aquinas, 1227–1274, tr. James Quinn, S.J., b. 1919, © 1969, James Quinn, S.J.,
Selah Publishing Co., North American agent. All rights reserved. Used with permission.
Music: PANGE LINGUA GLORIOSI, 87 87 87, Plainchant, Mode III.

127. PREPARE A ROOM FOR ME

1. "Pre - pare a room for me, your Sav - ior,
2. "This room we have pre - pared; the Ta - ble
3. "Where e - ven two or three have come the
4. "Lord Christ, we seek the food your grace a -
5. "My prom - ise I will keep; your hun - ger
6. "All thanks and praise to you, our Sav - ior,

1. Host and Priest, where I may gath - er
2. now is set. We wait your prom - ised
3. Meal to share, un - seen, but liv - ing,
4. lone can give. We come with emp - ty,
5. will be fed, for in this Meal I
6. Lord and Friend, that through this Loaf and

1. you, my friends, to cel - e - brate the feast."
2. pres - ence, Lord, where we once more are met."
3. lov - ing still, I sure - ly will be there!"
4. hun - g'ring hearts that we may eat and live."
5. of - fer you my - self, the liv - ing Bread!"
6. Cup you share your love that has no end!"

Text: Herman G. Stuempfle, Jr., 1923–2007, © 2000, GIA Publications, Inc.
All rights reserved. Used with permission. Music: SWABIA, Johann M. Speiss, 1715–1772.

128. JESUS, REMEMBER ME

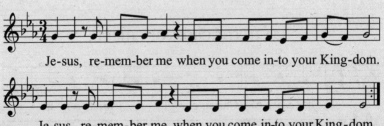

Je-sus, re-mem-ber me when you come in-to your King-dom.

Je-sus, re-mem-ber me when you come in-to your King-dom.

Text: Taizé Community, 1981. Music: Jacques Berthier, 1923–1994, © 1981, Les Presses de Taizé,
GIA Publications, Inc., agent. All rights reserved. Used with permission.

129. TREE OF LIFE

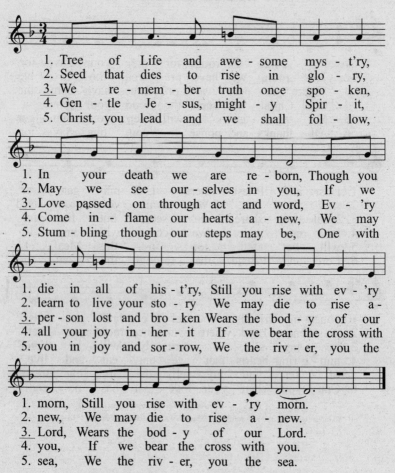

1. Tree of Life and awe - some mys - t'ry,
2. Seed that dies to rise in glo - ry,
3. We re - mem - ber truth once spo - ken,
4. Gen - tle Je - sus, might - y Spir - it,
5. Christ, you lead and we shall fol - low,

1. In your death we are re - born, Though you
2. May we see our - selves in you, If we
3. Love passed on through act and word, Ev - 'ry
4. Come in - flame our hearts a - new, We may
5. Stum - bling though our steps may be, One with

1. die in all of his - t'ry, Still you rise with ev - 'ry
2. learn to live your sto - ry We may die to rise a -
3. per - son lost and bro - ken Wears the bod - y of our
4. all your joy in - her - it If we bear the cross with
5. you in joy and sor - row, We the riv - er, you the

1. morn, Still you rise with ev - 'ry morn.
2. new, We may die to rise a - new.
3. Lord, Wears the bod - y of our Lord.
4. you, If we bear the cross with you.
5. sea, We the riv - er, you the sea.

Text: Marty Haugen, b. 1950. Music: THOMAS, 8 7 8 77; Marty Haugen, b. 1950.

130. IN THE CROSS OF CHRIST

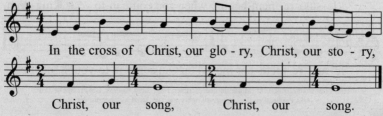

In the cross of Christ, our glo - ry, Christ, our sto - ry,

Christ, our song, Christ, our song.

131. FAITHFUL CROSS (CRUX FIDELIS)

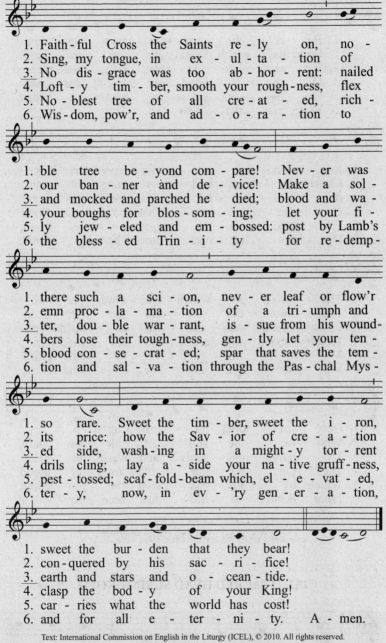

1. Faith-ful Cross the Saints re-ly on, no-
2. Sing, my tongue, in ex-ul-ta-tion of
3. No dis-grace was too ab-hor-rent: nailed
4. Loft-y tim-ber, smooth your rough-ness, flex
5. No-blest tree of all cre-at-ed, rich-
6. Wis-dom, pow'r, and ad-o-ra-tion to

1. ble tree be-yond com-pare! Nev-er was
2. our ban-ner and de-vice! Make a sol-
3. and mocked and parched he died; blood and wa-
4. your boughs for blos-som-ing; let your fi-
5. ly jew-eled and em-bossed: post by Lamb's
6. the bless-ed Trin-i-ty for re-demp-

1. there such a sci-on, nev-er leaf or flow'r
2. emn proc-la-ma-tion of a tri-umph and
3. ter, dou-ble war-rant, is-sue from his wound-
4. bers lose their tough-ness, gen-tly let your ten-
5. blood con-se-crat-ed; spar that saves the tem-
6. tion and sal-va-tion through the Pas-chal Mys-

1. so rare. Sweet the tim-ber, sweet the i-ron,
2. its price: how the Sav-ior of cre-a-tion
3. ed side, wash-ing in a might-y tor-rent
4. drils cling; lay a-side your na-tive gruff-ness,
5. pest-tossed; scaf-fold-beam which, el-e-vat-ed,
6. ter-y, now, in ev-'ry gen-er-a-tion,

1. sweet the bur-den that they bear!
2. con-quered by his sac-ri-fice!
3. earth and stars and o-cean-tide.
4. clasp the bod-y of your King!
5. car-ries what the world has cost!
6. and for all e-ter-ni-ty. A-men.

132. BEHOLD THE ROYAL CROSS ON HIGH

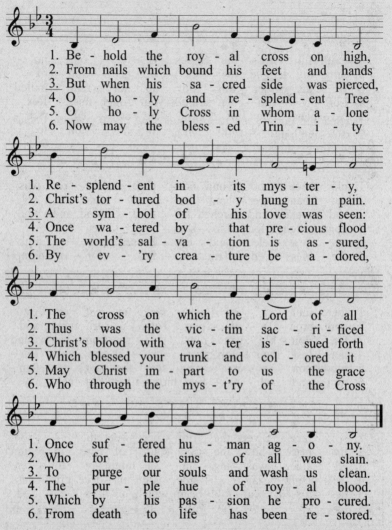

1. Be-hold the roy-al cross on high,
2. From nails which bound his feet and hands
3. But when his sa-cred side was pierced,
4. O ho-ly and re-splend-ent Tree
5. O ho-ly Cross in whom a-lone
6. Now may the bless-ed Trin-i-ty

1. Re-splend-ent in its mys-ter-y,
2. Christ's tor-tured bod-y hung in pain.
3. A sym-bol of his love was seen:
4. Once wa-tered by that pre-cious flood
5. The world's sal-va-tion is as-sured,
6. By ev-'ry crea-ture be a-dored,

1. The cross on which the Lord of all
2. Thus was the vic-tim sac-ri-ficed
3. Christ's blood with wa-ter is-sued forth
4. Which blessed your trunk and col-ored it
5. May Christ im-part to us the grace
6. Who through the mys-t'ry of the Cross

1. Once suf-fered hu-man ag-o-ny.
2. Who for the sins of all was slain.
3. To purge our souls and wash us clean.
4. The pur-ple hue of roy-al blood.
5. Which by his pas-sion he pro-cured.
6. From death to life has been re-stored.

Text: *Vexilla Regis prodeunt,* Venantius Fortunatus, 530–609; tr. Frank C. Quinn, OP, 1932–2008,
© 1989, GIA Publications, Inc. All rights reserved. Used with permission.
Music: DEUS TUORUM MILITUM, LM, *Grenoble Antiphoner,* 1753.

133. O SACRED HEAD SURROUNDED

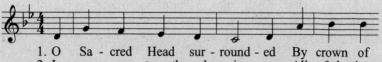

1. O Sa-cred Head sur-round-ed By crown of
2. I see your strength and vig-or All fad-ing
3. In this, your bit-ter pas-sion, Good Shep-herd,

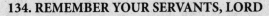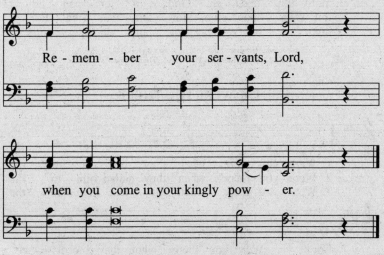

1. pierc - ing thorn! O bleed - ing Head, so wound - ed, Re-
2. in the strife, And death with cru - el rig - or, Be-
3. think of me With your most sweet com - pas - sion, Un-

1. viled and put to scorn! The pow'r of death comes
2. reav - ing you of life; O ag - o - ny and
3. worth - y though I be: Be - neath your cross a-

1. o'er you, The glow of life de - cays, Yet an - gel
2. dy - ing! O love to sin - ners free! Je - sus, all
3. bid - ing For ev - er would I rest, In your dear

1. hosts a - dore you, And trem - ble as they gaze.
2. grace sup - ply - ing, O turn your face on me.
3. love con - fid - ing, And with your pres - ence blest.

Text: *Salve caput cruentatum;* ascr. to Bernard of Clairvaux, 1091–1153; tr. by Henry Baker, 1821–1877.
Music: PASSION CHORALE, 76 76 D, Hans Leo Hassler, 1564–1612.

134. REMEMBER YOUR SERVANTS, LORD

Re - mem - ber your ser - vants, Lord,

when you come in your kingly pow - er.

Text: Russian Orthodox Liturgy; Matthew 5:3-12.
Music: BEATITUDES, Irregular with Refrain, Russian orthodox hymn; arr. Richard Proulx, 1937–2010,

135. AH, HOLY JESUS

1. Ah, ho - ly Je - sus, how hast thou of-
2. Who was the guilt - y? Who brought this up-
3. Lo, the Good Shep - herd for the sheep is
4. For me, kind Je - sus, was thine in - car-
5. There-fore, kind Je - sus, since I can - not

1. fend - ed that we to judge thee have in hate
2. on thee? A - las, my trea - son, Je - sus, hath
3. of - fered; the slave hath sin - ned, and the Son
4. na - tion, thy mor - tal sor - row, and thy life's
5. pay thee, I do a - dore thee, and will ev -

1. pre - tend - ed? By foes de - rid - ed, by thine
2. un - done thee. 'Twas I, Lord Je - sus, I it
3. hath suf - fered; for our a - tone - ment, while we
4. ob - la - tion; thy death of an - guish and thy
5. er pray thee; think on thy pit - y and thy

1. own re - ject - ed, O most af - flict - ed.
2. was de - nied thee; I cru - ci - fied thee.
3. noth - ing heed - ed, God in - ter - ced - ed.
4. bit - ter pas - sion, for my sal - va - tion.
5. love un - swerv - ing, not my de - serv - ing.

Text: Johann Heermann, 1585–1647; tr. Robert Bridges, 1844–1930, alt.
Music: HERZLIEBSTER JESU, 11, 11, 11, 5; Johann Crüger, 1598–1662.

136. WERE YOU THERE

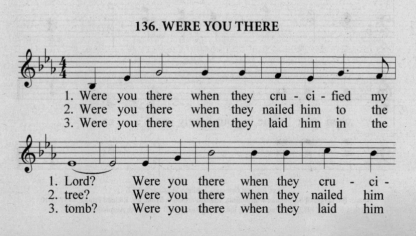

1. Were you there when they cru - ci - fied my
2. Were you there when they nailed him to the
3. Were you there when they laid him in the

1. Lord? Were you there when they cru - ci -
2. tree? Were you there when they nailed him
3. tomb? Were you there when they laid him

1. fied   my   Lord?   Oh!   Some-times   it
2. to   the   tree?   Oh!   Some-times   it
3. in   the   tomb?   Oh!   Some-times   it

1. caus - es me to   trem - ble,   trem - ble, trem - ble.
2. caus - es me to   trem - ble,   trem - ble, trem - ble.
3. caus - es me to · trem - ble,   trem - ble, trem - ble.

1. Were you there when they cru - ci - fied   my Lord?
2. Were you there when they nailed him   to   the tree?
3. Were you there when they laid him   in   the tomb?

Text: African-American spiritual. Music: WERE YOU THERE, irregular, African-American spiritual.

137. ADORAMUS TE CHRISTE

We adore You, O Christ, and we bless You
because by your Holy Cross You have redeemed the world.

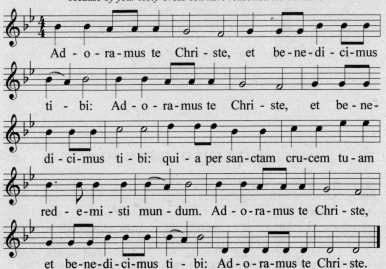

Ad - o - ra - mus te   Chri - ste,   et   be - ne - di - ci - mus

ti - bi: Ad - o - ra - mus te   Chri - ste,   et   be - ne -

di - ci - mus   ti - bi: qui - a per san - ctam   cru - cem   tu - am

red - e - mi - sti   mun - dum.   Ad - o - ra - mus te   Chri - ste,

et   be - ne - di - ci - mus   ti - bi: Ad - o - ra - mus te   Chri - ste.

Adapt. from antiphon of Good Friday Liturgy, Th. Dubois, d. 1924.

138. TAKE UP YOUR CROSS

1. Take up your cross, the Sav - ior said,
2. Take up your cross, let not its weight
3. Take up your cross, heed not the shame,
4. Take up your cross, then, in his strength,
5. Take up your cross, and fol - low Christ,

1. If you would my dis - ci - ple be;
2. Fill your weak spir - it with a - larm;
3. And let your fool - ish heart be still;
4. And calm - ly ev - 'ry dan - ger brave:
5. Nor think till death to lay it down;

1. Take up your cross with will - ing heart,
2. His strength shall bear your spir - it up,
3. The Lord for you ac - cept - ed death
4. It guides you to a bet - ter home
5. For on - ly those who bear the cross

1. And hum - bly fol - low af - ter me.
2. And brace your heart, and nerve your arm.
3. Up - on a cross, on Cal - v'ry's hill.
4. And leads to vic - t'ry o'er the grave.
5. May hope to wear the glo - rious crown.

Text: Charles William Everest, 1814–1877.
Music: BRESLAU, 88 88, Felix Mendelssohn-Bartholdy, 1809–1847, attr.

139. O LOWLY LAMB OF GOD MOST HIGH

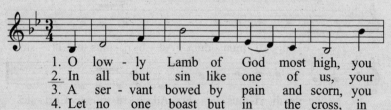

1. O low - ly Lamb of God most high, you
2. In all but sin like one of us, your
3. A ser - vant bowed by pain and scorn, you
4. Let no one boast but in the cross, in

1. clung not to di - vin - i - ty but
2. bod - y knew our ev - 'ry need. Lord,
3. gave your life up - on a tree. But
4. Je - sus Christ, the cru - ci - fied, whose

1. laid a - side your roy - al robes, em -
2. by your wounds we have been healed and
3. from the tomb God raised you up and
4. arms em - brace the u - ni - verse, whose

1. brac - ing our hu - man - i - ty.
2. by your death we have been freed.
3. we now share your vic - to - ry.
4. love is faith - ful, deep and wide.

Text: Delores Dufner, O.S.B., b. 1939; © 1982, 2003, GIA Publications, Inc. All rights reserved.
Used with permission. Music: DEUS TUORUM MILITUM, *Grenoble Antiphoner*, 1753.

140. O CROSS OF CHRIST, IMMORTAL TREE

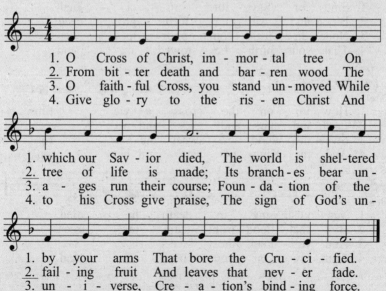

1. O Cross of Christ, im - mor - tal tree On
2. From bit - ter death and bar - ren wood The
3. O faith - ful Cross, you stand un - moved While
4. Give glo - ry to the ris - en Christ And

1. which our Sav - ior died, The world is shel - tered
2. tree of life is made; Its branch - es bear un -
3. a - ges run their course; Foun - da - tion of the
4. to his Cross give praise, The sign of God's un -

1. by your arms That bore the Cru - ci - fied.
2. fail - ing fruit And leaves that nev - er fade.
3. un - i - verse, Cre - a - tion's bind - ing force.
4. fa - thomed love, The hope of all our days.

Text: Stanbrook Abbey, © 1974. All rights reserved. Used with permission.
Music: ST. FLAVIAN, 86 86, adapt. from *John Day's Psalter*, 1562.

141. SING, MY TONGUE, THE SONG OF TRIUMPH

1. Sing, my tongue, the song of tri - umph,
2. He en - dured the nails, the spit - ting,
3. Faith - ful Cross, a - bove all oth - er,
4. Bend your boughs, O Tree of glo - ry!

1. Tell the sto - ry far and wide;
2. Vin - e - gar and spear and reed;
3. One and on - ly no - ble tree,
4. All your rig - id branch - es bend!

1. Tell of dread and fi - nal bat - tle,
2. From that ho - ly bod - y bro - ken
3. None in fo - liage, none in blos - som,
4. For a while the an - cient tem - per

1. Sing of Sav - ior cru - ci - fied;
2. Blood and wa - ter forth pro - ceed:
3. None in fruit your peer may be;
4. That your birth be - stowed, sus - pend;

1. How up - on the cross a vic - tim
2. Earth and stars and sky and o - cean
3. Sweet the wood and sweet the i - ron
4. And the King of earth and heav - en

1. Van - quish - ing in death he died.
2. By that flood from stain are freed.
3. And your load, most sweet is he.
4. Gent - ly on your bos - om tend.

Text: *Pange, lingua, gloriosi lauream certaminis;* Venantius Fortunatus, c. 530–609; tr. from *The Three Days,* 1981.
Music: PICARDY, 87 87 87, French carol, 17th cent.

142. THE ROYAL BANNERS FORWARD GO

1. The roy - al ban - ners for - ward go,
2. There while he hung, his sa - cred side
3. Ful - filled is now what Da - vid told
4. O tree of glo - ry, tree most fair,
5. Up - on its arms, like bal - ance true,
6. To you, e - ter - nal Three in One,

1. The cross shines forth in mys - tic glow,
2. By sol - dier's spear was o - pened wide,
3. In true pro - phet - ic song of old,
4. Or - dained those ho - ly limbs to bear,
5. He weighed the price for sin - ners due,
6. Let hom - age due by all be done:

1. Where he through whom our flesh was made,
2. To cleanse us in the pre - cious flood
3. How God the na - tions' king should be;
4. How bright in roy - al robe it stood–
5. The price which none but he could pay,
6. As by the cross you did re - store,

1. In that same flesh our ran - som paid.
2. Of wa - ter min - gled with his blood.
3. For God is reign - ing from a tree.
4. The pur - ple of a Sav - ior's blood!
5. And spoiled the spoil - er of his prey.
6. So rule and guide us ev - er - more.

Text: *Vexilla Regis prodeunt,* Venantius Fortunatus, 530–609; tr. John M. Neale, 1818–1866.
Music: VEXILLA REGIS, traditional chant, Mode I.

143. WHAT WONDROUS LOVE IS THIS

1. What won-drous love is this, O my soul, O my
2. To God and to the Lamb I will sing, I will
3. And when from death I'm free, I'll sing on, I'll sing

1. soul? What won-drous love is this, O my soul?
2. sing; To God and to the Lamb I will sing;
3. on; And when from death I'm free, I'll sing on;

1. What won-drous love is this That caused the Lord of
2. To God and to the Lamb Who is the great I
3. And when from death I'm free, I'll sing and joy-ful

1. bliss To bear the dread-ful curse for my soul, for my
2. AM, While mil-lions join the theme, I will sing, I will
3. be, And through e-ter-ni-ty I'll sing on, I'll sing

1. soul; To bear the dread-ful curse for my soul?
2. sing; While mil-lions join the theme, I will sing.
3. on! And through e-ter-ni-ty, I'll sing on!

Text: Alexander Means, 1801–1853.
Music: WONDROUS LOVE, 12 9 12 12 9, William Walher's *Southern Harmony*, 1835.

144. SOUND SALVATION'S MIGHTY TRUMPET!
Exsultet

1. Sound sal - va - tion's might - y trum-pet! An - gels, in
2. Sing, ex - ult, O ho - ly peo-ple, on you shines
3. On this night the He - brew peo-ple passed from slav -
4. On this night God's bound-less mer - cy t'ward the hu -
5. Lord, re - ceive this East - er can-dle, flame un-dimmed

1. glad cho - rus sing! All that lives, pro-claim in joy now:
2. the Ris - en One! With full hearts and minds and voic - es
3. 'ry through the sea; on this night the bap-tized faith-ful
4. man fam - i - ly shows the fault of our first par-ents
5. by giv - ing light; when your Son re - turns in glo - ry,

1. Je - sus is our Ris - en King! Earth, re-joice in shin-ing
2. praise the ev - er - last-ing Sun. Ask we now for one an -
3. share in Je-sus' vic - to - ry. Had he not come as re -
4. hap - py in its rem - e - dy. On this night the Star of
5. may he find it burn-ing bright. May the fire that Je - sus

1. splen-dor, all cre - a - tion bathed in light! Christ has
2. oth - er grace to pray this East - er song, faith in
3. deem - er, worth-less would our lives have been; but his
4. Morn-ing, Christ, is ris - en from the dead; rec - on-
5. kin - dled spread to earth's re - mot - est part; may the

1. con-quered, glo - ry fills you, ra-diance o - ver-comes the night.
2. Je - sus' res - ur-rec-tion, hope and love for - ev - er strong.
3. blood has paid our ran-som, free-ing us from chains of sin.
4. ciled is all cre - a - tion, and to heav-en earth is wed.
5. Star of Morn-ing find it still a - blaze in ev - 'ry heart.

Text: Delores Dufner, O.S.B., b. 1939, © 1991, 2003, GIA Publications, Inc.
All rights rseserved. Used with permission.
Music: HYMN TO JOY, 87 87 D, Ludwig van Beethoven, 1770–1827, adapt. Edward Hodges, 1796–1867.

145. THIS IS OUR FAITH

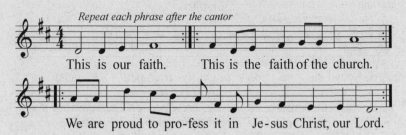

Repeat each phrase after the cantor

This is our faith.   This is the faith of the church.

We are proud to pro-fess it in Je-sus Christ, our Lord.

Text from the *Rite of Baptism for Children*, © 1969, ICEL. All rights reserved.
Music: Charles Gardner, b. 1947, © 2004, World Library Publications,
3708 River Road, Suite 400, Franklin Park, IL 60131-2158. All rights reserved. Used with permission.

146. SPRINGS OF WATER

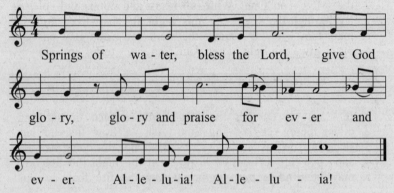

Springs of wa-ter, bless the Lord, give God

glo-ry, glo-ry and praise for ev-er and

ev-er. Al-le-lu-ia! Al-le-lu-ia!

Text: *Vidi aquam* and Psalm 118; tr. and music by Eric Holland, 1960–1991, © 1986.
Published and administered by Liturgical Press, Collegeville, MN 56321. All rights reserved.

147. VENI SANCTE SPIRITUS

Ostinato Refrain

Melody:

Ve-ni San-cte Spi-ri-tus.

Harmony:

Ve-ni San-cte Spi-ri-tus.

Text: Taizé Community, 1978. Music: Jacques Berthier, 1923–1994, © 1979, Les Presses de Taizé,
GIA Publications, Inc., agent. All rights reserved. Used with permission.

148. GREAT FLOWING RIVERS

Refrain

Al-le-lu-ia, al - le - lu-ia, al-le-lu - ia!

Verses

1. Great flow - ing riv - ers once sculpt - ed
2. Drink - ing pure wa - ter the earth springs
3. O'er deep, dark wa - ters the ark rode
4. Through part - ed wa - ters God's cho - sen
5. Saved from death's wa - ters Christ ev - er
6. In this blest wa - ter the Church comes

1. our land. Shaped by blest wa - ter and
2. a - live. Blest with this wa - ter our
3. se - cure. Sail - ing these wa - ters our
4. ones fled. Drowned in this wa - ter our
5. will reign. Washed in this wa - ter his
6. to birth. Born in this wa - ter, so

1. formed by God's hand, liv - ing stones fash - ion
2. spir - its re - vive. Seeds of God's good - ness
3. pas - sage is sure. Mak - ing life's jour - ney
4. old self is dead. In all that threat - ens,
5. new life we gain. Stead - fast in jus - tice
6. pre - cious our worth: Heirs of the God who

D.C.

1. the tem - ple God planned. Al - le - lu - ia!
2. with - in our hearts thrive. Al - le - lu - ia!
3. our hope shall en - dure. Al - le - lu - ia!
4. our faith con - quers dread. Al - le - lu - ia!
5. and peace we re - main. Al - le - lu - ia!
6. rules heav - en and earth. Al - le - lu - ia!

Text: Michael Kwatera, OSB, b. 1950. © 1993, Order of Saint Benedict,
administered by Liturgical Press, Collegeville, MN 56321. All rights reserved.
Music: O FILII ET FILIAE, 10 10 10 with alleluias; adapt. by Marty Haugen,
© 1986, GIA Publications, Inc. All rights reserved. Used with permission.

149. CHRIST IS ALIVE

1. Christ is a - live! Let Chris - tians sing. The
2. Christ is a - live! No long - er bound to
3. In ev - 'ry in - sult, rift, and war, where
4. Wo - men and men, in age and youth, can
5. Christ is a - live, and comes to bring good

1. cross stands emp - ty to the sky. Let
2. dis - tant years in Pal - es - tine, but
3. col - or, scorn or wealth di - vide, Christ
4. feel the Spir - it, hear the call, and
5. news to this and ev - 'ry age, till

1. streets and homes with prais - es ring. Love,
2. sav - ing, heal - ing here and now, and
3. suf - fers still, yet loves the more, And
4. find the way, the life, the truth, re -
5. earth and sky and o - cean ring with

1. drowned in death, shall nev - er die.
2. touch - ing ev - 'ry place and time.
3. lives, where ev - en hope has died.
4. vealed in Je - sus, freed for all.
5. joy, with jus - tice, love and praise.

Text: Brian A. Wren, b. 1936, © 1975, 1995, Hope Publishing Co., Carol Stream, IL 60188. All rights reserved. Used with permission. Music: TRURO, 88 88, *Psalmodia Evangelica*, Part II, 1789.

150. REGINA CAELI / O QUEEN OF HEAVEN

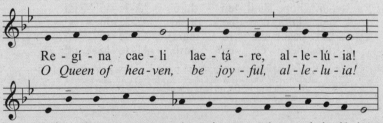

Re - gí - na cae - li lae - tá - re, al - le - lú - ia!
O Queen of hea - ven, be joy - ful, al - le - lu - ia!

Qui - a quem me - ru - í - sti por - tá - re, al - le - lú - ia!
For he whom you have hum - bly borne for us, al - le - lu - ia!

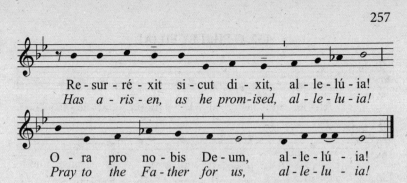

Re - sur - ré - xit si - cut di - xit, al - le - lú - ia!
Has a - ris - en, as he prom - ised, al - le - lu - ia!

O - ra pro no - bis De - um, al - le - lú - ia!
Pray to the Fa - ther for us, al - le - lu - ia!

Text: *Regina Caeli*; tr. by Winfred Douglas, 1867–1944, alt. Music: Plainchant, Mode VI.

151. THAT EASTER DAY WITH JOY WAS BRIGHT

1. That Eas - ter day with joy was bright,
2. His ris - en flesh with ra - diance glowed;
3. O Je - sus, King of gen - tle - ness,
4. O Lord of all, with us a - bide
5. All praise, to you, O Ris - en Lord,

1. The sun shone out with fair - er light,
2. His wound - ed hands and feet he showed;
3. who with your grace our hearts pos - sess
4. In this our joy - ful Eas - ter - tide;
5. Now both by heav - en and earth a - dored;

1. When to their long - ing eyes re - stored,
2. Those scars their sol - emn wit - ness gave
3. That we may give you all our days
4. From ev - 'ry wea - pon death can wield
5. To God the Fa - ther e - qual praise,

1. The a - pos - tles saw their ris - en Lord.
2. That Christ was ris - en from the grave.
3. The will - ing tri - bute of our praise.
4. Your own re - deemed for ev - er shield.
5. And Spir - it blest, our songs we raise.

Text: Latin, 5th cent.; tr. John M. Neale, 1818–1866, alt.
Music: PUER NOBIS, 88 88, Michael Praetorius, 1571–1621, adapt.

152. O FILII ET FILIAE

Al - le - lú - ia, al - le - lú - ia, al - le - lú - ia.

1. O fí - li - i et fí - li - ae
2. Et ma - ne pri - ma sáb - ba - ti,
3. Et Ma - rí - a Mag - da - le - ne,
4. In ál - bis sé - dens Án - ge - lus

1. Rex coe - lés - tis, Rex gló - ri - ae
2. Ad ó - sti - um mo - nu - mén - ti
3. Et Ia - có - bi, et Sa - ló - me
4. Prae - dí - xit mu - li - é - ri - bus

D.C.

1. Mor - te sur - réx - it ho - di - e. Al - le - lú - ia.
2. Ac - ces - sé - runt di - scí - pu - li. Al - le - lú - ia.
3. Ve - né - runt cor - pus ún - ge - re. Al - le - lú - ia.
4. In Gal - li - aé-a est Dó - mi - nus. Al - le - lú - ia.

5. Et Ioánnes Apóstolus
   Cucúrrit Pétro cítius,
   Monuménto vénit prius.
   Allelúia.

6. Discípulis astántibus,
   In médio stétit Chrístus,
   Dícens: Pax vóbis ómnibus.
   Allelúia.

7. Ut intelléxit Dídymus
   Quia surréxerat Iesus,
   Remánsit fide dúbius.
   Allelúia.

8. Víde Thóma, víde látus,
   Víde pédes, víde mánus,
   Nóli ésse incrédulus.
   Allelúia.

9. Quando Thómas Chrísti látus,
   Pédes vídit atque mánus,
   Díxit: Tu es Déus méus.
   Allelúia.

10. Beáti qui non vidérunt,
    Et firmiter credidérunt,
    Vítam aetérnam habébunt.
    Allelúia.

11. In hoc fésto sanctíssimo
    Sit laus et iubilátio,
    Benedicámus Dómino.
    Allelúia.

12. De quíbus nos humíllimas
    Devótas atque débitas
    Deo dicámus grátias.
    Allelúia.

Text: *O filii et filiae;* Jean Tisserand, d. 1494. Music: O FILII ET FILIAE, 888 with alleluias; Mode II.

153. O SONS AND DAUGHTERS

Al - le - lu - ia, al - le - lu - ia, al - le - lu - ia.

1. O sons and daugh - ters, let us sing!
2. That Eas - ter morn, at break of day,
3. An an - gel clad in white they see,
4. That night th'a - pos - tles met in fear;

1. The King of heav'n the glo - rious King,
2. The faith - ful wom - en went their way
3. Who sat and spoke un - to the three,
4. A - mong them came their Lord most dear,

D.C.

1. O'er death to - day rose tri - umph - ing. Al - le - lu - ia!
2. To seek the tomb where Je - sus lay. Al - le - lu - ia!
3. "Your Lord has gone to Gal - i - lee." Al - le - lu - ia!
4. And said, "My peace be with you here." Al - le - lu - ia!

5. When Thomas first the tidings heard,
   How they had seen the risen Lord,
   He doubted the disciples' word. Alleluia!

6. "My wounded side, O Thomas, see;
   Behold my hands, my feet," said he,
   "Not faithless, but believing be." Alleluia!

7. No longer Thomas then denied,
   He saw the feet, the hands, the side;
   "You are my Lord and God," he cried. Alleluia!

8. How blest are they who have not seen,
   And yet whose faith has constant been;
   For they eternal life shall win. Alleluia!

9. On this most holy day of days
   To God your hearts and voices raise,
   In laud and jubilee and praise. Alleluia!

Text: *O filii et filiae;* Jean Tisserand, d. 1494; tr. by John Mason Neal, 1818–1866, alt.
Music: O FILII ET FILIAE, 888 with alleluias; Mode II.

154. SING WITH ALL THE SAINTS IN GLORY

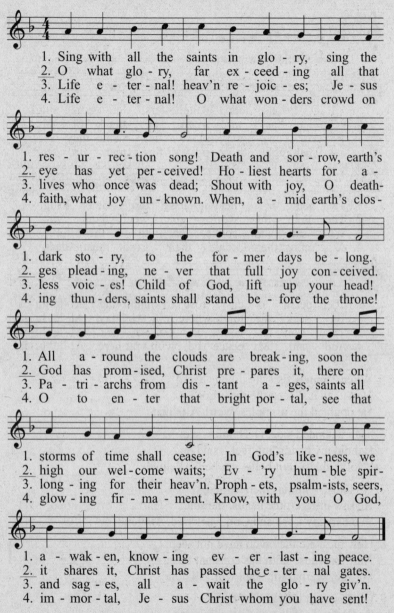

1. Sing with all the saints in glo - ry, sing the
2. O what glo - ry, far ex - ceed - ing all that
3. Life e - ter - nal! heav'n re - joic - es; Je - sus
4. Life e - ter - nal! O what won - ders crowd on

1. res - ur - rec - tion song! Death and sor - row, earth's
2. eye has yet per - ceived! Ho - liest hearts for a -
3. lives who once was dead; Shout with joy, O death -
4. faith, what joy un - known. When, a - mid earth's clos -

1. dark sto - ry, to the for - mer days be - long.
2. ges plead - ing, ne - ver that full joy con - ceived.
3. less voic - es! Child of God, lift up your head!
4. ing thun - ders, saints shall stand be - fore the throne!

1. All a - round the clouds are break - ing, soon the
2. God has prom - ised, Christ pre - pares it, there on
3. Pa - tri - archs from dis - tant a - ges, saints all
4. O to en - ter that bright por - tal, see that

1. storms of time shall cease; In God's like - ness, we
2. high our wel - come waits; Ev - 'ry hum - ble spir -
3. long - ing for their heav'n. Proph - ets, psalm - ists, seers,
4. glow - ing fir - ma - ment. Know, with you O God,

1. a - wak - en, know - ing ev - er - last - ing peace.
2. it shares it, Christ has passed the e - ter - nal gates.
3. and sag - es, all a - wait the glo - ry giv'n.
4. im - mor - tal, Je - sus Christ whom you have sent!

Text: 1 Corinthians 15:20; William Josiah Irons, 1812–1883, alt.
Music: HYMN TO JOY, 87 87 D, Ludwig van Beethoven, 1770–1827; adapt. Edward Hodges, 1796–1867.

155. CHRIST THE LORD IS RIS'N TODAY

1. Christ the Lord is ris'n to-day; Chris-tians,
2. Christ, the vic-tim un-de-filed, God and
3. Say, O wond-'ring Mar-y, say What you
4. Christ, who once for sin-ners bled, Now the

1. haste your vows to pay; Of-fer now your
2. sin-ners rec-on-ciled; When in strange and
3. saw a-long the way. "I be-held, where
4. first-born from the dead, Throned in end-less

1. prais-es meet At the Pas-chal Vic-tim's feet;
2. aw-ful strife Met to-geth-er death and life;
3. Christ had lain, Emp-ty tomb and an-gels twain;
4. might and pow'r, Lives and reigns for ev-er-more.

1. For the sheep the Lamb has bled, Sin-less
2. Chris-tians, on this hap-py day Haste with
3. I be-held the glo-ry bright Of the
4. Hail, e-ter-nal hope on high! Hail, our

1. in the sin-ner's stead. Christ the Lord is
2. joy your vows to pay. Christ the Lord is
3. ris-ing Lord of light. Christ my hope is
4. King of vic-to-ry! Hail, our Prince of

1. ris'n on high; Now he lives, no more to die.
2. ris'n on high; Now he lives, no more to die.
3. ris'n a-gain; Now he lives, and lives to reign."
4. life a-dored! Help and save us, gra-cious Lord!

Text: Wipo of Burgundy, c. 10th cent., attr.; tr. Jane Elizabeth Leeson, 1808–1881.
Music: VICTIMAE PASCHALI, 77 77 D, Wurth's *Katholisches Gesangbuch*, 1859.

156. BAPTIZED IN WATER

1. Bap-tized in wa - ter, Sealed by the Spir - it,
2. Bap-tized in wa - ter, Sealed by the Spir - it,
3. Bap-tized in wa - ter, Sealed by the Spir - it,

1. Cleansed by the blood of Christ our King:
2. Dead in the tomb with Christ our King:
3. Marked with the sign of Christ our King:

1. Heirs of sal - va - tion, Trust - ing his prom - ise,
2. One with his ris - ing, Freed and for - giv - en,
3. Born of one Fa - ther, We are his chil - dren,

1. Faith - ful - ly now God's praise we sing.
2. Thank - ful - ly now God's praise we sing.
3. Joy - ful - ly now God's praise we sing.

Text: Michael Saward, b. 1932, © 1982, Jubilate Hymns, Ltd. All rights reserved.
Administered by Hope Publishing Co., Carol Stream, IL 60188. Used with permission.
Music: BUNESSAN, 5 5.5 4 D, GAELIC MELODY.

157. THE STRIFE IS O'ER, THE BATTLE DONE

Refrain

Al - le - lu - ia! Al - le - lu - ia! Al - le - lu - ia!

Verses

1. The strife is o'er, the bat - tle done.
2. The pow'rs of death have done their worst,
3. On the third morn he rose a - gain
4. He closed the yawn - ing gates of hell,

1. The vic - to - ry of life is won;
2. But Christ their le - gions has dis - persed;
3. Glo - rious in maj - es - ty to reign;
4. The bars from heav'n's high por - tals fell;

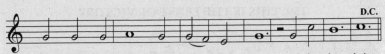

D.C.

1. The song of tri - umph has be - gun; Al - le - lu - ia!
2. Let shouts of praise and joy out - burst: Al - le - lu - ia!
3. O let us swell the joy - ful strain: Al - le - lu - ia!
4. Let hymns of praise his tri - umph tell: Al - le - lu - ia!

Text: Anon.; tr. Francis Pott, 1832–1909, alt. Music: VICTORY, 888 with alleluias,
Giovanni Pierluigi da Palestrina, c. 1525–1594; adapt. with alleluias William Henry Monk, 1823–1889.

158. CROWN HIM WITH MANY CROWNS

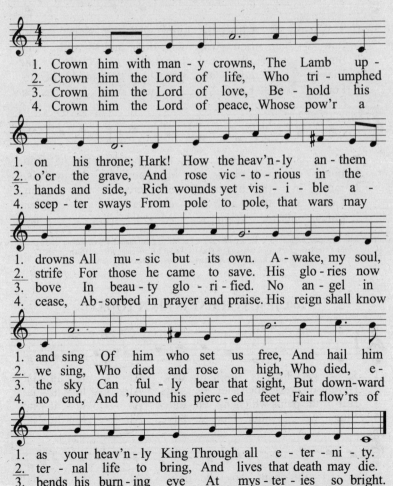

1. Crown him with man - y crowns, The Lamb up -
2. Crown him the Lord of life, Who tri - umphed
3. Crown him the Lord of love, Be - hold his
4. Crown him the Lord of peace, Whose pow'r a

1. on his throne; Hark! How the heav'n - ly an - them
2. o'er the grave, And rose vic - to - rious in the
3. hands and side, Rich wounds yet vis - i - ble a -
4. scep - ter sways From pole to pole, that wars may

1. drowns All mu - sic but its own. A - wake, my soul,
2. strife For those he came to save. His glo - ries now
3. bove In beau - ty glo - ri - fied. No an - gel in
4. cease, Ab - sorbed in prayer and praise. His reign shall know

1. and sing Of him who set us free, And hail him
2. we sing, Who died and rose on high, Who died, e -
3. the sky Can ful - ly bear that sight, But down - ward
4. no end, And 'round his pierc - ed feet Fair flow'rs of

1. as your heav'n - ly King Through all e - ter - ni - ty.
2. ter - nal life to bring, And lives that death may die.
3. bends his burn - ing eye At mys - ter - ies so bright.
4. par - a - dise ex - tend Their fra - grance ev - er sweet.

Text: Matthew Bridges, 1800–1894, vv. 1, 3, 4; Godfrey Thring, 1823–1903, v. 2.
Music: DIADEMATA, 66 86 D, George Job Elvey, 1816–1893.

159. THIS IS THE FEAST OF VICTORY

This is the feast of vic-to-ry for our God. Al-le-

lu - ia, al-le - lu-ia, al-le - lu-ia. lu - ia.

To verses *Last time*

1. ⸭ Wor-thy is Christ, the Lamb who was slain, whose
2. Pow - er, rich - es, wis - dom, and strength, and
3. Sing with all the peo - ple of God, and
4. Bless - ing, hon - or, glo - ry, and might be to
5. For the Lamb_____ who was slain has be-

1. blood set us free_____ to be peo-ple of God.
2. hon - or,_____ bless - ing, and glo - ry are his.
3. join in the hymn of all cre - a - tion.
4. God and the Lamb for - ev - er. A - men.
5. gun his_____ reign._____ Al - le - lu - ia.

160. JESUS CHRIST IS RIS'N TODAY

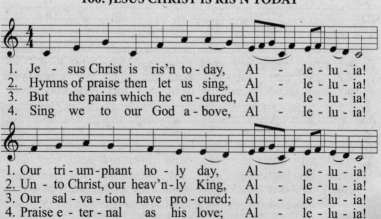

1. Je - sus Christ is ris'n to - day, Al - le - lu - ia!
2. Hymns of praise then let us sing, Al - le - lu - ia!
3. But the pains which he en - dured, Al - le - lu - ia!
4. Sing we to our God a - bove, Al - le - lu - ia!

1. Our tri - um-phant ho - ly day, Al - le - lu - ia!
2. Un - to Christ, our heav'n - ly King, Al - le - lu - ia!
3. Our sal - va - tion have pro - cured; Al - le - lu - ia!
4. Praise e - ter - nal as his love; Al - le - lu - ia!

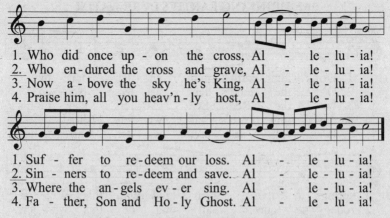

1. Who did once up - on the cross, Al - le - lu - ia!
2. Who en - dured the cross and grave, Al - le - lu - ia!
3. Now a - bove the sky he's King, Al - le - lu - ia!
4. Praise him, all you heav'n - ly host, Al - le - lu - ia!

1. Suf - fer to re - deem our loss. Al - le - lu - ia!
2. Sin - ners to re - deem and save. Al - le - lu - ia!
3. Where the an - gels ev - er sing. Al - le - lu - ia!
4. Fa - ther, Son and Ho - ly Ghost. Al - le - lu - ia!

Text: St. 1, *Surrexit Christus hodie,* Latin, 14th cent.; para. in *Lyra Davidica,* 1708, alt.;
sts. 2, 3, *The Compleat Psalmodist,* c. 1750, alt.; st. 4, Charles Wesley, 1707–1788.
Music: EASTER HYMN, 77 77 with alleluias, *Lyra Davidica,* 1708.

161. ALLELUIA! LET THE HOLY ANTHEM RISE

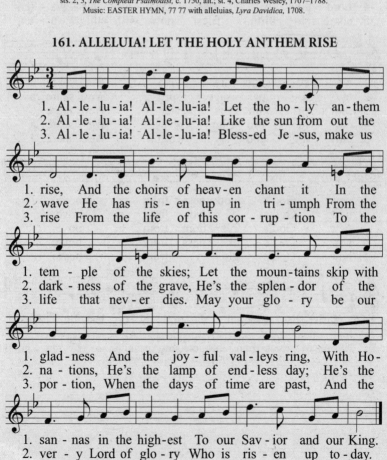

1. Al - le - lu - ia! Al - le - lu - ia! Let the ho - ly an - them
2. Al - le - lu - ia! Al - le - lu - ia! Like the sun from out the
3. Al - le - lu - ia! Al - le - lu - ia! Bless - ed Je - sus, make us

1. rise, And the choirs of heav - en chant it In the
2. wave He has ris - en up in tri - umph From the
3. rise From the life of this cor - rup - tion To the

1. tem - ple of the skies; Let the moun - tains skip with
2. dark - ness of the grave, He's the splen - dor of the
3. life that nev - er dies. May your glo - ry be our

1. glad - ness And the joy - ful val - leys ring, With Ho -
2. na - tions, He's the lamp of end - less day; He's the
3. por - tion, When the days of time are past, And the

1. san - nas in the high - est To our Sav - ior and our King.
2. ver - y Lord of glo - ry Who is ris - en up to - day.
3. dead shall be a - wak - ened By the trum - pet's might - y blast.

Text: Edward Caswall, 1814–1878. Music: HOLY ANTHEM, 87 87 D, traditional melody.

162. DRINKING EARTH'S PURE WATER

1. Drink - ing   earth's   pure   wa - ter,   na - ture
2. O'er   the   flood's   deep   wa - ters,   No - ah
3. In   the   Red   Sea   wa - ters,   Pha - raoh's
4. Saved   from   death's   dark   wa - ters,   Christ   the
5. In   this   sa - cred   wa - ter,   Chris - tians

1. springs   a - live.   Sprin - kled   with   this   wa - ter,
2. rode   se - cure.   Sail - ing   on   this   wa - ter,
3. hosts   were   slain.   Drowned   now   in   this   wa - ter,
4. Lord   now   lives.   Bap - tized   in   this   wa - ter,
5. come   to   birth.   Blest   now   with   this   wa - ter,

1. wea - ry   souls   re - vive.   We   share   a -
2. ours   a   pas - sage   sure.   We   share   a -
3. pow'r   of   sin   is   vain.   We   share   a -
4. ours   the   life   he   gives.   We   share   a -
5. ours   a   god - ly   worth.   We   share   a -

1. new   God's   good - ness   from   a - bove:
2. new   God's   fa - vor   from   a - bove:
3. new   God's   free - dom   from   a - bove:
4. new   God's   like - ness   from   a - bove:
5. new   God's   glo - ry   from   a - bove:

1.–5. Christ   has   won   sal - va - tion,   ev - er - last - ing   love!

Text: Michael Kwatera, O.S.B., b. 1950, and David Klingeman, O.S.B., b. 1955,
© 1991, Order of Saint Benedict, Collegeville, MN. All rights reserved.
Music: NOËL NOUVELET, 11 10 10 11, French carol.

163. CHRIST THE LORD IS RIS'N AGAIN

Cantor: / *All:*

1. Christ the Lord is ris'n a - gain, al - le - lu - ia,
2. Christ the Lord is ris'n in - deed, al - le - lu - ia.
3. Cry a - loud to God with joy, al - le - lu - ia;
4. Peo - ple of the Lord our God, al - le - lu - ia,
5. Faith - ful to the end of time, al - le - lu - ia,

Cantor: / *All:*

1. his hand on us to keep us safe, al - le - lu - ia.
2. All pow'r and glo - ry be to him, al - le - lu - ia.
3. let earth with glad - ness serve the Lord, al - le - lu - ia;
4. who made all things up - on the earth, al - le - lu - ia,
5. is God, whose mer - cy co - vers us, al - le - lu - ia,

Cantor: / *All:*

1. How his wis - dom is won - der - ful! al - le - lu - ia,
2. Praise his name to the end of time, al - le - lu - ia,
3. come to God with our songs of joy, al - le - lu - ia,
4. sing with praise and thanks - giv - ing, al - le - lu - ia,
5. and whose love is e - ter - nal, al - le - lu - ia,

1.–5. al - le - lu - ia, al - le - lu - ia!

164. VICTIMAE PASCHALI /
CHRISTIANS, TO THE PASCHAL VICTIM

Sequence for Easter

1. Ví - cti - mae Pa - schá - li lau - des im - mó - lent
1. *Chris - tians, to the Pas - chal vic - tim of - fer your*

Chri - sti - á - ni. 2. A - gnus ré - de - mit ó - ves:
3. Mors et vi - ta du - él - lo
thank-ful prais-es! 2. A Lamb re - deems the sheep:
3. Death and life have con - tend - ed

Chri - stus ín - no - cens Pá - tri re - con - cil -
con - fli - xé - re mi - rán - do: dux vi - tae
Christ who on - ly is sin - less, re - con - ciles
In that com - bat stu - pen - dous: the Prince of

li - á - vit pec - ca - tó - res. 4. Dic no - bis
mór - tu - us re - gnat vi - vus. 6. An - gé - li -
sin - ners to the Fa - ther. 4. Speak, Mar - y,
life who dies, reigns im - mor - tal. 6. Bright an - gels

Ma - rí - a, quid vi - dí - sti in vi - a?
cos te - stes, su - dá - ri - um, et ve - stes.
de - clar - ing what you saw, way - far - ing.
at - test - ing, shroud and nap - kin, rest - ing.

5. Se - púl - crum Chri - sti vi - vén - tis,
7. Sur - ré - xit Chri - stus spes me - a:
5. *"The tomb of Christ, who is liv - ing,*
7. *Yes, Christ my hope, is a - ris - en:*

et gló - ri - am vi - di re - sur - gén - tis:
prae - cé - det su - os in Ga - li - laé - am.
the glo - ry of Je - sus' res - ur - rec - tion;
To Gal - i - lee he goes be - fore you."

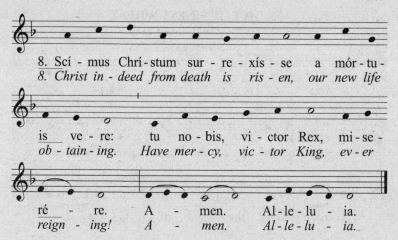

8. Scí - mus Chrí - stum sur - re - xís - se a mór - tu -
8. Christ in - deed from death is ris - en, our new life

is ve - re: tu no - bis, vi - ctor Rex, mi - se -
ob - tain - ing. Have mer - cy, vic - tor King, ev - er

ré - re. A - men. Al - le - lu - ia.
reign - ing! A - men. Al - le - lu - ia.

Text: Sequence for Easter, ascr. to Wipo of Burgundy, d. 1048; tr. by Joy Probst,
© 1975, Sisters of Saint Benedict, St. Joseph, MN, administered by Liturgical Press,
Collegeville, MN 56321. All rights reserved.
Music: VICTIMAE PASCHALI LAUDES, Plainchant, Mode I, ascr. to Wipo of Burgundy, d. 1048.

165. SACRED THIS BANQUET

Sa - cred this ban - quet, ho - ly our feast;

Here all find wel - come, great - est to least.

Food of the king - dom, gift from a - bove,

Pledge of our glo - ry, sign of God's love.

Text: Michael Kwatera, OSB, b. 1950, © 2010, Order of Saint Benedict,
published and administered by Liturgical Press, Collegeville, MN 56321. All rights reserved.
Music: Michael Joncas, b. 1951, © 2010, GIA Publications, Inc. All rights reserved. Used with permission.

166. GIFT OF FINEST WHEAT

Refrain

You sat-is-fy the hun-gry heart with gift of fin-est wheat; come give to us, O sav-ing Lord, the bread of life to eat.

Verses

1. As when the shep - herd calls his sheep, They
2. With joy - ful lips we sing to you Our
3. Is not the cup we bless and share The
4. The mys - t'ry of your pres - ence, Lord, No
5. You give your - self to us, O Lord; Then

1. know and heed his voice, So when you call
2. praise and grat - i - tude, That you should count
3. blood of Christ out - poured? Do not one cup,
4. mor - tal tongue can tell: Whom all the world
5. self - less let us be, To serve each oth -

D.C.

1. your fam - 'ly, Lord, We fol - low and re - joice.
2. us wor - thy, Lord, To share this heav'n - ly food.
3. one loaf, de - clare Our one - ness in the Lord?
4. can - not con - tain Comes in our hearts to dwell.
5. er in your name In truth and char - i - ty.

167. AT THAT FIRST EUCHARIST

1. At that first Eucharist before you died,
2. For all your Church, O Lord, we intercede;
3. So, Lord, at length when sacraments shall cease,

1. O Lord, you prayed that all be one in you;
2. O make our lack of charity to cease;
3. May we be one with all your Church above,

1. At this our Eucharist again preside,
2. Draw us the nearer each to each, we plead,
3. One with your saints in one unending peace,

1. And in our hearts your law of love renew.
2. By drawing all to you, O Prince of Peace.
3. One with your saints in one unbounded love.

1.–3. Thus may we all one bread, one body be,

Through this blest sacrament of unity.

Text: William Harry Turton, 1856–1938, alt.
Music: UNDE ET MEMORES, 10 10 10 10, with refrain; William Henry Monk, 1823–1889, alt.

168. PSALM 34: TASTE AND SEE

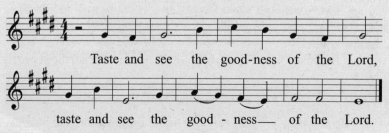

Taste and see the goodness of the Lord,

taste and see the goodness of the Lord.

169. TAKE AND EAT

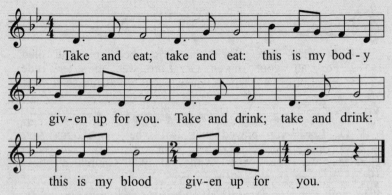

Take and eat; take and eat: this is my bod - y

giv - en up for you. Take and drink; take and drink:

this is my blood giv - en up for you.

170. LIFE-GIVING BREAD, SAVING CUP

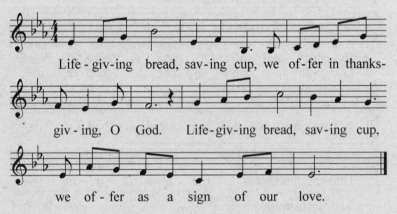

Life - giv - ing bread, sav - ing cup, we of - fer in thanks-

giv - ing, O God. Life - giv - ing bread, sav - ing cup,

we of - fer as a sign of our love.

171. BREAD OF LIFE, CUP OF BLESSING

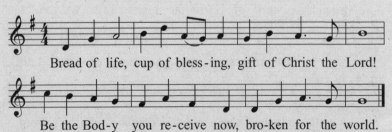

Bread of life, cup of bless - ing, gift of Christ the Lord!

Be the Bod - y you re - ceive now, bro - ken for the world.

172. EAT THIS BREAD

Eat this bread, drink this cup, come to him and
Je-sus Christ, bread of life, those who come to

nev-er be hun-gry. Eat this bread, drink this cup,
you will not hun-ger. Je-sus Christ, Ris-en Lord,

trust in him and you will not thirst.
those who trust in you will not thirst.

*Alternate refrain

Text: Robert J. Batastini, b.1942, and the Taizé Community. Music: Jacques Berthier, 1923–1994,
© 1984, Les Presses de Taizé, GIA Publications, Inc., agent. All rights reserved. Used with permission.

173. LORD, ACCEPT THE GIFTS WE OFFER

1. Lord, ac-cept the gifts we of-fer At this Eu-cha-
2. May our souls be pure and spot-less As the host of
3. Take our gifts, al-might-y Fa-ther, Liv-ing God, e-

1. ris-tic feast. Bread and wine to be trans-formed now
2. wheat so fine, May all stain of sin be crushed out,
3. ter-nal, true, Which we give through Christ, our Sav-ior,

1. Through the work of Christ our priest. Take us, too, O
2. Like the grape that forms the wine, As we, too, be-
3. Plead-ing here for us a-new. Grant sal-va-tion

1. Lord, trans-form us; be your grace in us in-creased.
2. come par-tak-ers In this sac-ri-fice di-vine.
3. to all pres-ent And our faith and love re-new.

Text: Mary Teresine Haban, O.S.F., b. 1914, © 1959, 1977, Order of Saint Benedict, Collegeville, MN.
All rights reserved. Music: SAINT THOMAS, 87 87 87, John Francis Wade, 1711–1786.

174. TRIDUUM: MORNING PRAYER HYMN

Two verses are sung on the assigned day.

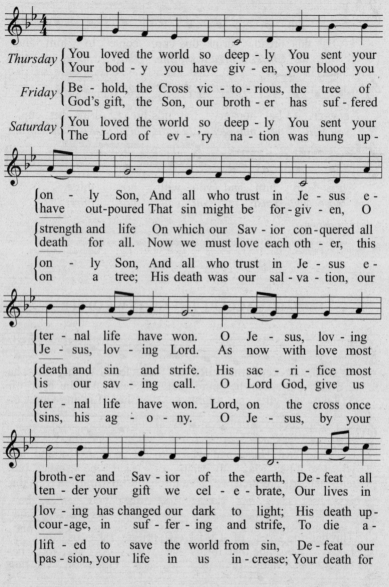

Thursday
You loved the world so deep-ly You sent your
Your bod-y you have giv-en, your blood you

Friday
Be-hold, the Cross vic-to-rious, the tree of
God's gift, the Son, our broth-er has suf-fered

Saturday
You loved the world so deep-ly You sent your
The Lord of ev-'ry na-tion was hung up-

on-ly Son, And all who trust in Je-sus e-
have out-poured That sin might be for-giv-en, O

strength and life On which our Sav-ior con-quered all
death for all. Now we must love each oth-er, this

on-ly Son, And all who trust in Je-sus e-
on a tree; His death was our sal-va-tion, our

ter-nal life have won. O Je-sus, lov-ing
Je-sus, lov-ing Lord. As now with love most

death and sin and strife. His sac-ri-fice most
is our sav-ing call. O Lord God, give us

ter-nal life have won. Lord, on the cross once
sins, his ag-o-ny. O Je-sus, by your

broth-er and Sav-ior of the earth, De-feat all
ten-der your gift we cel-e-brate, Our lives in

lov-ing has changed our dark to light; His death up-
cour-age, in suf-fer-ing and strife, To die a-

lift-ed to save the world from sin, De-feat our
pas-sion, your life in us in-crease; Your death for

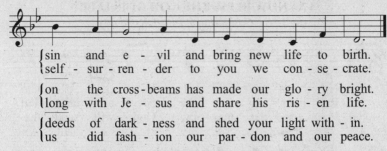

{ sin and e - vil and bring new life to birth.
{ self - sur - ren - der to you we con - se - crate.

{ on the cross - beams has made our glo - ry bright.
{ long with Je - sus and share his ris - en life.

{ deeds of dark - ness and shed your light with - in.
{ us did fash - ion our par - don and our peace.

Text: Vrs. 1, 5, Delores Dufner, OSB, b. 1939, © 1982, 1983, 1984, Sisters of Saint Benedict, St. Joseph, MN 56374.
Vr. 2, Gregory Murray, OSB, 1905–1992, © Downside Abbey.
Vrs. 3, 4, James Berry, © 1972, Crosier Fathers and Brothers, Phoenix, AZ.
Vr. 6, Arthur Russell, 1806–1874, alt.
All rights reserved. Used with permission.
Music: PASSION CHORALE, 76 76 D, Hans Leo Hassler, 1564–1612.

175. EASTER SUNDAY: MORNING PRAYER HYMN

Based on Psalm 95

1. Come, let us praise the Lord, with joy our
2. Our God of match - less worth, our King be -
3. In wor - ship bow the knee, our glo - rious
4. Come, hear his voice to - day, re - ceive what

1. God ac - claim, his great - ness tell a - broad and
2. yond com - pare, the deep - est bounds of earth, the
3. God con - fess; the great Cre - a - tor, he, the
4. love im - parts; his ho - ly will o - bey and

1. bless his sav - ing Name. Lift high your songs be -
2. hills, are in his care. He all de - crees, who
3. Lord our Right - eous - ness. He reigns un - seen: his
4. hard - en not your hearts. His ways are best; and

1. fore his throne to whom a - lone all praise be - longs.
2. by his hand pre - pared the land and formed the seas.
3. flock he feeds and gen - tly leads in pas - tures green.
4. lead at last, all trou - bles past, to per - fect rest.

Text: *Come, Let Us Praise the Lord,* Timothy Dudley-Smith, © 1984, Hope Publishing Company,
Carol Stream, IL 60188. All rights reserved. Used with permission.
Music: DARWALL'S 148TH, 66 66 88, John Darwall, 1731–1789.

176. NOW BLESS THE GOD OF ISRAEL
Canticle of Zachariah

1. Now bless the God of Is - ra - el, who
2. Re - mem - ber - ing the cov - e - nant, God
3. In ten - der mer - cy, God will send the

1. comes in love and pow'r, who rais - es from
2. res - cues us from fear, that we might serve
3. day - spring from on high, our ris - ing sun,

1. the roy - al house de - liv - 'rance in this hour.
2. in ho - li - ness and peace from year to year;
3. the light of life for those who sit and sigh.

1. Through ho - ly proph - ets God has sworn to
2. and you, my child, shall go be - fore to
3. God comes to guide our way to peace, that

1. free us from a - larm, to save us from the
2. preach, to proph - e - sy, that all may know the
3. death shall reign no more. Sing prais - es to the

1. heav - y hand of all who wish us harm.
2. ten - der love, the grace of God most high.
3. Ho - ly One! O wor - ship and a - dore!

177. BLESSED BE THE LORD, THE GOD OF ISRAEL
Canticle of Zachariah

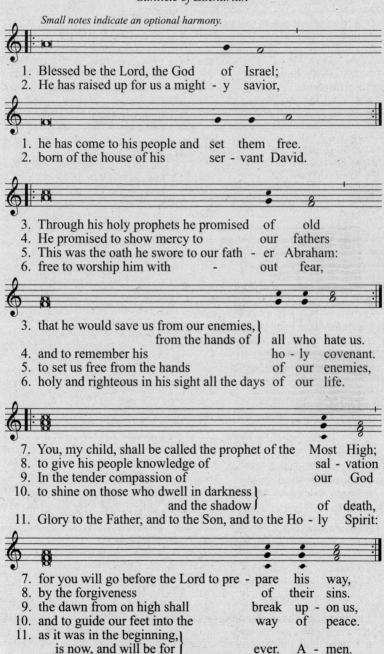

Small notes indicate an optional harmony.

1. Blessed be the Lord, the God   of   Israel;
2. He has raised up for us a might - y   savior,

1. he has come to his people and   set   them   free.
2. born of the house of his   ser - vant David.

3. Through his holy prophets he promised   of   old
4. He promised to show mercy to   our   fathers
5. This was the oath he swore to our fath - er   Abraham:
6. free to worship him with   -   out   fear,

3. that he would save us from our enemies,⎫
              from the hands of ⎰ all who hate us.
4. and to remember his   ho - ly covenant.
5. to set us free from the hands   of our enemies,
6. holy and righteous in his sight all the days of our life.

7. You, my child, shall be called the prophet of the   Most High;
8. to give his people knowledge of   sal - vation
9. In the tender compassion of   our   God
10. to shine on those who dwell in darkness⎫
              and the shadow⎰   of   death,
11. Glory to the Father, and to the Son, and to the Ho - ly Spirit:

7. for you will go before the Lord to pre - pare his   way,
8. by the forgiveness   of   their sins.
9. the dawn from on high shall   break up - on us,
10. and to guide our feet into the   way   of   peace.
11. as it was in the beginning,⎫
              is now, and will be for ⎰   ever.   A - men.

INDEX FOR MUSIC

Responsorial Psalms

Mass Settings

GUIDELINES FOR RECEIVING COMMUNION

For Catholics

As Catholics, we fully participate in the celebration of the Eucharist when we receive Holy Communion. We are encouraged to receive Communion devoutly and frequently. In order to be properly disposed to receive Communion, participants should not be conscious of grave sin and normally should have fasted for one hour. A person who is conscious of grave sin is not to receive the Body and Blood of the Lord without prior sacramental confession except for a grave reason where there is no opportunity for confession. In this case, the person is to be mindful of the obligation to make an act of perfect contrition, including the intention of confessing as soon as possible (Code of Canon Law, canon 916). A frequent reception of the Sacrament of Penance is encouraged for all.

For our fellow Christians

We welcome our fellow Christians to this celebration of the Eucharist as our brothers and sisters. We pray that our common baptism and the action of the Holy Spirit in this Eucharist will draw us closer to one another and begin to dispel the sad divisions which separate us. We pray that these will lessen and finally disappear, in keeping with Christ's prayer for us "that they may all be one" (Jn 17:21).

Because Catholics believe that the celebration of the Eucharist is a sign of the reality of the oneness of faith, life, and worship, members of those churches with whom we are not yet fully united are ordinarily not admitted to Holy Communion. Eucharistic sharing in exceptional circumstances by other Christians requires permission according to the directives of the diocesan bishop and the provisions of canon law (canon 844 § 4). Members of the Orthodox Churches, the Assyrian Church of the East, and the Polish National Catholic Church are urged to respect the discipline of their own Churches. According to Roman Catholic discipline, the Code of Canon Law does not object to the reception of Communion by Christians of these Churches (canon 844 § 3).

For those not receiving Holy Communion

All who are not receiving Holy Communion are encouraged to express in their hearts a prayerful desire for unity with the Lord Jesus and with one another.

For non-Christians

We also welcome to this celebration those who do not share our faith in Jesus Christ. While we cannot admit them to Holy Communion, we ask them to offer their prayers for the peace and unity of the human family.

Cover art: Detail from *Deposition from the Cross* by Fra Angelico, c. 1437–1440; courtesy of Wikimedia Commons.

Illustrations: Martin Erspamer, OSB, a monk of Saint Meinrad Archabbey. All rights reserved. Used with permission.

Back cover text: Paul Turner from *Glory in the Cross: Holy Week in the Third Edition of The Roman Missal*, © 2011 Order of Saint Benedict, Collegeville, MN 56321. All rights reserved.

Celebrating the Eucharist is a highly readable, calendar-dated quarterly missal and Mass guide published by Liturgical Press. With its classically beautiful cover, *Celebrating the Eucharist* includes the revised Order of Mass, readings from the *Lectionary for Mass*, prayer texts from *The Roman Missal, Third Edition*, and a repertoire of music rooted in the Catholic tradition. *Celebrating the Eucharist* is published quarterly with the approval of the Committee on Divine Worship, United States Conference of Catholic Bishops. For further information about this publication, call 800.858.5450.